DATE DUE

DEMCO 38-296

A SHORT HISTORY OF EUROPE

Also by Antony Alcock

GESCHICHTE DER SÜDTIROLFRAGE-SÜDTIROL SEIT DEM PAKET

HISTORY OF THE SOUTH TYROL QUESTION

HISTORY OF THE INTERNATIONAL LABOUR ORGANISATION

THE FUTURE OF CULTURAL MINORITIES (*editor with Brian Taylor and John Welton*)

UNDERSTANDING ULSTER

A Short History of Europe

From the Greeks and Romans to the Present Day

Antony Alcock
Professor of European Studies
University of Ulster at Coleraine
Northern Ireland

Foreword by J. E. Spence
Associate Fellow
Royal Institute of International Affairs
London

St. Martin's Press
New York

A SHORT HISTORY OF EUROPE
Copyright © 1998 by Antony Alcock
Foreword © 1998 by J. E. Spence
Maps © 1998 by Mary Alcock
All rights reserved. No part of this book may be used or reproduced
in any manner whatsoever without written permission except in the
case of brief quotations embodied in critical articles or reviews.
For information, address:

St. Martin's Press, Scholarly and Reference Division,
175 Fifth Avenue, New York, N.Y. 10010

First published in the United States of America in 1998

This book is printed on paper suitable for recycling and
made from fully managed and sustained forest sources.

Printed in Great Britain

ISBN 0–312–21003–5 clothbound
ISBN 0–312–21036–1 paperback

Library of Congress Cataloging-in-Publication Data
Alcock, Antony Evelyn.
A short history of Europe : from the Greeks and Romans to the
present day / Antony E. Alcock.
p.   cm.
Includes bibliographical references (p.   ) and index.
ISBN 0–312–21003–5 (cloth). — ISBN 0–312–21036–1 (paper)
1. Europe—History.   I. Title.
D20.A47 1997
940—dc21   97–34338
                                                          CIP

For Mary
whose idea this was

Contents

List of Maps

Foreword

During the last twenty years European studies has become a popular degree option for undergraduates and postgraduates alike. The subject is most profitably taught as an inter-disciplinary enterprise, combining language and literature tuition with exposure to the insights of the political scientist, the economist and the historian. This learning process has both academic and practical utility: on the one hand, the subject matter represents a major theme in the Western intellectual tradition, offering a rich and sustaining diet of scholarly literature. On the other, those inducted into European studies have every opportunity to prepare themselves for a variety of careers in which an understanding of Europe's past and present will be invaluable – even if its impact cannot be easily quantified.

Indeed, it might be argued that pioneers of European studies in Britain were more perceptive than their political masters, for many of whom the European idea was unfamiliar, indeed hostile terrain, scarred by memories of Europe's two civil wars. For them, to quote L. P. Hartley's famous remark. 'The past is a foreign country. They do things differently there'. But at least a younger generation – benefiting from Brussels-supported schemes of staff and student exchange – will be less insular.

Yet even the most ardent proponent of European integration would acknowledge the danger implicit in exploring the implications of the current debate about Europe's future at the expense of a proper and sophisticated understanding of Europe's past. It is not enough – in my view – to focus solely on events since 1945, important as they are in any explanation of the course of European integration and its institutionalisation in supra-national structures. A fuller appraisal requires a grasp of political ideas, social and economic process, and the evolving pattern of conflict and co-operation – the characteristic features of European history. Thus we must probe the experience of Greece and Rome, the medieval period and what followed as Europe began the long haul to modernity.

Crowded syllabuses, and the pressing need to combine disparate disciplines, often make it difficult to introduce students to Europe's seemingly remote past. Yet the effort must be made, if only to provide those we teach with a long view of the past in the hope that the present will be correspondingly better understood. For without such understanding, we will too easily assume that our current preoccupations are unique, that those who grappled with intractable issues in the past have nothing to tell later generations.

After all, the Greeks understood the balance of power as well as their eighteenth and twentieth century counterparts. Equally, those who seek some understanding of the role of ideology in the twentieth century can certainly learn from the experience of the religious wars of the seventeenth century. Similarly, those who wish to understand why the nation state continues to command loyalty and sacrifice might well find an answer in the historical record and – in particular – the rise of nationalism as perhaps the most potent of all ideologies.

Thus, historical study provokes the shock of recognition that we have been here before, that current debates over notions of equality, justice and sovereignty have historical antecedents.

It is in this spirit that I am delighted to commend Antony Alcock's *A Short History of Europe*. It offers a straightforward, meticulously researched account, one which provides the student with clear and detailed analysis. An experienced and perceptive teacher of European studies, Professor Alcock – in writing this account – has acknowledged the need for demonstrating how many of our current preoccupations derive from the past and the decisions of earlier generations of policy-makers. Edmund Burke may well have been right when he claimed that 'You cannot plan the future from the past'. But without some grasp of that past the student will all too easily be lost in the 'booming, buzzing confusion' of the present. Future generations of undergraduates and postgraduates alike will have cause to be grateful for a stimulating introduction to a major area of European studies.

J. E. SPENCE
Associate Fellow
Royal Institute of International Affairs

Not to know what happened before we were born is to remain perpetually a child. For what is the worth of human life unless it is woven into the life of our ancestors by the records of history.

Cicero

I said, 'Perhaps the Russians will explore some nice empty planet and allow people like us to go and live on it.'
'No good to me', said Valhubert. 'I wouldn't care a bit for oceans on which Ulysses never sailed, mountains uncrossed by Hannibal and Napoleon. I must live and die as a European.'

From *Don't Tell Alfred* by Nancy Mitford (Hamish Hamilton, 1960)

1 Ancient Greece 2000–280BC

With the exception of the Basques in Spain and the Ugro-Finnic group (Hungarians, Finns and Estonians), all European peoples speak Indo-European languages, which include Celtic, Germanic, Italic, Slavonic and Greek.

The home of the Indo-Europeans was in the region between central eastern Europe and southern Russia, and about 2000BC they began to migrate in two directions: westwards into Europe and south-eastwards into Asia Minor and India.[1]

It was in the period 1850–1600BC that the westward group penetrated what is now Greece, gradually infiltrating the area and merging with the original Mediterranean population mostly living in coastal areas.

The first Greek civilisation was that of Mycenae, based on a community in southern Greece, the Peloponnesus, although other communities were established in such places as Athens and Thebes as well as the islands of the Aegean sea and even along the coast of Asia Minor. These Mycenaeans were both warriors and traders and are believed to have overthrown in the fifteenth century BC the brilliant Minoan civilisation on Crete that had been founded by migrants from Asia before the second millenium. This opened the way for trade with Italy, Sicily and Egypt It was probably trade that brought the Mycenaeans into conflict with Troy, a city near the entrance to the Dardanelles. The sack of Troy in about 1200BC by the Mycenaeans under their king, Agamemnon, and the aftermath, provided the inspiration for Homer's eighth century BC epic poems, the *Iliad* and the *Odyssey*, the first works of European literature which in turn provided numerous themes for classical Greek tragedians and later European playwrights.

But hardly a century after the Trojan War the Mycenaeans were themselves overthrown by new-comers from the north. These were Dorian and Ionian Greeks who were militarily superior to the Mycenaeans because they had weapons of iron whereas the latter only had bronze.

Over the next three centuries these Dorian and Ionian Greeks not only took over the Mycenaean settlements on the mainland but also those on the islands, including Crete, and along the coast of Asia minor.

1

It was from these settlements that city-states or '*polis*', developed, small self-contained communities, areas for common security, perhaps around a fortress on a hill and controlling the local countryside in order to be as self-sufficient as possible in food.

What was important about these city states was that the ways they governed themselves provided the foundation of European political thought and experience. At various times some were ruled by one person, a king or a tyrant, (Sparta even had two kings), some by an aristocratic or wealthy élite, and others by the citizenry as a whole.

But although all these city-states were Greek, that did not prevent bitter rivalry, frequently ending in armed conflict. By the sixth century BC two city-states had become prominent – Sparta and Athens.

Sparta developed a society that was based on a military-style disciplinary education in which male children were taken from their families at the age of five. It enabled Sparta to have the largest army and become the most efficient – and feared – military power in Greece and to dominate the Peloponnese. It was probably the Spartans who developed the characteristic army of the ancient Greeks, infantrymen heavily armed with a shield, short sword and a nine-foot long thrusting spear, formed into phalanxes eight ranks deep. Athens, on the other hand, had gained a reputation for the arts, through the holding of drama festivals and games open to all Greeks (the Olympic Games were started in the seventh centuryBC) and by the construction of splendid buildings and temples.[2]

From 750–550BC Greek civilisation spread around the coasts of the Black Sea, North Africa, Italy, and southern France. One important reason for this expansion overseas in large numbers was the poor soil in Greece, which was unable to provide for a growing population. Another was the need to develop maritime trade and commerce. Colonies were established at places ideal for trade and where raw materials, particularly metals, could be obtained. A colony would be founded by a mother-city. Although politically autonomous, the colony usually retained contact with its parent.

It was in this period too that an economy based on money rather than barter was introduced, due to the development of coins by the rich and cultured Kingdom of Lydia which controlled the western coast of Asia Minor.

What was important about city-state culture was the basic belief of its citizens that they owed their personal and spiritual development to their city-state; that they would be better off in their own city-state than in another. This required that the city-state should aim to improve the lot of the individual citizen; that the purpose of the government should be to help the citizens in the search for a harmonious happy life.

This fostered four things:

The first was an ethos of the rule of law. Rule by the known laws of the city-state, commonly agreed upon by its citizens and applicable equally to all, was better than rule by the whims of despots accountable perhaps to the Gods but to no one else. The expression of this can be seen in *The Politics* of Aristotle in which the author provided a list of six forms of government, three good and three bad. The good forms aimed at satisfying the general interest; the bad forms related only to the advantages to be gained by the individual or group concerned.

Thus under monarchy, or kingship, there was rule by one person, pre-eminent because of his virtues and political capacity. He might be above the law but ruled according to it. Under aristocracy (from the Greek *aristoi* – the best) rule was by a small group of pre-eminent virtuous persons who nevertheless respected the law. Under polity, or what might be called 'constitutional democracy' (from the Greek *demos* – the many) there was rule by the many, the majority, but again respecting the constitution of the state.

The converse of monarchy was tyranny, rule by one man, not required to give an account of himself and governing in his own interest. Tyrants could be elected to govern a city-state – and some were – but they were nevertheless tyrants rather than kings because rule was according to their personal decisions. Under oligarchy, rule was by the (usually wealthy) few in their own interests, their chief concern being to preserve their position and wealth. The converse of polity was democracy, condemned as destructive rule by the mob, manipulated by demagogues.[3]

Second, there was the emphasis on the individual liberty of the citizen. The Greeks were the first to realise that liberty was an essential for the development of an individual's imagination and intellect.

Third, and following on from the previous two, the city-states provided a framework for freedom of thought and speech leading to an intellectually enquiring, questioning society unlike any other in the Ancient World. Anything could be investigated with no consideration except the logic of facts to determine the outcome.[4] Greeks therefore pursued astronomy, medicine, mathematics, physics and philosophy in the attempt to find and explain the universe. They also discussed social issues. Aristotle, for example, examined whether punishment for a crime should be the same for all, or depend on the standing of the person committing it. He discussed the advantages and disadvantages of private and communal property.[5] It was this freedom of thought and speech that promoted the relatively democratic way of life in Greece as opposed to the rest of the known world rather than *vice versa*.[6]

Fourth, for all the above reasons these city-states fostered not only a Greek national consciousness but one based on feelings of superiority over other societies. It has been said that national consciousness awakens when a group feels two things: that membership of the group gives the individuals concerned a personal dignity; and that the group has a spiritual identity which distinguishes it from other groups, giving it a special mission. Greeks had a feeling of common destiny. They might fight each other, but still looked upon each other as equals. They considered themselves free men imbued, because of that freedom, with personal dignity. A Greek was free, not because he governed himself but because he was governed by a known law which respected him and his rights. The Middle Eastern Empires of Assyria, Persia and Egypt might be wealthier but the peoples in them were not a community but a mass of individuals subject to the despotic whim of kings and priests. The kings and priests were not part of a community but apart from and above the rest. The kings did not fulfil the law – they were above it, ruling like tyrants by arbitrary personal will. They were not responsible to the Gods – in many of the Middle Eastern Empires they *were* Gods. The subjects of such masters were considered by the Greeks as slaves.

This somewhat ideal description of Greek society must not, of course, be exaggerated. The *polis* was really there only for its citizens, those who could participate by right of birth in its administration, rather than for all its inhabitants, because that would include foreigners and slaves. And the *polis* was not only an unequal but a demanding society. The belief that a man would only be able to fulfil his potential as part of a *polis* implied the subordination of the individual to the good of society as a whole, an implication that would find an echo in later philosophies and in the policies of some twentieth century dictators. The family was not considered highly, being seen as a possible rival to the *polis* for its affections. The place of women was certainly not equal to that of men. They were not there to help run the city-state but to be domestic drudges with their main duty to produce children so that these could perpetuate the race, provide labourers for society and protect their fathers in old age. For all intents and purposes they could not own property (except for personal clothes, jewellery and slaves) or do business. At all times they had to be under the protection of a guardian. The foreign resident might have the protection of the law but he did not have the same rights as a citizen and at least in Athens he needed a citizen protector. And the city-states were slave societies. In Athens, for example, the number of slaves might equal the number of free men.[7]

And perhaps a more serious drawback to the city-state syndrome was the fostered devotion to one's city-state. This civic patriotism ensured that if the Greeks had a national consciousness and superiority complex based on language and culture they would find it difficult to sacrifice the independence of the individual city-state and come together voluntarily to unite in one single state.

This individuality and superiority complex would be put to the test when the expansion of the Indo-European Greeks brought them into contact with the other peoples of the eastern Mediterranean.

One such were the Phoenicians, a semitic people who had established a chain of city-states in today's Syria and Lebanon – Tyre, Sidon and Beirut being the most prominent. As seafaring traders these Phoenicians had profited from the collapse of Crete and Mycenae to take a prominent position in the Mediterranean. More than that, their alphabet had been adapted by the Greeks around 1000BC. These Phoenician city-states had also founded colonies. One of them, Tyre, was the mother-city to what was to become the important city-state of Carthage, near today's Tunis. By 650BC and for the next four centuries Carthage would be the dominant commercial and military power in the western Mediterranean, sending traders through the Straits of Gibraltar even to Britain and establishing colonies of its own in Spain.

But there were also the despotic kingdoms and empires of the Middle East. With Lydia, whose control of the western coast of Asia Minor included a number of important Greek city-states, relations were good. It was a very different story with the Persians who were also an Indo-European people but from the south-eastern migration of 2000BC.

In 546BC the Persians overthrew the Kingdom of Lydia, and by the turn of the century had not only captured the entire Middle East, including the Phoenician cities, Egypt and North Africa up to Cyrenaica, but had crossed the Hellespont into Europe and penetrated as far as Thrace. This brought the Greeks face to face with an aggressive and imperialistic power which surrounded them on three sides For the next two centuries Graeco-Persian relations would dominate the policies of the eastern Mediterranean.

In 499BC the Greek cities in Asia Minor revolted against the harsh rule of the Persians and appealed to Greece for help. Athens provided help but because of political differences Sparta did not. Feeling that he would never be able to subdue the Greeks in Asia Minor unless their support from Athens was crushed, the Persian King Darius I decided to strike at Athens. In 490BC he sent an army of 50 000 men by sea which landed at Marathon, twenty-five miles from Athens, and there the Athenian heavy infantry inflicted a crushing defeat on the Persians, pushing them back to their boats with little loss to themselves. The news was brought to Athens by a runner, Pheidippides, and his feat is commemorated today in the footrace of that name.

Ten years later the Persians tried again. Darius's son Xerxes arranged for Carthage to attack the Greeks in Sicily, while, having built a bridge of boats across the Hellespont, he himself marched into Greece at the head of a huge army. At the same time the Persian fleet was sent to manoeuvre off the Greek coast.

This second attempt likewise met with disaster. In Greece itself there was agreement to bury differences, and a defensive alliance was concluded by the city-states under the leadership of Sparta, the only state which could be said to have a professional army.[8] Although the Persians defeated a small Spartan army at Thermopylae and went on to sack Athens, that was the limit of their success.

During the previous ten years the Athenians had not been idle. They had been building a navy (the so-called 'wooden walls' of the city), and it sank the Persian fleet off Salamis while the Carthaginians were defeated in Sicily. The following year the

Spartan army got its revenge at Plataea and the Athenians won at sea again at Miletus. The Greek city-states in Asia Minor were liberated.

For the Greeks there were three results of the war with Persia. First, the political and intellectual independence of the Greeks in Europe was secured. Second, there was a tremendous rise in Greek morale at what was seen as the triumph of the Greek way of life, of freedom over despotism. Third, these victories signalled the rise of Athens. Its central position, excellent harbour and powerful fleet enabled the city to take over the commercial and cultural leadership of the Greeks. This was the start of the 'Golden Age' of Greek civilisation, in tragedy and comedy, history and philosophy, architecture and sculpture.

The three most famous Greek tragedians were Aeschylus (525–456BC), Sophocles (496–406BC) and Euripedes (485–406BC). Their plays explored such problems still of relevance today as the nature of good and evil, the conflict between spiritual values, the demands of the state or family, the rights of the individual and the nature of divine forces and human beings. Comedy, particularly by Aristophanes (444–380BC) was used to ridicule politicians or too clever intellectuals or even to deliver a political message. The History of the Persian Wars by Herodotus (484–425BC) took as its theme conflict between Europe and Asia and was the first work of European history. These were the years when Socrates (469–399BC) developed his method of challenging ideas through logically constructed questions; when the Parthenon was constructed on the Acropolis of Athens (447–438BC) and the Temple of Zeus was built at Olympia.[9]

However, if Athens was admired for its cultural leadership, it became so powerful and arrogant in the fifty years following the defeat of the Persians as to cause fear and resentment. To guard against a revival of the Persian threat Athens formed a naval confederacy of most of the maritime city-states of the Aegean based on the island of Delos. The members of this Delian League had to provide money, ships and men. But when Naxos wanted to leave the League on the grounds that the danger from Persia was over Athens treated the threatened secession as a rebellion and crushed it. Other Aegean States were forced to join the League. Athens then had transferred to itself the League's headquarters and its treasury and required all commercial disputes between members of the league to be settled in Athenian courts. Athenian coins, weights and measures were gradually introduced into the other cities of the League.

But inter-city-state rivalry was still playing an important part in Greek politics. When Athens discontinued the anti-Persian alliance with Sparta and made a treaty instead with one of Sparta's enemies not only Sparta but its allies Thebes and Corinth felt threatened, and tried to exploit the resentment of Athens in the Delian League.

After some preliminary skirmishing in the 450s, war between Athens and Sparta broke out in earnest in 431. The Pelopennesian War, chronicled by Thucydides, lasted for twenty-seven years, and in many ways was like a contest between a whale and an elephant. The Spartans could invade the Athenian hinterland but since the Persian war the Athenians had built the so-called 'Long Walls' of fortifications enclosing both their city and its port of the Piraeus and making it impregnable. On the other hand the Athenians used their fleet to attack the Spartan coast and ensure food supplies. Victory came to Sparta in the end when it built a fleet which defeated the Athenians at Aegospotami in the Dardanelles in 405BC. Athens was besieged by land and sea and, facing starvation, surrendered in the following year. Sparta now assumed the leadership of Greece.

Unfortunately Spartan leadership was even more unhappy than that of Athens. Rulers governing in Sparta's interests were installed in most Greek cities. When some of the cities – Athens, Thebes, Corinth – rebelled they invoked Persian help and Sparta was defeated. But the potential resurgence of Athens alarmed Persia into switching sides. Peace between Athens and Sparta was brokered by Persia but the price was the surrender of the Greek cities in Asia Minor to Persia. Sparta then turned against Thebes but was defeated. Thebes, however, did not enjoy its supremacy for long. The continual wars had exhausted the city-states and the days of their independence were coming to an end. For in the north of Greece a new power was rising that would conquer them all.

Macedonia had hardly counted as a part of Greece. The Greeks considered it wild and primitive but the royal family claimed to be Greek. In 359BC Philip II became King of Macedonia. He dealt swiftly with internal and external enemies, in the process gaining Macedonian access to the Aegean. The striking force of his army was strengthened by the introduction of a long pike to replace the traditional thrusting spear, a heavy cavalry arm and siege artillery.

He then found a pretext to intervene in the Greek inter-city-state conflicts to the south.

His victories, including the capture of Thessaly, and Thrace with its gold mines, as well as pressure on the allies of Athens and Thebes to come over to him, led the two to form a League against him, but Philip crushed it at Chaeronea in 338BC. The following year at Corinth he formed a league of all the Greek city-states except Sparta under his leadership.[10]

Now the great debate in the decade before Chaeronea was whether the Greeks should unite to drive out the Macedonians, as advocated by the great Athenian orator Demosthénes, or unite with Macedonia against the Persians and liberate the Greek cities of Asia Minor, as advocated by another Athenian, Isocrates, and Philip himself. The victory of Chaeronea resolved this argument and in 337BC the decision was taken to attack the Persian Empire. But the following year Philip was assassinated and the leadership of Macedonia, the League of Corinth and the Persian campaign devolved onto the shoulders of his son, Alexander, aged twenty.

Accordingly in 334BC Alexander, at the head of an army of 50 000 which included a number of non-Macedonian Greeks, crossed the Hellespont into Asia Minor and advanced on the Persian Empire.

A Persian army hurriedly gathered together by the western satraps (provincial governors) was immediately defeated at the river Granicus after which the Greek cities of Asia Minor were liberated and the area put under Macedonian rule. But a problem for Alexander was the danger from fleets under Persian control operating out of the coastal cities of the Levant. Accordingly he headed for Syria and Lebanon. In November 333BC a second Persian army led by King Darius III in person got behind him and tried to cut him off at Issus but was routed, leaving Alexander free to take the Phoenicean cities one by one and continue on to Egypt which submitted peacefully. To guard the mouths of the Nile Alexander founded the city that bears his name. Retracing his steps Alexander entered Mesopotamia and in October 331BC at Gaugamela on the Tigris he vanquished the Persian army for a third time, Darius fleeing from the field. Alexander then had himself proclaimed King of Asia and, on capturing Persepolis, the capital of Darius, burnt it in revenge for the sack of Athens in 480BC.

When Darius was found dead a few months later, murdered by one of his satraps, Alexander proclaimed himself as his legal successor. But instead of settling down, his energy and will to dominate

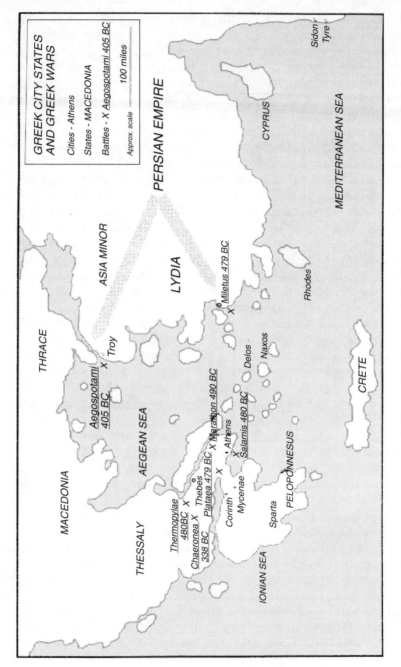

1 Greek City States and Greek Wars

led him to spend the next five years marching the length of the former Persian empire, through the mountains and deserts of Parthia, Bactria and Afghanistan, to Samarkand and as far as the Indus river in today's Pakistan, winning remarkable victories over the local inhabitants. He even wished to go further into India but by then his soldiers were weary of the continual campaigning and absence from home and mutiny forced his return to Persia.

Alexander was now head of three political groupings – Macedonia, the rest of Greece (Sparta had joined the Corinthian League after its attempt to spark a revolt had been suppressed), and the former vast Persian empire. But how was he to bind them – particularly the peoples of the Middle East – to him? Alexander's great significance was his vision of all these territories and the multitude of peoples in them as one community.

One thing that had struck the Greeks about the peoples of the Middle East was their religiosity. Alexander realised that if his power there was to rest on a popular basis that basis must be religious.[11] Accordingly, wherever he went he identified himself with the chief God of the area, and therefore claimed worship. To this end he even re-introduced Persian court ceremonial which included prostration before the King-God. His Greek followers and subjects did not like these developments. They were free men; they resented acknowledging as a God (let alone being obliged to bow down before him) a man many had known personally as a comrade in arms.

The second step in Alexander's plan was to fuse Greeks and Persians so as to create a ruling class for his empire. To that end he organised a multiple marriage ceremony between 10 000 of his Greek officers and soldiers with Persian women. He had already led the way by marrying a Persian princess. Persians were given equal rights with Greeks and taken into the Greek army. But the Greeks were not enthusiastic about the loss of their separate identity, let alone the challenge to the feelings of cultural superiority, which fusion implied.

Alexander's empire was thrown open economically. The hoarded wealth of the eastern empires was melted down and turned into coin which was used as the basis for a common currency. Barriers to trade and the movement of peoples were removed; markets were put in touch with one another. In the next generation thousands of Greek traders and artisans would enter this wider world to seek their fortunes.[12]

There were three consequences of the implementation of Alexander's vision by him and his successors.

The first of these was the expansion of Greek civilisation throughout the Middle East. Greek became the great international language. Towns and cities were established not only as garrisons but as centres for the diffusion of Greek language, literature and thought, particularly through libraries as at Antioch and the most famous of all, at Alexandria in Egypt which would be the finest in the world for the next thousand years.

Second, this internationalism spelt the end of the classical Greece of the city-state and everything it stood for. Most city-states had been quite small in terms of citizenry and this was considered to be a good thing. The focus of life was the *agora* the open market place where assemblies could be held and where the issues of the day, as well as more fundamental topics such as the purpose of government or the relationship between law and freedom, could be discussed and decisions taken by individuals in person. Plato felt that the ideal city-state should have about 5000 citizens because to the Greeks it was important that everyone in the community should know each other. In decision-making the whole body of citizens together would have the necessary knowledge in order generally to reach the right decision, even though the individual might not be particularly qualified to decide. Aristotle, who lived in the third century BC, when the city-state system was declining, believed that a *polis* of 100 000 simply would not be able to govern itself.

But that implied that the city-state was for the amateur, the all-rounder, the jack-of-all-trades but not necessarily the master of any one. It implied a respect for the wholeness of life and a consequent dislike of specialisation. It implied economic and military self-sufficiency.

At Alexander's birth city-states like Athens, Sparta and Thebes seemed to the Greeks large and powerful. When he died mainland Greeks looked out on an Empire which stretched from the northern shores of the Black Sea to southern Egypt; from Sicily in the west to the Indus river in the east. But with the development of trade and commerce came the growth of cities. It was no longer possible to be a jack-of-all-trades. One now had to specialise, and with specialisation came professionalism. There were getting to be too many persons to know; an easily observable community of interests was being replaced by a multiplicity of interests. The city-state was simply too 'small-time'.

Third, Greek philosophy was opened up to the religiosity of the East.[13] In the heyday of the city-state religion played an important part. Not only were there the famous Gods on Mount Olympus, Zeus, father of the Gods and Hera his wife, Aphrodite (Goddess of Love), Apollo (God of Light), Ares (God of War), Athena (Goddess of Wisdom), Dionysus (God of Wine and Entertainment), Poseidon (God of the Sea), but there were the spirits which obeyed Zeus, like the Furies and the nine Muses. And each city-state might have local deities as a protector or protectress.

But these Gods were made very much in Man's image. They were considered in supermen/women terms. Their worship was linked to the rituals connected with one's progress through life, birth, marriage, death, invoking protection against danger, in the taking of oaths, prophecy and healing, rather than to any code of behaviour.[14] Nor was there much of a theory of an after-life.

After the Peloponnesian War, a life spent in the service of their city-state no longer seemed ideal to Athenians. Socrates was the first person in Greece to propound a morality based on an individual conscience rather than the demands of the state. For this he was accused of not believing in the city's Gods and so corrupting the youth, and was condemned to death by drinking hemlock. Although given every opportunity to recant and even to escape, he refused to do so.

Greek philosophy – even conscience – might complement religion but was no substitute for what has been described as an instinctive and profound craving of Mankind for God. It was becoming difficult for reason alone to fulfil the spiritual void, and that made Greeks receptive to the religious systems of the Middle East, even if they never succumbed to them completely.[15]

The combination of the religious instinct of Asia with the philosophic spirit of Greece created what would be become known as 'Hellenism', to which the two greatest Greek contributors were the Epicureans and the Stoics.

The search for harmony with nature that was so much part of the Greek philosophical ideal led the Epicureans to insist that Nature behaved according to natural laws and no one, Gods or not, could interfere with these.

The idea of harmony with nature was also taken up by the Stoics, founded by Zeno of Cyprus c.320–270BC. Man proposes but the *Logos* (divine reason governing the universe) disposes. To the stoics the *Logos* fashioned the universe into one purposeful, rational, living whole of which human beings were an integral part. It was the substance of a human being's soul. The wise person realised that nature was divine and all that happened was part of a rational plan. Humans should therefore not only bow to the inevitable but welcome it as part of divine providence.

Stoics rejected the City and the State as the source of a person's significance or dignity. All were citizens of the world. Social distinctions were meaningless since everyone carried out the intentions of this divine reason. It was the Stoics, therefore, who gave the world the idea of the brotherhood of man which complemented Alexander's political vision. It was they who postulated the idea that natural law was superior to man-made law. They posed a number of questions that are of relevance today:

> If everything is ordered by the *logos* how can man be held responsible for what he does?
> How does one reconcile divine will with evil?
> Should a good person try to improve society by participating in it, or should one stand aside and criticise?
> Should one take action when another was being wronged, or pass by on the other side?

During the next three centuries Mithraism and a number of Asiatic and Egyptian cults gradually moved westwards to occupy the Greek spiritual vacuum while Greek philosophical ideas moved eastwards to supplement the religions of western Asia. The intensification of contact between the two under Alexander's successors would prepare the way for Christianity.[16]

There is no doubt that Alexander intended to become master of the known world and unite it. With only one part of that world was he unfamiliar – the western Mediterranean. But while preparing for a campaign against Carthage malaria took hold of his already exhausted frame and he died in Babylon in 323BC aged thirty-three. Asked on his deathbed to name his successor Alexander is alleged to have replied, 'the strongest'. So for the next forty years his kin, his generals and their relatives and descendants fought it out amongst themselves for his inheritance.

By 280BC Alexander's empire had disintegrated into a number of independent but fragile monarchies; amongst the most prominent being Macedonia, ruled by the family of Antigonus; Egypt, ruled by the family of Ptolemy; and the territories of much of the former Persian empire, ruled by the family of Seleucus.

Nor was Alexander's vision pursued. He may have wished to fuse Greek and Middle East society but his successors in the Middle East were more interested in the maintenance of Greek cultural supremacy over 'barbarians'. Thus, for example, they staffed their state administrations with Greeks and non-Greeks would only be employed if they learned Greek. The Middle East was not, therefore, assimilated.[17]

Nevertheless, for all the imperfections of their society in practice, the postulation of individual freedom under a known law and a rational approach in all matters were the great contributions of the ancient Greeks to European civilisation, providing a firm foundation upon which to build for their successors, the Romans.

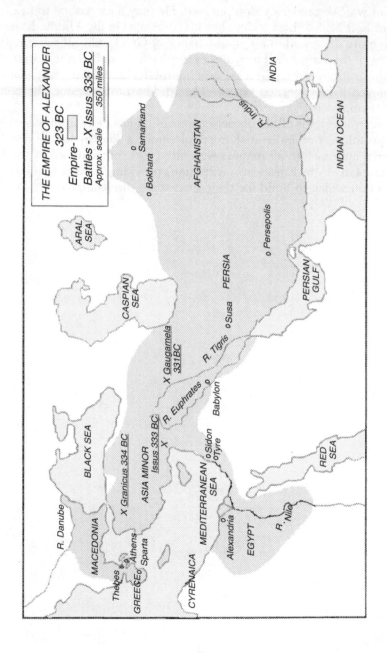

THE EMPIRE OF ALEXANDER
323 BC

Empire-

Battles - X *Issus 333 BC*

Approx. scale   350 miles

INDIA

R. Indus

AFGHANISTAN

o Samarkand

o Bokhara

INDIAN OCEAN

ARAL
SEA

PERSIA

o Persepolis

CASPIAN
SEA

PERSIAN
GULF

X *Gaugamela*
331BC

R. Tigris   o Susa

R. Euphrates   o Babylon

BLACK SEA

X *Granicus 334 BC*

ASIA MINOR

Issus 333 BC
X

o Sidon
o Tyre

MEDITERRANEAN
SEA

RED
SEA

R. Danube

MACEDONIA

Thebes o   o Athens
GREECE o Sparta

CYRENAICA

Alexandria
o

EGYPT

R. Nile

2 The Empire of Alexander

2 Rome: Republic and Empire 753BC 565AD

Legend has it that the city of Rome was founded on the plain of Latium by the twin brothers Romulus and Remus in 753BC. It was merely one city among many in the Italian peninsula, surrounded by a number of tribes, Etruscans to the north in today's Tuscany, Sabines in the centre east of the Tiber, Samnites in the central Apennines and Campania to the south.

The initial development of Rome as a city and militarily was influenced most by the Etruscans, who themselves had learned the art of pottery, military organisation and the alphabet from the Greeks. The original government of Rome was monarchy, but in 509BC the last king was ousted and a republic established.[1]

For the next 250 years Rome was involved in a struggle for control of Italy south of the river Po. Having made allies with the other city-states of Latium, Rome proceeded to take the Etruscan capital in 396BC, suppress a revolt by its Latin allies in 338BC and fight three wars against the Samnites between 343BC and 290BC, subduing them. The only setback was when Rome was sacked in 387BC during a brief incursion into Italy of Celts, whom the Romans called Gauls. But the conquest of the Samnites in Campania brought the Romans into contact with the Greek coastal trading cities of southern Italy. Alarmed at the rise of Rome these cities called for help from King Pyrrhus of Epirus, in mainland Greece. The so-called Pyrrhic War lasted from 287–267BC and the Romans were again victorious, taking all southern Italy.

Rome had been successful. But how was this success consolidated so as to lay the foundation for the state that was soon to take over the Mediterranean world?

First, in all territories they conquered, the Romans planted colonies in strategic locations. Second, these colonies were linked to Rome by road. Third, Italy was divided into territory either directly administered by Rome, which included the colonies and towns with privileges of private and/or public citizenship and amounting to one-third of the peninsula, or ruled by 'allies' of Rome whose relations with Rome were determined by special treaty but who were allowed their own municipal administrations. Fourth, all those

17

involved in what amounted to a Roman confederation had to provide a military (and in the case of Greek cities, naval) service. Fifth, Rome decided all questions of war, peace, foreign policy and the coinage.[2]

Rome was undoubtedly helped by the fact that these tribes had no common consciousness like that of the Greeks.[3] It would be for Rome to provide it. But other factors were also helpful. One was determination, particularly to learn from failure. The other was opportunism. Rome did not set out to conquer the world; it merely took advantage of the opportunities that presented themselves. The result was that if it took Rome 250 years to conquer Italy south of the Po it took half that time to become mistress of the Mediterranean world.

The great power in the western Mediterranean was Carthage, which controlled most of the African shore, southern and eastern Spain and the islands of Corsica and Sardinia and the western part of Sicily. And it would be support for rival Greek cities in Sicily that would bring Rome and Carthage into conflict in three wars.

Rome appreciated the agricultural wealth of Sicily and its strategic importance to the security of southern Italy. Rome, like Sparta before it, had an army but lacked a fleet, without which it would not be possible to get to grips with Carthage. The problem for the Carthaginians was that behind their navy the army was mostly made up of mercenaries. Rome therefore followed Sparta's example and built a fleet which, in the First Punic War (264–261BC), despite initial defeats, eventually triumphed. Sicily was captured and Rome established control over the western Mediterranean sea. Three years later, taking advantage of domestic troubles in Carthage, Rome seized Corsica and Sardinia.

The Second Punic War (218–201BC) rose from rivalry in Spain. To compensate for the loss of the islands Carthage had expanded its empire in Spain in order to get manpower for its armies and to exploit copper and silver mines in the south to get revenue. Carthage and Rome had, however, divided Spain into spheres of influence but soon fell out. Denied control of the sea, the Carthaginian leader Hannibal led an army of 40 000, including elephants, from Spain through southern France, over the Alps and into Italy. But though he defeated three Roman armies – at the Trebia and Lake Trasimene in 217BC and Cannae in 216BC, he lacked the means to capture cities. Almost all Rome's allies stood firm, and after the defeats the Romans refused to meet him again in pitched battle, adopting the delaying tactics of the consul Quintus Fabius Maximus. Hannibal was thus left to wander frustrated around Italy.

When the Romans, under the command of Publius Cornelius Scipio, drove the Carthaginians out of Spain, Hannibal was recalled home but Scipio pursued him and in 202BC at Zama, utterly defeated the Carthaginian general outside his capital. In the peace treaty Carthage gave up Spain, which became a Roman province, and promised not to go to war without Rome's permission. Rome was now the dominant power in the western Mediterranean.[4]

The opportunity for triumph in the eastern Mediterranean came through the support offered to Carthage in the Second Punic War by Macedonia. During the period 215–148BC Rome took advantage of Greek inter-state rivalry to fight four wars against Macedonia and its allies as a result of which the Macedonian and Seleucid kingdoms became Roman provinces and were divided up. Only the Ptolemies in Egypt from Alexander's successors, together with Numidia and the reduced Carthage now remained independent, and Carthage was soon to go. Arguing that it had gone to war against an ally of Rome without the latter's permission the Romans took the opportunity to raze Carthage to the ground during the Third Punic War (149–146BC), and turn its hinterland into another Roman province called Africa, one furthermore also rich in agriculture.

During this period of the Republic the government of Rome was effectively in the hands of the Senate. This was a body of three hundred members from old landed aristocratic families. It was from the ranks of the Senate that the Republic's chief magistrates or executive officers, Consuls and Praetors, were chosen. There were two Consuls, chosen annually, who administered the government by joint decision and commanded the armies. The Praetors administered justice. The Senate was not, however, a legislative body. What it did do was to give advice to the Consuls and Praetors, advice which was not lightly to be disregarded. There were also a number of popular assemblies. One, the *Comitia Centuriata*, the people organised in army units, actually elected the Consuls; another, the *Comitia Tributa*, was the people organised by areas of domicile and would later develop into the Assembly of the People. The officials of these assemblies were known as Tribunes, who became for all practical purposes officials of the Republic.[5]

These were the years when Rome gained a reputation for rectitude and conscientiousness in public life.[6] But would these virtues survive the changes inevitably consequent upon Rome's transformation in status from city-state to world power? The answer was no.

In the century following the end of the Second Punic War not only the character but the moral fibre of the Roman Republic changed. For this there were a number of reasons:

First, as Rome expanded to control the Mediterranean it became the centre for trade and commerce. There was a massive inflow of wealth. Formerly Rome had been comparatively poor; now, a new class of plutocratic businessmen would rise, the 'Knights'. Their wealth gave them a political influence that would be one source of challenge to the Senate, but they were more interested in personal power and profit than in civic virtue, and insinuated a climate of greed, indolence and luxury far removed from the stern spartan patriotism that had defeated Hannibal. Their interests were in financial speculation and control of the government agents involved with the contracts for construction, supplying the army, mining operations and the collection of taxes. This climate of greed spread to the government of the increasing number of provinces. Those sent out to govern the provinces had an absolute control of local armed forces, the administration and justice. But they only had a limited time in office. They might be made to answer charges of corruption on their return, but in the meantime Rome was far away and there was no trained bureaucracy to control them.[7]

Second, there was the rise of a dispossessed and poor class that would also come to pose a challenge to the Senate. Many small yeoman farmers would find their holdings taken over by large estates – *Latifundia* – owned by rich absentee landlords who saw that grazing paid better than growing corn. Dispossessed, they would drift to the cities, especially Rome, to swell the numbers of those unable to find work and often starving. Riots would begin to become a feature of life in Rome. In the meantime slaves were imported to work the land they had left, and corn was imported from Sicily and Africa to feed and appease the Roman populace; games to entertain it would come later.[8]

Third, there was the professionalisation of the Roman army. As the territory under the control of the Republic expanded more men were required, and required for long periods of service. The days of contingents from Rome and its allies, raised from those who had spare time from farming, could no longer be sustained. And armies needed commanders. Ambitious persons, ex-consuls in far off provinces, would ensure that the army would henceforward be the key factor in Roman politics until the end of the Empire.

During the years 113–100BC the Consul Gaius Marius, who had conquered Numidia, introduced a number of military reforms. Traditionally the Roman army was a conscript one of small landowners. Marius, however, recruited volunteers from the landless proletariat. These volunteers swore an oath of loyalty to the general rather than the Senate, thus paving the way for a professional army at the whim of its leader rather than the state. Marius also developed the six thousand man legion in ten cohorts of six hundred as the backbone of the increasingly formidable Roman army.[9]

For the next hundred years Roman history would be characterised by the struggle for power between a number of successful political leaders backed by troops loyal to them.

Three such prominent men were Marcus Crassus, who had crushed the Spartacus slave revolt; Gnaeus Pompeius (Pompey), who had eliminated piracy in the eastern Mediterranean, ended a long-standing anti-Roman revolt by Mithradates, King of Pontus, annexed Syria, and reorganised Asia Minor by installing client rulers favourable to him; and Gaius Julius Caesar, governor of Spain.

These three formed the First Triumvirate, 60–53BC. Caesar became Consul and was given command of the armies in Illyria and Gaul; Pompey became governor of Spain; Crassus received command of the army in Syria, where a new and dangerous threat to Rome had appeared, the Parthians.

It was Caesar who had the most spectacular success. It was only in 118BC that the Romans established themselves solidly in southern France, annexing today's Provence and Languedoc in order to ensure communications with Spain. Taking advantage of requests from some Gaulish tribes for help against the invading Helvetii, he marched north into Gaul and in 58–52BC conquered today's France and Belgium, setting the frontiers of the Roman state on the Rhine.

Crassus was defeated and killed at Carrhae by the Parthians in 53BC, and the following year Pompey was elected sole consul. However, he was manoeuvred into a breach with Caesar by the latter's enemies in the Senate. Caesar resolved to settle matters for once and for all with the Senate, and in 49BC with his army crossed the river Rubicon, which marked the boundary between his command and the Roman state, and marched on Rome, thus inaugurating a second civil war. Pompey withdrew, first to Greece, where he was pursued by Caesar and defeated at Pharsalus, and then to Egypt. But on landing there he was murdered by the advisers of Ptolemy XIII, co-ruler of Egypt with his sister Cleopatra, with whom he was also at war. When Caesar arrived shortly after, he took Cleopatra's side, defeated her brother and installed her as queen after which he enjoyed a famous love affair with her from which a son, Caesarion, was born. But Pompey's sons and supporters were still alive and it would be three years before Caesar defeated them in North Africa and Spain.[10]

In 45BC Caesar returned to Rome where four years previously he had been proclaimed dictator for life. His first object was to consolidate his hold on power. He began by uniting in his person a number of the Republic's offices, including the Consulate and the Tribunates. Magistrates and provincial governors loyal to him were appointed, and the Senate increased to nine hundred members, also on that basis. His supporters abroad were rewarded by receiving Roman citizenship. He introduced measures of economic and agrarian reform, extended the franchise to provincial cities and legislated on municipal government. Cisalpine Gaul was admitted to citizenship as were colonies of veterans planted in Greece, Africa, Gaul and Spain.[11]

Although he had also been magnanimous to his opponents in Rome there were still many who resented his dictatorship, especially those who feared not only for the survival of the Republic and its institutions but wished for the return of its values. Their particular exponent was the former Consul Marcus Tullius Cicero, a formidable orator, but with a considerable literary reputation as well. He believed the political system was blameless, merely degraded by its participants, and had been a reluctant supporter of Pompey in the civil war. He was joined by two other Pompey supporters, Marcus Junius Brutus and Gaius Cassius. The Liberators, as they called themselves, believed that with the death of Caesar the Republic would be saved. Accordingly they and a number of conspirators assassinated him in the Senate on the Ides of March in 44BC.

The Liberators had, however, miscalculated the level of their support in Rome. Fleeing abroad to rally their support, they were pursued by Caesar's heirs, his nineteen-year-old great nephew

Octavian, his chief military commander Mark Antony and the governor of Provence, Marcus Lepidus. These three formed the Second Triumvirate, which defeated the Liberators at Philippi in Greece in 42BC. Brutus and Cassius committed suicide. Cicero was proscribed and later murdered.

The triumvirs then divided the Roman world between them. Octavian took the west, Antony the east, and Lepidus was given Africa. But it was the first two who were the strong men and it would be between them that the struggle for control of the Roman world would lie. The outcome would be significant for European history.

In the east Antony soon came under the spell of Cleopatra. Egypt was a wealthy kingdom, and Antony became increasingly attracted to life there, rather than Rome. The Romans were afraid that if Antony won, the centre of the Roman world would switch to Alexandria, and Octavian accused Antony of giving away Roman territory to Cleopatra.

In the war that followed, the naval forces of Antony and Cleopatra were decisively defeated at Actium off southern Greece in 31BC. The celebrated couple fled back to Egypt and committed suicide on the approach of Octavian's army. The following year, Cleopatra's son and heir by Caesar, Caesarion, was killed, and Egypt was annexed as a Roman province. The Mediterranean had, at last, become a Roman lake.

Had Antony and Cleopatra won at Actium they might indeed have transferred the capital of the Mediterranean world from Rome to Alexandria, a better strategic and commercial site, and in place of a Rome-dominated empire there would have arisen a cosmopolitan world empire as dreamt of by Alexander. What made Actium one of the decisive battles of the world was that it prevented Europe from changing its cultural axis.[12]

It was in 27BC that the Senate conferred on Octavian the title of Augustus by which he is better known. For someone who was to be the first Roman emperor Augustus was careful to have himself seen merely as the 'first citizen' of the state, seeking to maintain republican institutions and ensuring that the powers that he received were approved by them. But these powers were considerable and laid the foundation for the change not only to imperial but even to divine status. From 31–23BC he was Consul and thereafter received further powers which made the consulship unnecessary, including control of the armed forces and the provinces. The army now took the oath of allegiance to him directly. As Tribune he controlled Rome, with the power to propose laws and veto any item of public business. In 12BC he was appointed Pontifex Maximus, head of Rome's state religion.[13]

At home he tried to create an Italian patriotism by getting all the people of the peninsula to look on Rome as part of their heritage and to take pride in its achievements. The Knight class was expanded on a property evaluation basis, and together with freed men it was brought into the government and civil service, thus opening careers to men of talent. Augustus's position made it difficult to challenge his choice of candidates for election, but the result was that the role of the popular assemblies declined.

Rome's religion was really based on the pantheon of Greek deities. As Pontifex Maximus, Augustus was determined to revive Rome's religion and make it into a focus for national patriotism. A temple-building programme was begun. The title of Augustus implied a semi-divine nature, and on his death he was voted divine honours, a precedent for future emperors.

It was also in the reign of Augustus that the now considerable frontiers of the Empire were basically fixed and arrangements made for their control and defence. The army consisted of twenty-eight legions, some 150 000 men (later it would be raised to thirty-three), but this was clearly not enough, and so another 130 000 auxiliary troops were raised from among the subject peoples, sometimes from those along the frontiers, which would also be a cause for problems in the future. In addition, Augustus created a force upon which he could rely for his protection and use to control Rome, the nine thousand-strong Praetorian Guard. Eight legions each were placed to guard the three most vulnerable frontiers – those of the Rhine, the Danube and Syria.[14] Attempts to extend the boundaries of the Empire met with mixed fortunes. Under Augustus, an attempt to extend the frontier from the Rhine to the Elbe ended in the disastrous defeat of the Teutoburger Forest in 9AD when three legions under Publius Quintilius Varus were annihilated by the German tribes under Arminius (Hermann). This battle too was one of the most significant in European history. It has been claimed that had the Romans conquered Germany European history would have been very different. One culture, not two in unending conflict, would have dominated the western world.[15] As it was, the defeat struck a blow at Roman prestige, and made Rome apprehensive of what the German tribes could and might do. On the other hand, if the German tribes could not then appreciate the phenomenon of German nationalism, their successors would always look on the victory of the Teutoburger Forest as the first proof of German greatness, and see Hermann as their first hero. And thus the failure of Varus ensured that the problem of the German people and their place in Europe would dominate the Continent's history for the next two thousand years.

More success was had with Dacia, trans-Danubian Romania today. The Emperor Trajan annexed it in 106AD. But of greater importance was the conquest of today's England, begun under the Emperor Claudius in 43BC and finally accomplished by the Emperor Hadrian who built the boundary wall which bears his name in 120AD along the line of the Tyne and the Solway to keep out the tribes to the north. An attempt to push the frontiers even further north to the line of the Forth and the Clyde, the Antonine Wall, was shortlived (142–185AD), because of tribal pressure.

With the frontiers well protected by the legions, the Mediterranean controlled by the Roman fleet, and the Empire bound together by an excellent system of roads, Rome introduced a world of peace, security and order. Trade restrictions between the various parts of the Empire were gradually abolished and this Romano-Mediterranean world fostered the intermingling of peoples, creeds and cultures.

This generally agreeable situation would last for two centuries after the death of Augustus in 14AD. But there were a number of danger signals. Between 162 and 168 the frontiers were penetrated by the Persians in Syria, the Germans crossed the Danube and the Moors of Mauretania invaded Spain. Only with difficulty were they repulsed. Henceforth the Empire would be on the defensive, and by the end of the second century the army had to be increased to 400 000 men. More significant, the principle of imperial succession changed. Rather than members of Augustus's family becoming Emperor, by the end of the second century AD the Emperor was adopting the person he considered most fit to govern, and that meant the person who could control the loyalty of the various armies – on the Rhine, on the Danube, facing the Persians, in Egypt or in Africa. But if the candidate was not generally acceptable, civil war might ensue. However, this emphasis on the military meant increasing expenditure on defence, not only to raise armies but also to retain the loyalties of the troops. The increased expenditure was met by increasing taxes, and soon the burden of taxation would become crushing for all who had to pay. In order to provide a sense of cohesion and instil loyalty to the Empire as well as raise revenue for the army, the Emperor Caracalla introduced two reforms in 212AD. First, he granted citizenship to all free persons. Hitherto, if Roman citizenship had been open to all without distinction as to race, language and religion, it was usually obtained under particular circumstances, such as for persons becoming freedmen or being adopted as an heir, or for outstanding services. Towns or areas might also obtain it as a reward. The new rule meant an end to distinctions between the ruling class of Romans and the rest; all could now aspire to the highest ranks in government and the army; all were subject to the same body of law. Second, except for those in Italy, Roman citizens, who hitherto had not paid direct, but only indirect taxes, now had to pay them in full.

But it was not enough.

The so-called 'crisis of the Ancient World' began about 235AD as a result of attacks on all the frontiers of the Empire, with the Germanic tribes assaulting the lines of the Rhine and the Danube. Saxons, Franks and Alemans attacked the former, Visigoths (western Goths) and Ostrogoths (eastern Goths) the latter. The Persian Empire renewed its attacks on Armenia, Mesopotamia and Syria, while in the south Moors and Berbers attacked in Africa, Numidia and Mauretania. Once again the tribes were thrust back, although trans-Danubian Dacia had to be abandoned.

In order better to defend the Empire, including providing the money, and indeed to ease the burden of its administration the Emperor Diocletian (284–305) carried out a dramatic reform which was to have a historic long-term significance. The Empire was divided into two, with an emperor called an Augustus in charge of each half. Each of these emperors would adopt their successors, called Caesars, who would succeed them after twenty years, and so on. The dividing line between the two halves of the Empire was the southward turn of the Danube at the town of Var in today's Hungary, extended straight through today's Yugoslavia and the Ionian Sea to Benghazi in today's Libya, dividing Cyrenaica and Tripolitania. But the Augustii decentralised further, dividing their territories with their Caesars so that the Empire was really divided into four. Diocletian set up his capital in Nicomedia (Izmit in present day Turkey); his Caesar, Galerius, had his administrative centre at Sirmium (near today's Belgrade), and was in charge of the Balkans. In the West, the Augustus Maximian controlled Italy and

North Africa, setting up his capital in Milan, while his Caesar, Constantius, was in charge of Britain, Gaul and Spain, with his administrative centre at Trier on the Mosel and with a second centre at York. All these centres were chosen because of their proximity to potential danger-spots. But an important consequence of this decentralisation was that Rome ceased to be the political capital of even the western part, let alone the whole Empire. The Roman Senate lost all say in the government of the Empire.

Under Diocletian and later Constantine, the Army was increased to nearly one million men, but even this did not save the Empire as a whole. The western half, heavily penetrated by the Germanic tribes, collapsed, although continuing in theory until 476. The eastern half, on the other hand, continued for another thousand years. So why did the western half of the Empire collapse and the eastern half survive?

Basically the western Empire fell because it was over-extended and there was a palpable collapse in public spirit and morale.

First of all the frontiers in the west were vulnerable. Once the tribes broke through across the Rhine or Danube there was no second line of defence except the Alps and the Pyrenees

Second, the west – Britain, Gaul and Spain – was less populated, less cultivated and less rich than the east. Much of Britain and Gaul was uncleared forest. And whereas the east numbered nine hundred cities, together with hundreds in North Africa, there were only twenty-eight in Britain and one hundred and fourteen in Gaul. The Germans beyond the frontiers eyed these open spaces with envy. They were familiar with agricultural techniques and stock-breeding and wanted to share Rome's prosperity and security, particularly since they were in turn coming under pressure from tribes to their north and east. What they wanted was to share the empire rather than overthrow it. The result was that with a decline in the population and the need for more troops Germans were increasingly invited within the Empire from the end of the second century onwards to provide farmers and soldiers. By the fourth century the emperors were allowing whole tribes to settle and be given land. Many 'German' regiments were raised, commanded by their own chiefs as 'Roman' generals to resist the next invasion, possibly by their own kin.[16]

Third, there was the army itself. The Emperor was the paymaster of the army. On the one hand there was the principle of the adoption of a successor to the emperor; on the other hand, there

28

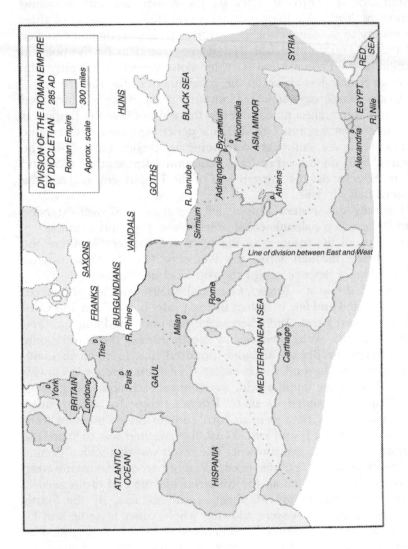

3 Division of the Roman Empire by Diocletian

DIVISION OF THE ROMAN EMPIRE
BY DIOCLETIAN 285 AD

Roman Empire

Approx. scale ——— 300 miles

HUNS

SAXONS

FRANKS

BURGUNDIANS

VANDALS

GOTHS

BRITAIN

York

London

Paris

Trier

R. Rhine

GAUL

Milan

Rome

ATLANTIC
OCEAN

HISPANIA

MEDITERRANEAN SEA

Carthage

R. Danube

Sirmium

Adrianople

Byzantium

Nicomedia

Athens

ASIA MINOR

BLACK SEA

SYRIA

EGYPT

Alexandria

R. Nile

RED
SEA

Line of division between East and West

was his autocratic authority which effectively cut him off from his subjects. To the extent that the emperors were weak in the role (and most of them were) the real power lay with the generals. Most emperors owed their position to the loyalty of the army. But that did not stop generals from wanting to become emperor. From 150–306 no less than eighty generals were hailed as emperor, thirty alone in the years 247–270.[17] The conflicts arising from these rivalries were, of course, an incentive to the Germans to intervene, quite apart from the damage to cities and crops which alienated the civilian population.

And the civilian population, squeezed between the demands of the army and the demands of taxpayers to pay the army was indeed being increasingly alienated.

Diocletian went beyond Caracalla by applying direct taxation to Italy. Ninety per cent of state revenue came from a tax on land, so that the burden fell on the agricultural population. But the tax was not progressive, and if it could not be paid in coin had to be paid in kind. There was a regular conscription system but it was not enforced. People could pay cash to avoid the draft, and there were numerous exempted categories. The inhabitants of cities were considered useless as soldiers so the burden fell on small farmers and peasants. A key class was that of the rich influential landowners, many of them Senators, who now had no part to play in government, and who were accordingly quite openly against the State, preferring to withdraw from public life and concentrate on developing their wealth.

In order to maintain their estates landlords either refused to let men go to the army or sent the worst, conniving at evasions of the draft and even giving shelter to deserters. They also not only evaded taxes but connived at tax evasion by the agricultural population. Many villages voluntarily chose landlords to protest them from official tax collectors, and many small farmers fled to these estates to escape the tax collector, and the landowners were glad of their labour. The state had to tolerate this, being obliged to strike a deal by which the landowners levied taxes on their labour force. But increasingly in their areas the big landowners set up self-sufficient administrations acting as the law, forcibly ejecting the official tax collectors. Since tax collections failed to meet their target and alienated the population, the only alternative for the government was to cut taxes. But if taxes were cut the only sector where expenditure could be reduced was the army, which no government could afford to alienate. The decline in revenue fed through to the civil service and to the extent that it was badly paid the way was opened to rapaciousness and corruption.[18]

Neither did it help that Christianity, increasingly powerful in the fourth and fifth centuries, for reasons given below, was hostile both to army and state. St. Ambrose condemned military service for being not an obligation for all but akin to slavery.[19] Nor did it help that Romans never assimilated their German defenders and, in particular, their governing classes rejected contemptuously the idea that the Germans could be their equals in the Empire. Some of the Germans, who had only wanted to share the Empire, reacted by not becoming Roman after all.[20]

The Empire was therefore in a parlous state when in 375 a two-hundred-year migratory onslaught against it was begun by the German tribes.

The immediate cause was the Huns, an aggressive nomadic people living in central Asia. In that year they invaded the territory of the Ostrogoths in southern Russia. The Ostrogoths moved west and put pressure on the Visigoths, who in 376 were allowed to settle within the Empire in Thrace with promises of food and land. Unfortunately they were shortchanged and treated with contempt by Roman officials. Desperate and on the brink of starvation they united with the Ostrogoths and defeated and killed the eastern Emperor Valens, at Adrianople in 378.[21] The Emperor Theodosius (379–95) bought off the Visigoths and Ostrogoths but after he died nothing could restrain the Visigoths and their leader Alaric. He ravaged the Balkan peninsula and then invaded Italy. In 410 he took Rome.

Although the western Roman Empire is popularly believed to have fallen in 410, Emperors continued until 476 when the commander of the army Odoacer, chief of the Heruli, a tribe with Scandinavian origins, sent the last Emperor, Romulus Augustulus, into a pleasant retirement. Odoacer was well aware that having an Emperor in the west only added to political difficulties for German commanders. Accordingly the western imperial insignia were sent to the eastern Emperor, Zeno, who was recognized as the sole ruler of 'the one and indivisible Empire'.[22] The Empire was theoretically one again, but in fact this was not to be.

Truth to say, the end of the western Roman Empire was an event that was hardly noticed. There was no sudden collapse of Roman resistance against external barbarians. The barbarians had long been providing the army – Alaric's main opponent in the Balkans and Italy had been Stilicho, a Vandal (the Vandals were a Germanic tribe then in today's Hungary), so why should they not assume the real authority as well?

For the one hundred and fifty years following the fall of Rome the migratory penetrations of the western Roman Empire continued. Some of them were spectacular.

After sacking Rome the Visigoths left Italy and established themselves in south-western France and northern central Spain, setting up a kingdom of their own with their capital at Toulouse. It would last from 419 until 507.

The Ostrogoths, after Adrianople, left the lower Danube, and moved to northern and central Italy. In 492 their King Theodoric overthrew Odoacer of the Heruli and set up a kingdom which would last until 563, taking as its capital Ravenna, which had become the capital of the western Empire in 404.

The Vandals crossed the Rhine, passed through France and into Spain where they set up a kingdom in the south. Ejected by the Visigoths they developed a naval capacity which enabled them to cross to North Africa and set up a second kingdom near Carthage from which they seized the islands of the western Mediterranean and even landed and sacked Rome in 455.

The Burgundians, from central Germany, entered the empire and settled around Worms in about 400. After a crushing defeat at the hand of the Huns in 436 they moved to what is now Burgundy and established a kingdom there.

Saxons, Angles and Jutes crossed over from northern Germany and Denmark into England, driving back its Celtic populations into the west and Wales, and establishing kingdoms there (Essex, Wessex, Anglia, Mercia, Northumberland) that would last until the tenth century.

However, undoubtedly the most significant of these Germanic tribes was the Franks. Starting out on the northern Rhine, they entered northern France, establishing a kingdom between the Somme and the Loire under their most famous King, Clovis, and then expanded south. In 507 Clovis defeated the Visigoths at Vouillé and thus took all western and south-western France. He made Paris his capital. Clovis died in 511 but his successors defeated the Burgundians and forced the Ostrogoths to surrender southern France as well, so that by the first quarter of the seventh century the country, with the exception of the Celtic kingdom of

Brittany founded by migrants fleeing England from Anglo-Saxon pressure, was united under the Merovingian dynasty.

Far less successful were the most feared barbarians of all, the Huns. By 430 they had built up a large empire stretching from southern Russia to the Danube. Angered at the refusal of the eastern Emperor, Marcian, to continue paying subsidies, their leader Attila invaded the west, first overthrowing the Burgundians and then advancing on, but failing to take, Paris. In 451 at Chalons-sur-Marne he was brought to bay by a 'Roman' army of Franks, Burgundians, Visigoths and Ostrogoths in a battle described by Gibbon as one in which 'the nations from the Volga to the Atlantic were assembled'.[23] Forced to withdraw, Attila first ravaged northern Italy and then continued east, going back to Hungary. But when Attila died his sons quarrelled over the inheritance; the Germanic tribes in his empire revolted and the Hunnic Empire dissolved, the remnants merging with Ugrian tribes to form part of a Bulgar state in southern Russia, their end unlamented.

In the meantime, the eastern Empire had survived with a certain confidence.

First of all, it was better placed strategically compared to the west. Once the line of the Danube had been broken, the invaders would have to face the Bosphorus and one of the largest and best fortified cities of the Empire, Byzantium, later named Constantinople after the Emperor Constantine who, as sole ruler, moved the capital of the Empire there in 330. The only way round that obstacle and into Asia Minor was by sea, and generally the tribes did not extend their operations in that direction, although the Goths did so, invading Bythinia and ravaging the north coast of today's Turkey (256–270). But these expeditions could not be sustained and the Emperor Aurelian drove them out.

Second, the eastern Empire possessed a sounder social and economic structure than the west. Being more populous, with far more trading cities and better cultivated, it was far more wealthy. To a much larger extent people felt they had a stake in society, and therefore were more ready to pay their taxes, so that the resources of the east were much greater than the west, and the capacity for defence, whether against Persians or barbarians, was thus enhanced.

Third, the eastern Empire was more stable politically. In the period 364–476 there were only two usurpations, both easily suppressed.[24]

Fourth, for reasons that will be explained, the Christian church had a much more positive attitude towards the state in contrast to its hostility in the west.

From 527–565 reigned the eastern Empire's most famous ruler, the Emperor Justinian. His ambition to reconquer the western Empire was nearly successful. After defeating the Persians his great general Belisarius first attacked and destroyed the Vandal kingdom of North Africa in 534, and then crossed to southern Italy, defeating the Ostrogoths, capturing Rome, then their king, and finally their capital, Ravenna.

But the eastern Empire was not able to hold its Italian conquests. In 568, another Germanic tribe, the Lombards, invaded the peninsula. They set up a Kingdom that would consist of all northern, most of central, and even part of southern Italy. Only an enclave round Ravenna, Calabria, Sicily and the area round Naples would remain under the control of what would henceforth be known as the Byzantine Empire. And only sixty years after the death of Justinian another far more formidable threat would arise – Islam.

There was one other consequence of Justinian's failure to re-conquer the west. Justinian could be said to be the last truly Roman emperor. Until his day Latin was regularly used in the civil service, the army and the law, even though few in the eastern Mediterranean spoke it. In 641 the Emperor Heraclius decreed that Greek, the language of the people and the Church, should henceforth be the official language of the Empire. Within a generation, even among the educated classes, Latin became virtually extinct.[25]

The western Roman Empire might have fallen, but despite its degeneration in the last one and a half centuries, those living in the ensuing Dark Ages would retain the memory of a framework which had nevertheless held in relative peace and stability a large number of different peoples and civilisations. The framework may have been held together by the army and civil service but it was built on law.[26]

According to tradition, around 452bc three commissioners were sent by Rome to Athens and other Greek city-states for the purpose of finding out what was most useful in their legal systems. The result was the Twelve Tables of Laws, so called because the laws were engraved on bronze tablets and placed in the Forum. These formed the basis of subsequent Roman law. The tablets only existed in fragments, having been destroyed by the Gauls during the sack of Rome in 390bc.

In the beginning, under the Republic, besides the Twelve Tables, law was founded on custom, that is, customs long observed and sanctioned by the consent of the people over time. Thereafter it was systematically developed by edicts of the tribunes and the formal opinions of jurists when asked specifically on points of law.

Roman law was divided, on the one hand, into '*ius civile*', or civil law, which applied to Roman citizens. Under the Republic all citizens were subject to the law, and citizenship conferred both civil (family and property) rights and political (election and employment) rights. On the other hand, foreigners did not have the rights of Roman citizens and were subject to *ius gentium*, which provided for their protection and generally governed their relations with the Roman state. The distinction between the two would end when the Emperor Caracalla made all inhabitants of the Empire Roman citizens.

Under the Empire, apart from ordinances of the Senate and the edicts of magistrates the most prolific sources of law were the imperial 'constitutions', of which there were three branches. Edicts were general laws ordered by the Emperor. Rescripts were formal answers to questions put to him either by private individuals or public bodies. Decrees were judgements or decisions given by the Emperor in lawsuits brought before him as supreme magistrate either in first instance or appeal.

From the beginning Roman law laid down a number of principles that are the basis of justice today: that every citizen is equal before the law; that he or she must know the charge against him or her; that the accused has the right to defend him or herself or be defended at public expense if need be; that the burden of proof should lie with the plaintiff rather than the defendant; that people of unsound mind could not be held legally responsible for their actions; that there should be a statute of limitation (twenty years for criminal offences); that the notion of intent in the commission of a crime was important.

Roman law laid down court procedure, including the competency of tribunals, summonses (including penalties for non-compliance), the rule under which the plaintiff opens a case and the defendant speaks last, rules of evidence, rules for jury systems (including verdicts by majority, the right to challenge jurors, perjury, verdicts of guilty, not guilty, and non-proven, in which latter case there would have to be a new trial).

Roman law laid down comprehensive family law. One was a minor up to the age of twenty-five. Roman law covered degrees of

consanguinity, marriage contracts, divorce, adoption, the legitimisa-
tion of bastards, laws on the management of minors and the insane.
With regard to inheritance, Roman law dealt with testate and
intestate, debts, disinheritance or exclusion (under Roman law at
least a quarter of one's estate had to be left to one's children, if any),
property left in trust and the revocation or annulment of wills.

Roman law was equally comprehensive in regard to property,
including its acquisition, servitudes, and usufruct; contracts and
their fulfilment; debts and debtors, loans, interest, sequestration,
warranty, partnership relations and the principle of *caveat emptor.*

Roman law gave legal personality to corporations in order to
ensure continuity since the rights of individuals died with them.
Corporation law applied to city councils, schools, hospitals and
business firms. It gave corporations the right to hold property, to
sue and be sued, and laid down rules for the election of office
bearers and the winding up of the institution.[27]

It was in 438 that the eastern Emperor Theodosius II collected all
the constitutions since the time of Constantine (d. 337) and arranged
them in sixteen books covering every aspect of law in what became
known as the Theodosian Code. This was promulgated as law in the
east and adopted in the west by Valentinian III.

A far more ambitious attempt to reform and codify Roman law
was undertaken a century later by Justinian. He sought to remove
all contradictions and repetitions and also to see that laws were
compatible with Christian teaching. A commission was therefore set
up to examine all legislation and imperial constitutions still in force,
with powers to make changes so as to adapt these laws to the
existing state of society. Justinian's *Codex* appeared in 529 and was
the supreme authority for every law court in the Empire. In 530
appeared the Digest, a fifty book codification of all the principal
writings of Roman jurists. Thereafter all previous works were prohibited in courts or schools of law.[28]

However, it would be some time before Justinian's codes became
known in the West.

In the West it was the Theodosian Code that was admired by the
three Germanic kingdoms which had replaced the western Empire,
the Ostrogoths, the Visigoths and the Burgundians. After Justinian's
victories his codes were introduced into Italy and Africa, but in
Gaul and Spain the Theodosian extracts continued. However, while
the Germans allowed Roman law to continue, and drew from it,
they did not allow it to supersede their own laws, which were based

on custom. The two systems existed side by side, and the individual was subject to the one or the other, depending on birth, or even choice.[29]

It would not be until the tenth century that Justinian's codes became fully known in the West and replaced the Theodosian extracts, thus laying the foundation for the legal systems of the countries of western Europe. The chief instruments in their transmission were the Christian Church, which followed Roman rather than German customary law, and the Universities, particularly Bologna, Ravenna and Montpellier.

In England, because the Anglo-Saxon invasions of the fifth century broke the link with Rome, a 'primitive confusion' of Germanic customary law governed society until Roman law returned with the Norman conquest in the eleventh century, contributing, with pre-conquest French and Anglo-Saxon law, to the development in the twelfth and thirteenth centuries of English common law. This common law was based not on codes but on case law following the principle of *stare decisis*. The principle was designed to overcome arbitrary decisions by justices, and the consequences were not only that a uniform legal system was obtained by the ruling of justices rather than Roman law, but the rulings formed the basis of the system of precedent in decision making which would henceforward underlie the development of the English legal system,[30] differentiating it from developments on the continent.

In Germany, because the Holy Roman Empire in the Middle Ages was a mosaic of principalities, bishoprics, free cities, and small territories ruled by Imperial Knights, and different laws applied to municipalities, guilds, knights and peasants, the same legal confusion applied. But since customary law could hardly settle disputes between such disparate institutions recourse to Roman law gradually spread via the Church and the Universities. Nevertheless it would not be until 1495 that the High Court of the Empire adopted Roman law as its guide to the common law of the Empire, and this was followed by the courts of the various principalities and towns.

3 Christianity 100BC–1200AD

The Greeks may have been the first to realise the worth of individual liberty, the Romans the value of discipline and authority, but in both these fields the spirit of man is doomed to anarchy and waste unless inspired by faith.[1] The third great pillar of European civilisation is the Christian religion.

So why did Christianity succeed?

The Gods of Rome were really the Gods of Greece transported and given Roman names. Up to the end of the first century AD traditional Roman religion had an important role to play. It provided, through its rituals, a sense of order and cohesion and was essential in the building of patriotism. The weakness of this religion was that it could do nothing to relieve concern about a world in which everything depended upon oppressive, whimsical chance or fate. It could not fill the vacuum in the soul. So while retaining the forms and attending the ceremonies of the official cults, many people turned elsewhere in the search for strength to endure life on earth and find a happy life in the hereafter. Some sought the answers in astrology. Others turned to the many mystery cults coming to Rome from the Middle East. And thus an epoch began, lasting until the seventeenth century, when people's chief anxieties concerned the after-life.[2]

Magic might alter one's fate, but initiation lifted one beyond, in order to 'be saved' through personal union with a Saviour God who was believed, in many cases, himself to have died and risen again. The initiations leading to this end provided an intense emotional experience. Purifications, sacramental banquets, purged human sin through *ecstasis* (the soul leaving the body) and *enthousiasmos* (the God entering and dwelling within his worshippers). Through the medium of these experiences each Mystery religion gave its initiates comforting promises of immortality. The knowledge that was sought now had to come not through reason but by revelation through union with God, for that alone could provide the secret which would defeat the stars, or chance.[3] And thus Belief came to supplant Reason.

Among the more famous of these Mystery religions was Manichaeism, which sought to get round the problem of how a Good Creator could allow Evil to exist by postulating the co-existence of good and evil powers.

37

A much larger and more popular cult was that of the Egyptian god-dess Isis, with its theme of death and resurrection. According to Egyptian legend the husband of Isis, Osiris, a mythical King and bringer of Egyptian civilisation, was murdered by his brother Seth. His dismembered body was reassembled by Isis who posthumously conceived their son Horus, who fought and overcame Seth. Osiris was then resurrected as King of the Underworld and a symbol of immortality.

The cult of Isis thus promised immortality in an afterlife. The cult was open to all people – Roman citizens, freedmen and slaves. But Isis was, above all, the woman's goddess, 'Holy Mother', and her statues would usually be with the infant Horus in her arms.

A third cult was Mithraism, whose origin was Persian. Mithraism stressed the struggle in the world between the forces of good and evil. The hero of the good, and identified with the light or the Sun, was Mithra. Mithraism – and its theme of struggle – particularly appealed to the military in the Empire.

There were many resemblances between these Mystery cults and Christianity, which sought to answer the same needs – mutual support, posthumous guarantees, a protector who was above Fate,a privileged status such as the world could not give, and ritual and revelation.[4] But there were also great differences between them:

The belief among Christians that the Saviour would come again caused them to view their earthly lives as something transient, that what they did on earth should really be related to the life hereafter.

Second, whereas the Mystery cults provided hope for the individual, Christians believed that Jesus died, not to save any one person, but Mankind as a whole.

Third, Christianity, being originally a sect of Judaism, was uncompromisingly monotheistic. The Mystery cults were not exclusive. People often belonged to several, and they did not demand unconditional allegiance. This gave the devotees of Christianity a unique confidence and fanaticism.

Fourth, again from Judaism, came other pillars of Christianity: the principle of authority; the belief that its followers formed a chosen Race, transcending tribal or national or linguistic divisions; and a binding code of moral conduct, continually stressed in preaching.

But the real strengths of Christianity, the features which in the end caused it to outstrip all its rival religions, were, on the one hand, its Founder's message of faith, hope and charity, extending to women, children, the destitute, those ill or rejected by society, criminals, even one's enemies. This was the message of the Beatitudes: concern for others rather than self. On the other hand, the early Christians were aggressively evangelistic. They wanted to share their new-found life in Christ with other less fortunate. And they were certain that they were right and that they had found ultimate truth and values in Jesus and his teachings.[5]

Christianity was able to spread throughout the Empire for the same reasons as the Mystery religions – the peace and good order of the Empire up to the middle of the third century, made travel easy and safe. And in the eastern part of the Empire, as well as in the educated sections of society in the west, there was the common language – Greek – the language in which the New Testament was originally written.

In its organisation in the first three centuries, Christian communities, usually in towns, would elect Bishops as their spiritual leaders, and these Bishops had the power to choose priests and ordain them, could admit and expel members. Initiation into a community was through baptism and the symbol of participation in the community was Holy Communion.

The activities of these early communities usually involved acts of charity, particularly tending the sick. Financial means of support were mostly obtained through donations to the Church. These were the days when the Church had very little property, and meetings were held in members' houses.

These were also the days when Christianity was persecuted. The refusal of Christians to accept any other Gods, and thus refuse to worship the Emperor or the traditional Gods, made them an easy target. Some emperors were bitterly anti-Christian, none more so than Diocletian, in whose reign the divine nature of the Emperor was stressed.

But shortly afterwards Christianity got its first real major boost, and from the hands of a ruler of the Empire at that, the Emperor Constantine. When Diocletian divided the Empire, Constantine's father, Constantius, was the Caesar in the West, in charge of Britain, Spain and Gaul. When he died in 306, his armies proclaimed his son not Caesar but Augustus, that is, supreme ruler rather than deputy. For the next eighteen years war was waged throughout the Empire before Constantine defeated first of all his western rival Maxentius at the Milvian Bridge before the walls of Rome and then the eastern Augustus Licinius and his Caesar to become, in 324, sole ruler. He would rule alone until his death in 337.

In 313 Constantine promulgated the Edict of Milan, which forbade persecution of all forms of monotheism and, to the extent that this included Christianity, saved Christian congregations from harassment. Why did he do this?

Constantine's account of his favourable attitude to Christianity is quite well-known. In 312, just before the battle of the Milvian Bridge, Constantine, alarmed by reports of Maxentius' mastery of the magical arts, prayed to the 'Supreme God' for help and saw a vision, a cross in the noon-day sky above the sun and with it the words '*In hoc signo vinces*' (By this sign you will conquer). As a result Constantine ordered his troops to emblazon their shields with the Christian monogram made by combining the two Greek letters *chi* and *rho*, and shortly afterwards Maxentius unwisely left the safety of the walls of Rome to be defeated and killed.

Note that Constantine did not declare Christianity to be the official religion of the Roman Empire. He wanted to rule his Empire in peace and if Christians were now very numerous there was no reason to offend those, still in the majority, who were not. Nor was Constantine himself converted to Christianity until his death-bed. He had been a worshipper of the Unconquered Sun. If the story of the cross in the sky is true, Constantine may have interpreted it to mean that his own God was recommending worship of the Christian God, and he therefore continually identified the Sun with the Christian God, a belief made easier by the tendency of Christian writers and artists to use sun imagery in portraying Christ. For them Christ was the source of light and salvation, and a mosaic from a third-century tomb found under St. Peter's, Rome, even showed him as the Sun God in his chariot.[6]

It was Constantine who, in 321, ordered that 'the venerable day of the Sun' be the rest-day in the week. Previously Christians had held the Jewish Sabbath, a Saturday, sacred. When the pagan symbols eventually disappeared, the Unconquered Sun was the last to go.

What Constantine did do was treat Christianity as his favoured religion. He lavished gifts on the Church. The clergy was exempted from taxation and the jurisdiction of secular courts if accused of civil crimes. He allowed high church dignitaries to become part of the civil administration. And he donated the Lateran Palace in Rome to the Bishop of Rome.

It was Constantine who changed the date of Christmas Day, originally celebrated on 6 January, to 25 December, the most important day of the year for the cult of the Unconquered Sun, since it was from then on that the sun began to be reborn as the days grew longer.

There can be no doubt that the Christian church took over many ideas and images from paganism and the Mystery Cults. The Roman winter festival of Saturnalia, 17–21 December, was the period for merrymaking, the giving of gifts and the lighting of candles. The veneration and portrayal of the Blessed Virgin Mary, the mother of Jesus, stemmed from Isis, and particularly from images of the goddess holding her son Horus. The cult of saints and martyrs was developed so that chapels would be built over their tombs and they themselves would be adopted by cities just as previously Greek and Roman cities had a god or goddess as a patron.[7]

But Constantine's significance did not lie merely in his support for Christianity. His decision to move the capital of the Roman Empire to Byzantium would have profound and unforeseen circumstances both for the history of Europe and the development of the Christian religion. In the West the Church, Roman and Catholic, would become a rival to the state and engender one of the most enduring debates in political history, one that would dominate the Middle Ages, namely, which one was superior? In the East the Church, Greek and later Slavonic Orthodox, would be not a rival to the state but an integral part of it, an institutional tradition that would outlast the eastern empire and be continued in the states where Orthodoxy flourished right up to the present day.

Constantine's decision to choose Byzantium as the capital of his Empire was based on a number of reasons: the greater danger to the Empire perceived as coming from the Persian Empire and the Germanic tribes of the lower Danube; the greater economic resources of the East compared to the decline in the West; and the city's splendid defensive position, being surrounded on three sides by water. But there was also a religious factor. As someone who believed, after the Milvian Bridge, that he was responsible for the protection and development of the Church, he was affronted by the traditional paganism of Rome, whose élites despised Christianity.

He would try to counter this by an extensive programme of church building, and indeed saw Rome as the chief shrine of the Christian faith, but he was never happy there.[8]

And near Byzantium a crisis in the Christian church was calling for his attention.

As the Church expanded it began to include people and ideas from many different backgrounds. It had to fight pressures from paganism and Judaism, to sort out attitudes to contemporary customs and culture, and decide between beliefs and opinions about issues on which there were no precedents to guide its thinking.

When Constantine became master of the East in 324 he found a dispute raging between Alexander, bishop of Alexandria and his presbyter, Arius. The issue was the relationship of God the Father to God the Son. Arius maintained that the Son was created by the Father, and therefore could not truly be divine like the Father. Alexander and his bishops considered this view heretical and excommunicated Arius, but Arius found plenty of support elsewhere.

The Church, or rather Alexander, asked Constantine for help and Constantine was delighted to intervene. After all, the Roman Emperor was *Pontifex Maximus*, and had prime responsibility for maintaining good relations between his people and their Gods.

Constantine therefore called a Council at Nicaea in 325. This was the first 'ecumenical' (general) council, and he often presided over its sessions. Indeed it was he who proposed the reconciling phrase *homousios* (Greek: 'of one essence': today's version is 'of one substance') to describe Christ's relationship to God the Father.[9]

Arius, however, refused to accept the word, and even worse, Alexander's successor, Athanasius refused to accept repentant Arians back into the fold, so church unity was frustrated and the Arian controversy dragged on after Constantine's death, troubling his sons who succeeded him. Generally the eastern part of the Empire was inclined to support Arius while the western part supported the Nicaean solution. Where the Arians scored a big success was with the conversion of the Goths and Burgundians on the borders of the empire in 340, through the mission of Ulfilas. He translated the Bible into Gothic, a task for which he had to invent a Gothic alphabet.[10] That the Goths were Arians would have an unexpected consequence a century and a half later.

Constantine's intervention established, at least in the East, the rule that the Emperor had everything to do with the Church. He believed that it was just as important to achieve and maintain a uniform tradition as it was to decide what the correct tradition was. Thus whatever church leaders agreed upon in an ecumenical council was immediately pronounced as law by the Emperor. Those who dissented were labelled as 'schismatics', deprived of office and banished.

In practice, in the East, the Emperor was considered the living image of Christ, and he was head of the Church. Constantine was seen as God's chosen deputy. The Imperial power was seen as the earthly reflection of God's heavenly power. The Emperor not only presided at Church Councils, he had the right to approve all candidates for the post of Patriarch of Constantinople, the eastern equivalent of the Bishop of Rome. It was up to the Emperor to set out official religious policy, especially in regard to forms of religious behaviour and attitude to sects and cults. In the East, therefore, once the doctrine was established that the Emperor was above the Church it was never challenged.[11]

In the West matters developed very differently.

The political decline in the status of Rome as a result of Diocletian's division of the Empire and the decision of Maximian to move the western capital to Milan was further accelerated by Constantine's decision to make Byzantium the new, sole capital of the Empire. But paradoxically it contributed to the rise and independence of a strong western Church.

The divorce in the West between the temporal and spiritual powers arose from the attitude of the Church to the State and its values. To begin with the western Church accepted the idea of temporal supremacy but it soon moved to propounding equality, before claiming outright church superiority.

Thus when the Emperor Constantius, Constantine's son, and a follower of Arius insisted on having western bishops condemn Athanasius, who was still refusing to accept Arians back in the Church, the bishops replied on the basis of the Biblical text 'Render unto Caesar the things which are Caesar's and unto God the things which are God's', that God had put into the Emperor's hands the affairs of state but to Church leaders He had entrusted the affairs of His Church.[12]

The hostility to the state arose from the severity of the Christian moral code. Many amusements of everyday life, such as the theatre, horse-racing, the baths, gladiator and wild beast fights were condemned; some held that a soldier who killed in battle, a judge who sentenced someone to death, the executioner, were all guilty of murder. Divorce was forbidden. It was therefore very difficult to avoid sin, and indeed it was generally felt that those who acquired secular power and administered secular justice could not be free from sin. A career in the public service was thus so fraught with temptation as to be morally dangerous.[13]

Indeed, St. Augustine (354–430), Bishop of Hippo (Carthage) and the first great Christian theologian, although grudgingly admitting that a secular state was necessary for the preservation of religion, was very hostile to states in general and to the Roman state in particular. He taught that people should disobey governments which commanded anyone to do something against their conscience. 'For' he said, 'the Christian is subject to a higher authority and will obey the lower ones only when there is no conflict between them.' However, this disobedience was to be passive, not revolutionary. Government might be bad but it was still ordained by God, and therefore should be borne as part of God's will. However bad things were physically they need not affect one's soul. One should endure the bad things and give thanks that another world existed where all would be free and without pain.[14] As will be seen, these same arguments would be put forward by Martin Luther more than a thousand years later.

Faced with this, there were two choices for the Christian.

One was to plead that man was sinful and the flesh was weak, and to rely on divine grace, mechanically interpreted as being baptised and doing penance for one's misdeeds. It was this attitude that caused a British monk, Pelagius, to preach the doctrine that people could achieve a state of grace by their own efforts, such as being charitable and doing good works. Pelagius equated grace with conscience, and said that people could distinguish between good and evil, and with free will, could choose. For this he was condemned as a heretic through the influence of St. Augustine, who held that Man was from the beginning utterly and hopelessly sinful, and that the only way one could be saved was through the Grace of God. St. Augustine's reasoning was that if Pelagius was correct, then there would be no reason for Christ to redeem Mankind by his crucifixion. However, this also carried the implication of predestination – that God alone could choose to save someone or not. This was another way of trying to reconcile evil creation with a perfect Creator, and divine omnipotence with human responsibility.[15]

The alternative was simply to withdraw from this sinful world and seek a more intimate union with God, far from temptation. People who did this became hermits, living alone in the desert or caves, or forming Christian communities. It was through the latter kind of activity that the monastic movement was started in Egypt at the beginning of the fourth century – monks living in common under an Abbot adhering to a strict discipline. By the end of the century it had reached the West, and found its first great expression in the Monastery of Monte Cassino, south of Rome, founded by St. Benedict in 529.

Monastic life was regulated by the Saint's famous rule. It emphasised the values of agricultural labour, the holding of property in common and the importance of a self-enclosed spiritual world detached from the disintegrating imperial and social life around it. The Rule organised the monastic day, dividing time according to the Scriptures rather than the Roman day or the working day of early medieval man. For example, the division of the day into seven parts derived from the statement by David in the Psalms, 'Seven times a day I will praise thee.' The Rule provided the conditions for an ascetic life: prayer, silence, manual labour, obedience and humility. It arranged the internal organisation of the monastery – discipline, penances, recruitment, and practical rules on dress, food, drink, visits by outsiders. Silence was considered as essential to prayer. Excessive speech increased the possibility of error and sin. The Master should speak and the disciples listen. Manual labour was lauded because 'indolence is the enemy of the soul'. Obedience to the Abbot was the core of Benedictinism, and was held to be the principle sign of humility. Humility was seen as self-abnegation, and consisted of twelve steps, including thinking of nothing but God and allowing His will to replace that of the monk; suffering in silence and accepting the minimum of material comforts; being patient and enjoying all humiliations; dressing simply and finding pleasure in the performance of simple tasks.

But of seminal importance was the insistence on reading, leading to literacy in monasteries and the foundation of libraries in them. One by-product was the collection, preservation and copying of manuscripts and treatises, including texts by Roman – even if pagan – authors such as Cicero, Virgil, Ovid, Tacitus, as well as the translation of medical and scientific works.[16]

The triumph of Christianity came when in 391 the Eastern Emperor Theodosius I, a convinced Christian, ordered all pagan and mystic places of worship to close and forbade people to give donations to these cults so that Christianity became the sole, and thus official, religion of the Empire. Even the Olympic Games were discontinued in his reign on the grounds of their pagan associations, not to be renewed for over fifteen centuries.

But by then the spiritual and political decline of the Roman state allowed bishops to play an active – and often independent – role in government. Indeed, a number of powerful bishops had sufficient authority to weather the collapse of Roman imperial government in the West. One of these was Ambrose, bishop of Milan 374–97, who, as governor of a province had experienced Roman political service before entering the Church.

Ambrose was the first of a long line of Christian prelates who would not only defend the independence of the Church against the power of the state but also argue that in spiritual matters the church was superior to the state. When Theodosius ordered the massacre of some citizens in Greece for refusing to obey his demands Ambrose denounced the massacre and refused to let the Emperor participate in Church ceremonies.[17]

And with the end of the Western Roman Empire the Church became even less inclined to accept theoretical equality between the two institutions.

In the mid-490s the Pope in Rome, Gelasius, would write to the Emperor Anastasius in Constantinople about the so-called Doctrine of the Two Powers stating in no uncertain terms that the spiritual power was superior to the temporal since the Emperor had to look to the Church for salvation and that he should rule for the good of God's people under the guidance of the Pope.[18]

But Church versus State was not the only issue. Parallel to the emerging hostility between the spiritual and temporal powers was the emerging hostility between Rome and Constantinople for the spiritual supremacy itself.

The Christian church in the early centuries had its roots in the cities.[19] In theory all bishops were equal but some were more important than others because of the importance of their cities. The Council of Nicaea had recognised as pre-eminent Rome, Alexandria and Antioch, but in 381 Constantinople was added to the list when the Church Council declared it second to Rome. The bishop of Rome, Damasus, objected on the grounds that it implied that the status of a bishop depended on the status of his city in the Empire. It was he who developed the so-called Petrine Doctrine that the pre-eminence of Rome depended not on its status as the imperial capital but to the bishop of Rome's position as successor of the first bishop, Peter, the rock upon whom Christ had promised he would build his Church. But this doctrine was rejected by the Council of Chalcedon in 451 precisely on the grounds that civil status should govern ecclesiastical status, and the Council went on to declare that the church of the new Rome (i.e. Constantinople) had a legal position similar to that of old Rome. The delegates from Rome left the Council in protest.[20]

Inevitably the question of authority spilled over into doctrine.

After the controversy surrounding the relationship of God the Father to God the Son came that of the relationship between the divine and human nature of Christ. The churches of the Eastern Empire – Antioch, Alexandria and Constantinople were bitterly divided between themselves and within each other. The so-called Monophysites believed that Christ had only one nature, and that although He was both the Son of God and the son of the Virgin Mary yet the Divine absorbed the Human nature and made it one. Rome, however, held that Christ was of both natures but that these were indivisible, exercised through one will. At Chalcedon the Council was inclined to accept Rome's interpretation but the issue did not go away. Over the next two centuries successive Byzantine Emperors persecuted or supported the Monophysites, increasingly to be found in the Egyptian, Syrian and Armenian churches. The issue was finally settled at the sixth ecumenical Council, held at Constantinople in 681, which condemned Mono-physitism, declaring that in Christ there were 'two natural wills and modes of operation without division ... His Human will followed in subjection to his Divine will.'[21]

But there was a price to be paid for alienating the Monophysites. There was no Eastern church unity when it came to facing the rise of Islam after 622, and after Islam overran the Middle East the Monophysites broke away from the Eastern church and set up their own independent churches of which today the Copts in Egypt are the most notable descendants.

Rome and Constantinople may have come together – to their loss – over Monophysitism, but soon afterwards they were to be divided again over Iconoclasm.

In 726 the Emperor Leo III attacked icons, condemning their use in worship as idolatry, and demanding their removal or destruction in all public places and churches. The Pope not only rejected the ban but wrote to Leo to tell him that dogma was not the business of Emperors but of Popes. In reply Leo ordered the removal of Byzantine territories under the authority of the Patriarchate of Rome – Sicily, southern Italy and the western Balkans – to that of the patriarchate of Constantinople. The iconoclasts wanted to replace the icons with traditional Christian symbols such as the Cross, the Bible and the elements of the Lord's Supper. But their views were by no means widely accepted, and many areas of the Empire rejected them. The result was that the issue would bedevil relations with Rome and within the Byzantine Empire itself for another hundred years, providing yet another cause of division in the latter in the face of the increasingly vigorous onslaughts of Islam.[22]

Not, of course, that the Western church had no problems with uniformity. In the west the crucial area was the British Isles. Christianity had existed in England but had been driven back, like its Celtic population, to the west following the collapse of Roman rule and conquest by the pagan Saxons, Angles and Jutes. Christianity had come to Ireland, where Druidism was the main form of worship, in the fourth century brought by missionaries from monasteries in Gaul. It would not be until the fifth century that St. Patrick broke the power of the Druids and founded the so-called Celtic Church in Ireland which, during the next hundred years, thanks to persons like St. Columba, brought the Gospel to Scotland and Northern England.

In 597 Pope Gregory I, determined to convert the pagan Anglo-Saxon kingdoms in England to Christianity, dispatched there a mission headed by his prior, Augustine. Gregory hated heretics (he saw the Eastern church as heretical) and he was determined to secure Christian unity. For him unity was synonymous with uniformity, and in many respects the practices and administration of the Celtic church differed considerably from those of Rome, and would thus need to be brought into line together with the pagan Anglo-Saxons.[23]

To begin with, there was the view held by some influential sections of the Church that the conversion of the Irish to Christianity had been conducted by someone unqualified.[24]

The different administrative structure of the Celtic church was a particular source of criticism. As previously mentioned, Christianity in the Roman Empire had been an urban phenomenon. The key person in this urban community was the bishop. Although monasteries were expanding, and were controlled by an abbot, in the hierarchy of the Roman church they still came under the authority of the bishop, and the bishop himself was part of the central organisation of the Papacy. But Ireland, which had never been part of the Roman Empire, had no centralised organisation – political or clerical. Nor was there anything remotely resembling an urban society. In tribal, rural Ireland monasteries were more suitable as ecclesiastical centres, and that meant that bishops, responsible for spiritual values, were under, and considered less important than, abbots. But there were other issues involved, particularly property and celibacy. Aristocratic families might found monasteries and maintain material rights in them. As for celibacy, which had begun as a voluntary practice in the fourth century and had never been adopted in the East but now faced moves in the West to make it obligatory, the Irish objected, arguing that the heralds of the Gospels were husbands and fathers. But Rome was displeased that Irish abbots were generally not celibate and abbatial succession sometimes passed from father to son.[25]

Other practices which offended Rome included the different Celtic way of calculating Easter (Pope John IV would condemn it as heretical); that in the Celtic church communion was given in both kinds; and that a Celtic bishop could be consecrated by one bishop acting alone whereas Rome required three.[26]

Pope Honorius (625–38) was the first to warn the Celtic church that it did not have a monopoly of wisdom.[27]

In 664 a Synod was held at Whitby in the kingdom of Northumbria between representatives of the Celtic and Roman churches. According to the Venerable Bede's account, the spokesman of the Roman delegation regarded conformity as a matter of belief.[28] The result was acceptance of a number of Roman practices and the Romanisation of Christianity – in England, but not (then) in Scotland or Ireland.

Indeed the Irish showed themselves remarkably reluctant to accept Roman domination. The Celtic church may well have maintained the light of Christianity in the Dark Ages in the West but this soon ceased to be of any account once Rome began to accuse the Irish of ignoring its decisions. Soon church councils on the European mainland were resolving not to recognise Irish prelates and ordering that no one should receive baptism or the Eucharist from them.[29]

The Roman church had been trying to penetrate Ireland from the seventh century onwards but would enjoy little success until the second half of the tenth century when the invasions of the island were undertaken by Norsemen who, back home, had been converted by missionaries loyal to Rome. The Norse towns such as Dublin, Waterford and Limerick elected 'Roman' bishops on the advice of Rome's most powerful agent in the British Isles, the See of Canterbury. The two churches would exist uneasily side by side until in 1156 Pope Adrian IV in his Bull *Laudabiliter* urged King Henry II of England to go to Ireland and root out its 'nurseries of vice', the monasteries whose teaching was unfavourable to Rome, and complete the Romanisation of Ireland.[30]

King Henry's action in doing so in 1171 was the first step in the domination of Ireland by Britain. But although it was crushed at the time, some of the traditions of the Celtic church (communion in both kinds, right of the clergy to marry) would be taken up at the time of the Reformation four centuries later, when the Protestant Church of Ireland would look upon itself as the true church, the restored independent national church founded by St. Patrick, and destroyed by Rome. The consequences of that inter-church hostility haunt the Irish people today.

In Scotland the agent of the Romanisation of the church was Queen Margaret, the half-Hungarian wife of King Malcolm Canmore (1058–93), the conqueror of Macbeth who was the last King of Scotland to be crowned under the rites of the Celtic Church. Brought up at the Anglo-Saxon court of Edward the Confessor of England, she saw it as her mission to eliminate the Gaelic language and culture and replace it by the Anglo-Saxon, and eliminate the Celtic religion and replace it by the Roman. The latter was accomplished during the reign of her youngest son David, 1124–53, when the Roman form of rule and the monastic institutions sanctioned by Rome became the recognised religious institutions of Scotland. For her efforts Margaret was canonised.[31]

4 The Papacy and the Foundation of the Holy Roman Empire 700–1000AD

It has been said that the two great ideas that the Age of Antiquity bequeathed were those of a world religion and a world monarchy; that the doctrine of the unity of God required the unity of the community of those faithful to him, a Holy Empire, one universal temporal state to control and promote that spiritual unity.[1]

In the years following the collapse of the western Roman Empire, amid the economic disruption and the economic uncertainty, one remembered – and yearned for – the restoration of order, an order providing for spiritual and psychological as well as physical security.

But who could provide it? Certainly the Church could not provide it. It had no armies. Furthermore, the position of the Papacy itself was very weak and dangerous. Although the clergy might be widespread, the Pope himself merely lived in a large unruly city, nominally the capital of a duchy of the Byzantine Empire but controlled by its Senate and nobility. And he faced two formidable adversaries, Islam and the Lombards, at a time when his relations with his putative defender, the Emperor in distant Constantinople, were bad.

The prophet Mohammed was born in Mecca in 570. He was a wealthy businessman when he received the call to establish Islam. In Arabia the population was polytheist and for twelve years Mohammed preached monotheism to them in vain. In 622 he was forced to flee to the city of Medina, and it was from this flight that the Islamic calendar began. Rallying his supporters he eventually overthrew the opposition in Mecca, where he returned in 630 to organise the establishment and expansion of Islam.

The essentials of Islam were that there was but one God, and Mohammed was his prophet. There was no priesthood because there was no need for a mediator between a person and his or her God. There were no graven images. There was no distinction

51

between church and state – there was only one society. Moslems had duties of prayer (four times daily), charity, fasting, to go to Mecca at least once in their lifetime, and to know the Holy Book, the Koran. Moslems also believed in predestination – all that was needed was submission to the will of God who had marked out everyone's destiny. To a Moslem Christ was not the Son of God but a mortal. He was, nevertheless, a recognised prophet. Islam recognised both Christians and Jews as 'people of the book', worshippers of the one God, although each religion had its own prophets.[2]

The Arabs were fuelled with fanatic enthusiasm for this new religion. Mohammed died in 632, but by 634 Islam had swept through Arabia, Palestine, Syria and Egypt; by 644 the Persian Empire had been overthrown; from 674–78 Islamic forces overran the main part of the Byzantine Empire, even besieging Constantinople before being forced to withdraw. By 695 Islam had taken over all North Africa. And then in 711 the Moslems crossed the Straits of Gibraltar into Europe. By 720 the Visigoth Kingdom had been destroyed and almost all Spain was theirs. The Pyrenees were then crossed and France penetrated as far north as Poitiers where, in 732, the Franks under Charles Martel defeated the Moslem army and the Islamic expansion into western Europe was halted. Territories under Islamic control were governed by leaders called caliphs, or 'successors' (to Mohammed), and caliphates were established, first in Damascus, and then Bagdad. The first European caliphate was that of Cordoba.

The triumphal progress of Islam had been made easy for two reasons. First, the Byzantine and Persian Empires were very weak, as a result of a long war between them from 606–28, in which the Byzantines had been victorious but both had been exhausted. Second, because of the persecution of the Monophysites as heretics, the Christians of Egypt, Palestine and Syria had little reason to be loyal to the Byzantine Empire. When the time came to choose between Islam and Constantinople, they opted for the former. Islam was tolerant of Christianity. As long as Christians paid their taxes and accepted an inferior status, their lives, property and freedom of worship were guaranteed. For the Pope, however, the Islamic control of the southern shores of the Mediterranean and Spain meant that attacks on Christian Italy and southern France were inevitable.[3]

The Lombards had arrived in Italy from Pannonia in 568 to find a political vacuum. The Ostrogoth kingdom had just been destroyed by Justinian but the Byzantine Empire had not been able to reimpose domination of the peninsula. The Lombard leader was actually related by blood to the Ostrogoth royal line and thus found it easy to step into Ostrogoth shoes.[4] From their capital at Pavia the Lombards took over much of northern Italy and then spread south to the so-called duchies of Spoleto (the Marche and Umbria) and Benevento (Molise, Basilicata, Campania and northern Puglia and Calabria) so that more than half the Italian mainland was in their possession. But the Lombards also wanted the Byzantine territories of Rome and Ravenna, and were misusing church property and revenues in their lands, but despite the threat to both of them, because of the Pope's denunciation of iconoclasm and Ravenna's rejection of it, the Emperor refused to come to their aid. In 751 Ravenna fell to the Lombards. Rome would surely be next. To whom should the Pope turn?

There was only one answer: the most successful military power in western Europe, the Kingdom of the Franks.

The ruling house of the Franks was the Merovingian dynasty, founded by Merovech of the Salian Franks, commander of the Frankish contingent at Chalons-sur-Marne. And of particular pleasure to the Pope was that the true founder of the Frankish state, Merovech's grandson Clovis, had been baptised in 496 by Remigius, bishop of Rheims, who was loyal to the Roman church rather than to the Arianism to which the other Germanic tribes had converted. Under the Merovingian system of government the King chose royal officials (counts) from the property owners of the territories of his kingdom. The Royal household, however, was controlled by the King's chief retainer who was known as the Mayor of the Palace, or *major domo*. As dynastic disputes and weak leadership led to the decay of the Merovingian state so the power and authority of the Mayors of the Palace rose until by the beginning of the eighth century the King was a figurehead and it was the Mayors of the Palace who held the kingdom together.

What drew the attention of the Pope to the Franks was the victory of the Mayor of the Palace, Charles Martel, over the Arabs at Poitiers in 732. With the agreement of the Pope, Pepin, the son of Charles, dethroned the last of the Merovingians and in 751 was anointed King of the Franks. In 754 the Pope personally journeyed to France to ask Pepin for help against the Lombards, with the result that in return for being named a Patrician of Rome (a right which was not in the Pope's gift) Pepin agreed to give any land taken from the Lombards to the Papacy. Following the victory of the Franks over the Lombards that same year the Papacy received Ravenna and the Emilia Romagna, the foundations of the Papal States that would last until Italian unification in the mid-nineteenth century.[5] Twice more the Lombards threatened Rome, and twice the Franks descended into Italy to defend it. On the last occasion, in 774, Pepin's son Charles, the future Emperor Charlemagne, captured Pavia, the Lombard state came to an end, and it was in its capital that Charlemagne had himself crowned King of Italy, with the Iron Crown of Lombardy, said to contain material from the Holy Nails, and this would pave the way for institutionalised Germanic interference in Italian affairs.

During the next twenty-five years Charlemagne waged war on three adversaries. First, to the east the pagan Saxons were bloodily subdued and christianised, with Charlemagne pushing his frontier to the Elbe and establishing bishoprics throughout his new territories. Next was the turn of the Avars, fierce horsemen from Asia but now settled in Pannonia. Their attacks on the eastern Empire had led to them being bought off in gold annually for nearly a century. But when they turned their attentions to the west Charlemagne ordered a crusade against them which ended with their elimination from the political scene. Equally important, the Avar hoard of bullion fell into Charlemagne's hands. Not until the Spanish conquest of the Americas would Europe see so much gold, and it paid for the Carolingian renaissance in architecture, manuscript illumination and sculpture, besides providing a lift for the western European economy.[6] Finally, to the south, following another Arab incursion over the Pyrenees, Charlemagne retaliated, pushing Islam back to the frontier of the Ebro river in Spain itself.

So for the Pope in Rome, looking around for a temporal power to play the part of Roman Emperor and protect Christianity from all that threatened it, there was not much of a choice.

At Christmas in 800 Charlemagne was visiting Rome. The Pope could continue to acknowledge the Byzantine Emperor as the one Emperor, or he could do otherwise. The Byzantine Emperor at that time was actually an Empress, Irene, someone with a very unsavoury reputation – she had even had her own son murdered.[7] Who would want to rely on an imperial family that was proving itself weak and incompetent, with very different views about the Roman church's position *vis-à-vis* the state, and with very different doctrines? On the other hand, present in the city was its Protector, a warrior in the Roman church tradition with a formidable record of victory, whose domains stretched from the Elbe to the Ebro, from Brittany to Pannonia, from the North Sea to Rome.

Accordingly, on Christmas Day 800 Pope Leo III took the opportunity to crown Charlemagne (rather to his surprise) as Roman Emperor, and in doing so he sealed the division of Christian Europe between the East and the West.

The Pope's action was met with astonishment and anger in Constantinople. Since the deposition of Romulus Augustulus in 476 there had been but one Emperor – in Constantinople – and therefore there was only one Empire. In Byzantine eyes civilisation was the union of the temporal Roman Empire with the Christian faith. That union was symbolised by the Emperor himself, as the successor of Augustus and God's ruler on earth. Just as there was one ruler in Heaven so – although he might agree to share his throne for purely administrative reasons – there could be but a single Emperor on earth. As the Empire in the West declined, even before its fall in 410, it was the Emperor in the East who was the true Emperor, and to challenge his authority was not merely treason but blasphemy.

To Charlemagne, brought up under the Salic Law of the Franks, according to which no woman could wear the crown except as her husband's consort, all the Pope had done was to arrogate to himself the right to appoint the Emperor of the Romans, a right which for nearly five centuries had been exercised by the East, and therefore as far as he was concerned the Roman Empire was still one with himself as the Emperor.[8]

Charles offered to heal the rift by marrying Irene. With all the Imperial domains in East and West under one crown the Empire would once again be one. But Irene's ministers refused to surrender their Empire to, as they saw it, an uncouth and illiterate barbarian. When Irene showed signs of accepting the offer she was deposed.[9] It was not until 812 that the Eastern Emperor grudgingly agreed to recognise Charlemagne as Emperor in the West, and thus the Roman Empire was again divided into two. On the one side was Constantinople. If it saw itself as the inheritor of Roman traditions nevertheless its ethos was entirely Greek, having nothing in common with either language or religion in Europe beyond the Adriatic.[10] Indeed, it now exercised power in the West only in southern Italy and Sicily. On the other side was an Empire ruled by Germans, Frank to begin with, Saxon later an Empire that would later become known as the Holy Roman Empire of the German Nation.

The Empire that Charlemagne had created disintegrated soon after his death in 814. His successor was his son Louis the Pious, who ruled until 840, but he was unable to control his three sons, who fought each other while he was alive and after his death. In 843 by the Treaty of Verdun the three agreed to divide the Empire. Charles II (the Bald) obtained the lands in the west, Louis (the German) took the lands in the east, while Lothar, the new Emperor, got the centre – today's Belgium and Holland, the Rhineland, Alsace-Lorraine, Burgundy, Provence and Northern Italy. But the territories of the centre soon became a target of acquisition for the other two, foreshadowing a pattern of political struggle that would last well into the twentieth century. And indeed in 870 by the Treaty of Mersen the Treaty of Verdun was revised, with Lothar's son the Emperor Louis II keeping Northern Italy, but the rest of the centre being divided between the eastern and western Frankish kingdoms.

For the next hundred years these three institutionally weak areas were involved in endemic conflict, not only between but within each other. But two patterns emerged. One was the politico-cultural separation of the East and West Franks. By the end of the ninth century inhabitants of the west Frankish area were speaking a Romance language derived from Latin, that would become French. In the east the Franks continued to speak German. The other was the rise of aristocratic nobilities to replace the power slipping from the hands of weak rulers of the eastern and western Frankish territories. In the east the leaders of the Germanic sub-tribes, the Dukes of Saxony, Thuringia, Bavaria, Swabia, Franconia and Lorraine would develop autonomous powers that in many cases would provide the foundation for future quasi-independent states. In the west the same occurred with the Counts of Paris, Aquitaine, Britanny, Burgundy, Flanders, Toulouse and Normandy.

But the political anarchy in the heartland of western Europe was compounded by attacks on its periphery. The depredations of Islam continued in the south, with Sicily, still part of the Byzantine Empire, being invaded in 827 and finally falling in 878, but being used in the meantime as a springboard for attacks on southern France and the rest of Italy. Rome itself was threatened in 843. In the north and west Vikings from Scandinavia battened on the hapless populations of the British Isles and the West Frankish

57

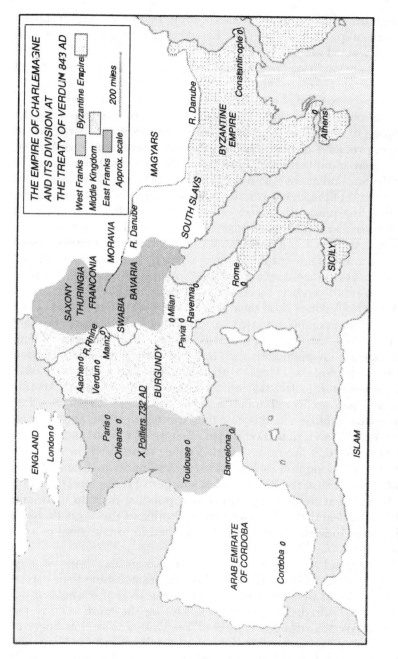

4 The Empire of Charlemagne and its Division at the Treaty of Verdun 843AD

Kingdom, while from the east columns of fierce Magyar horse-archers swept regularly over the East Frankish realm, also penetrating Italy and France.

Until the sixth century Scandinavians had merely been part of the general *Volkerwanderung*, the most notable example being the Heruli whose chief, Odoacer, had deposed Romulus Augustulus. For the next century and a half there was a period of respite for the peoples of mainland Europe. There were domestic struggles at home, problems of land shortage and overpopulation in Scandinavia's cold mountains and northern flatlands had been eased by migration, and there was more concern with the Baltic area. But by the end of the eighth century Viking incursions picked up again. In this first phase the object of raids was loot from areas with a higher civilisation, a particular target being the riches of monasteries, such as Lindisfarne, sacked in 793. These Vikings looked for adventure, fame, profit, danger, women, but also for comradeship. Access to the target area and escape from it was easy. Then, in the mid-ninth century, things changed dramatically.[11]

Hitherto Vikings used their ships for sailing along coasts. Then new techniques, and in particular the ability to fix latitude, enabled them to cross the open sea in relative safety. With problems of land shortage and overpopulation recurring at home, this was the period when in general the Danes came to England and northern France, the Norwegians to Ireland and the islands of the northern Atlantic (Iceland was discovered in 860) and the Swedes to Russia. But they came with a difference: this time they wanted to settle, and a period of conquest and residence began, first in England and then in France. Not that the raids ceased: Vikings penetrated the Mediterranean, attacking and sacking cities in Aquitaine, in Islamic Spain and North Africa, the Balearic Isles, southern France, and even Pisa in Italy. What made things easier was political division in Britain and Ireland and the disintegrating authority of the West Frankish Kingdom. Indeed, Vikings would be invited in to take sides in local conflicts.[12]

In England the Danes overran the Saxon kingdoms of East Anglia, Northumbria and most of Mercia, establishing their capital at York. They were prevented from taking over the whole of the country by Alfred, King of Wessex. During the tenth century the King of Wessex regained control of England, and in 959 Edgar of Wessex was crowned as first King of all England. But the Danes did not give up and sought help from Svein, King of Denmark. Edgar's successor, Ethelred (nicknamed The Unready), tried to buy off Svein's attacks, with money raised by heavy taxes on his subjects. In 1013 Svein mounted a massive attack on England and Ethelred fled to France. But Svein died at the moment of his triumph and final Danish victory over a returning Ethelred was secured at Ashingdon in Essex in 1015 by his son Canute. When Ethelred's son died that same year the people of England accepted Canute as their king, Canute himself taking to wife Emma, the widow of Ethelred who had died in 1016. But Danish England, seemingly secure, would only last until 1042.

In the meantime the Danes, who had been pillaging northern France, sailing up the Seine and its tributaries and even besieging Paris, settled in Normandy. By the Treaty of St. Claire-sur-Epte in 911 their leader Rolf did homage to the king of the West Franks, Charles the Simple (who was also Emperor) and was confirmed in possession of the land as first Duke of Normandy, promising to defend it against other Vikings. In 912 Rolf was baptised. During the rest of the century ties with Denmark were loosened as the Normans became involved in domestic French politics.[13]

In 896 Magyar nomads from the Russian steppes had seized the land between the Tisza and the Danube rivers in today's Hungary. For the next sixty years they launched from there devastating raids throughout the East and West Frankish states, Italy, and on one occasion even penetrating Spain. The Moravian Kingdom was destroyed in 906, Pavia burnt in 924, and Magyar forces appeared outside Rome, Paris and Orleans.

In 911 the last direct descendant of Charlemagne died and for a few decades it looked as if the idea of a restored Roman Empire would disappear too. In the vacuum the Germans began electing a King from among their ducal leaders. In 937 they chose Otto of Saxony and it was he who, in 955, inflicted such a crushing defeat on the Magyars on the Lechfeld near Augsburg that they returned home and settled down, establishing the Hungarian state and, under their ruler Stephen (997–1038), accepting Christianity. For the next five hundred years Hungary would be an important European state.

Otto, too, benefited from his victory. As a result of his military and political reputation, and because the Pope needed his services, the Pope reactivated the Roman Empire by crowning Otto as the first Holy Roman Emperor. Thereafter the Emperors were almost always from the Germanic world, while the Western Franks drifted out of the orbit of the Empire and began the process that would lead, in 987, to the election of the Count of Paris, Hugues Capet, as King, and the establishment of the Kingdom of France.

In the meantime these invasions by Islam, the Vikings and the Magyars had brought about the complete collapse of the western European economy. Society became withdrawn upon itself. The prosperity of Europe in the days of the Roman Empire had depended on the unity and freedom of trade in the Mediterranean. Even after the collapse of the western Empire the economic influence of the Byzantine Empire made itself felt via its Italian possessions in terms of trade and the input of coin, particularly gold. This was now destroyed by the Arabs who, by the end of the ninth century controlled almost all the western Mediterranean except the Italian peninsula, and all the eastern Mediterranean outside the Greek islands of the Aegean, defended by the Byzantine fleet. The west was thus more or less cut off from the Byzantine Empire by sea, while contact by land was hazardous.

But there were many other disincentives to trade. Roads had been built under the Roman Empire mainly for military rather than trade purposes, but as a result of the invasions since the fall of the western Empire these had fallen into disrepair and as trade declined there did not seem much point in repairing them. Travel itself – to fairs – was slow, expensive and dangerous, with transportation by ox rather than horse and with brigandage widespread. Few rivers in the west were navigable for much of a distance from the sea, apart from those in northern France, the Low Countries, the Rhine, the Rhône and the Po. And where was one to travel to? With the destruction of so many towns – and ports – on important trade routes by the invaders, the interdependency of town and countryside under the Roman Empire was destroyed, and as economic activity dried up many towns ceased being centres for fairs and lost their meaning. The bedrock of the western European economy was thus a subsistence, barely self-sufficient agriculture based on the two-field system under which fields would lie fallow in alternate years. Eighty per cent of the population lived on the land.

In any case, what was there to trade? If areas were barely self-sufficient in food there was no reason to trade in food, and such perishable goods hardly travelled well. As for trade in manufactured goods like agricultural or domestic implements, since trade was slow, expensive and dangerous, one aimed for self-sufficiency at home. That only left luxury goods, but what was there to pay for them? With the drying up of the monetary input from the east coins became debased with clipping or minting with an inferior metal and so exchange and barter substantially replaced a monetary economy.

And a declining population ravaged by war and undernourishment and with only primitive medicines to combat disease provided no incentive or demand. A final demoralising blow was the widespread belief that the world would end with the year 1000, so there was no need to bother about anything.[14]

It was in these desperate days that a system of society was created that would be the foundation of western Europe for seven hundred and fifty years – feudalism.

The root of the system was simply the need for peace and order so that society could be restored, at a time when neither the state nor towns could provide adequate protection, when control of society was loose, with few institutions and few officials to administer them.

The basis of feudalism was the marriage between, on the one hand, the old tribal Germanic practice whereby a leader gathered around him a group of companions for whom he was responsible, providing them with food, clothing and arms in return for their loyalty, and on the other hand the landed estates which had developed in the last days of the Roman Empire.[15] The aim of feudalism was to restore and enhance the power of central government by establishing and institutionalising a network of protective relationships, and to establish order and a Christian peace by creating armed forces capable of dealing with Saracens, Vikings and Magyars.[16]

The feudal system was developed by the Carolingian Frank successors to the Merovingians. The threats posed by fast moving mounted Magyars and sea-borne Arabs and Vikings from different quarters meant that the day of the infantryman, the decisive force on the battlefield since the days of Greek phalanxes and the legions of Rome was, for the time being, over. What was wanted was mobility and that could only be provided by the horse. When, during the eighth century the stirrup was adapted by the Franks and riders had a stable platform from which to couch their spears (rather than throw them) and charge home through the ranks of the enemy, a new fighting man was born, the armoured knight.[17]

In order to control his state in the absence of a corps of officials, Charlemagne continued the Merovingian practice of dividing it up into territories(counties), over which he placed nobles (counts, a word derived from the '*comites*' or companions of the old Germanic warrior bands), both to defend and administer them. As the royal deputies they were absolute in their domains, with powers of justice and taxation. The nobles received from the king land in return for military service and the obligation to put into the field a required number of knights. The nobles themselves distributed the land given to them by the king to their knightly followers in the form of manorial estates, and in their turn the knights had to provide soldiers from the estates. The key was land. The manorial estate provided the services and income which a knight needed to arm and equip himself – a string of horses; smithies to forge weapons, armour and horseshoes; a staff of squires and grooms; and labourers to till the soil, harvest the crops and keep the estate in food. From the point of view of the defence of the realm castles were built at strategic points – river crossings, at the mouths of rivers, at important trading places – and put in the hands of the nobles or knights.

From the king downwards to the humblest agricultural worker the system was institutionalised on the basis of oaths of loyalty – by the superior to protect, by the inferior to obey. The noble paid homage, pledging his loyalty to the king, placing himself in his service, becoming his vassal and receiving in return his 'fief', the appropriate amount of land. Likewise the knight paid homage to his superior for his manorial estate. As for the agricultural population, whereas in the eighth century there were still peasants who held land on the old Roman principle that if they were free they had to cultivate that land but not leave it, while others held land in return for labour services, the need for protection in the upheavals of the ninth and tenth centuries led to these semi-independent farmers offering their labour and freedom of movement and that of their children to the lord of the estate, becoming hereditary serfs, bound to the soil. Indeed, a serf whose daughter married outside the estate would have to pay a fine to his lord since the labour of her descendants would be lost to the estate for ever.[18] Feudal relationships were thus personal ones, and were dissolved only on the death of one of the two participants in the act of homage, the lord or his vassal.[19]

The advantage of the system was that it was psychologically comforting. The powerful needed subordinates for their survival and prestige; the protected gained status by being protected by someone powerful. Theoretically coherent, feudalism nevertheless presented a number of problems:

First, in theory on the death of a vassal his fief returned to his lord. But this was a controversial issue. The lord might wish to take the land back on the death of the incumbent, perhaps because the incumbent's son was too young and the territory needed to be given to someone militarily stronger or more capable or even as a reward. On the other hand, to refuse hereditary succession might upset local loyalties and alarm other vassals. Soon fiefs became more or less hereditary, and one consequence was a loosening of the ties between nobility and rulers.[20]

Second, there was the issue of divided loyalties. What should a vassal do if, holding lands from two superiors, these were at war?[21] This problem would become acute when, following the Norman conquest of England in 1066, and later possession of considerable parts of France by the Kings of England, nobles held land in fiefdom to the kings of both France and England.

Third, a very rigid hierarchical society developed in which everyone had his place and social mobility was difficult, if not actually frowned upon. The best chances of social improvement for those at the lower end of the scale lay either in the Church, or by outstanding service in war leading either to promotion or enrichment at the sack of a city or by capturing an enemy knight and holding him to ransom.

All this really demonstrated that war was the hallmark of the feudal age. Society's leaders were associated with being warriors rather than men of learning or trade. The successful leader was the successful warrior.

Feudalism also meant attachment to things local and regional. If it had been introduced to strengthen society, the number of local and regional powers, military and judicial, was nevertheless a factor for weakening rather than strengthening the public authority, the state (to the extent that the word had much meaning in the early Middle Ages) particularly in its ability to protect those for whom it was theoretically responsible.[22]

5 Eastern Europe 600–1100AD

At the time of the fall of the Western empire its Eastern counterpart seemed so strong – strategically more difficult to attack, wealthier and with a higher morale. There were far fewer internal disputes over the leadership; church and state enjoyed good relations as opposed to their mutual hostility in the West; there was a considerable free peasantry in contrast to the serfs on the big landed estates in the West. But it was not long before the political and economic patterns of the West repeated themselves in the East.

The seventh century was a disastrous one. The Islamic conquest of Syria, Palestine and Egypt was doubly shattering. On the one hand, these were the most economically advanced and densely populated areas of the Empire, and their loss meant the loss of considerable tax revenue. The loss of Egypt was particularly significant because it was from there that corn was imported to provide for the large, often unemployed and unruly mob of Constantinople. On the other hand, important religious and cultural centres had been lost – Alexandria, one of the most powerful centres of Greek culture, Antioch, and the holiest Christian city of all, Jerusalem. And the Islamic advance continued. In the 650s the Arabs took Cyprus and Rhodes and the Byzantine fleet was defeated. Constantinople itself was besieged from 674–78 by land and sea (and would be again in 717–18), the city surviving thanks to the invention, during the siege, of Greek Fire, a composition of sulphur, nitre, naptha and asphalt which took fire when mixed with water and was thus particularly effective in naval engagements. Armenia would fall in 691 and North Africa in 697. In the meantime Arab assaults on Asia Minor led to the decline of many hitherto prosperous cities.

The loss of Egypt meant that the corn for Constantinople now had to be obtained from Thrace, but the seventh century also saw deep penetration of the Balkans, including Greece, by Slavs and Avars, who even besieged Constantinople in 626, but above all, by the Bulgars so that Byzantine control of Macedonia and mainland Greece was reduced to a few coastal cities.[1]

As the Germanic tribes moved westwards and broke through the barriers of the Roman Empire their places in the Balkans, Danubian basin and eastern central Europe were taken by Slavonic

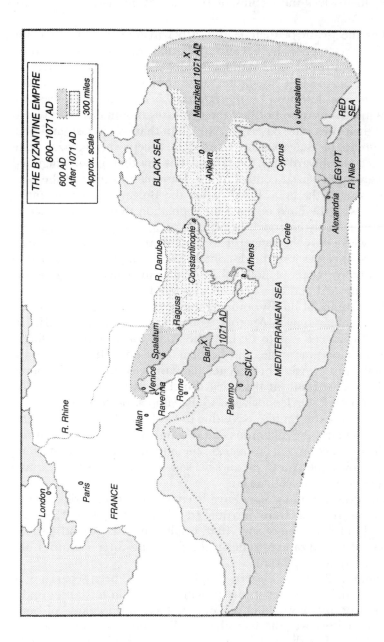

The map shows:

THE BYZANTINE EMPIRE 600–1071 AD

600 AD
After 1071 AD
Approx. scale ___ 300 miles

London
Paris
FRANCE
R. Rhine
Milan
Venice
Ravenna
Rome
Spalatum
Ragusa
Bari X 1071 AD
Palermo
SICILY
R. Danube
Constantinople
Athens
Crete
BLACK SEA
Ankara
X Manzikert 1071 AD
Cyprus
MEDITERRANEAN SEA
Jerusalem
RED SEA
Alexandria
EGYPT
R. Nile

5 The Byzantine Empire 600–1071AD

tribes, themselves the victims of pressure by nomadic tribes from western Asia.

After the death of their leader Attila in 453 in Pannonia, the Huns were set upon by a Germanic tribe, the Gepids, and their kingdom destroyed. The remnants, mixed with a tribe of Ugrian stock, set up the first 'Bulgarian' state round the sea of Azov. But this state was destroyed by the Khazars, a semi-nomadic blend of Turks and Huns from north of the Caucasus mountains, who would set up their own state based on Astrakhan that would last until 969. One group of Bulgars who refused to accept this Khazar state migrated northwards up the Volga, but another group migrated westwards and seized control of the Danubian basin and the Slav populations of the area. It was when the Bulgar upper class inter-married with the mass of the Slav population that the Slav race of Bulgarians finally emerged. In 681 the area of today's Bulgaria was formally ceded by the Emperor to the Bulgarians.[2] When, ten years later Armenia was lost, the discontent in the Empire led to a period of twenty-five years of political instability in which two emperors were dethroned and one of them murdered.

The fortunes of the Byzantine Empire revived when, in 717, the general commanding in Anatolia assumed the purple as Leo III. His first achievement was to destroy the Arab naval and land forces besieging Constantinople, and he then went on to drive the Arabs out of the rest of Asia Minor, feats that paralleled the triumph of the Franks against Islam in the West. But Leo was the Emperor who was responsible for Iconoclasm. Quite simply, he believed that the misfortunes of the Empire were due to God's wrath at society's sins, and particularly the idolatrous cult of icons. When, after inaugurating the destruction of icons in 726, the imperial forces won startling victories over the Arabs, he and his son, the Emperor Constantine V, were even more convinced.[3]

The seventh century may have been a disaster militarily but two important reforms were introduced by the Emperor Heraclius (610–41) and his successors that would lay the ground for the success of the Byzantine state in the following three centuries, the zenith of imperial power.

Traditionally in the Eastern Empire there had been separation of civil and military power in the provinces. Only in territories under prospect of attack was one person, an Exarch, in charge of both. Such a territory was the Exarchate of Ravenna. Beginning in Asia Minor Heraclius divided territory into military districts – *themes* –

under the command of a general, who also was in charge of the civil government. Soldiers in these *themes* were given inalienable grants of land and freed from taxation in return for service. On the death of the owner of the land his eldest son inherited both it and the obligation of military service. Other sons were given land that became available or had fallen out of cultivation because of the invasions, and thus increased the number of tax-paying free peasant farmers. Together with the decline of the cities this reform changed the Empire from an urban to a rural society. It also changed the structure of the countryside. Because of the invasions large estates with serf relations were broken up and transformed into small ones with free farmers. In addition to the *theme* armies of soldier-peasants a central mobile army of full-time soldiers was based on Constantinople.

The second reform involved taxes. Under Diocletian the unit of taxation was an area of land and he who cultivated it paid the tax. But no tax was paid on uncultivated land, nor by those who were neither landlords nor tenants. Under the new system the land tax was payable even if the land was not cultivated. Indeed, the tax on uncultivated land would have to be paid by neighbours, who could, however, take over and cultivate the land. There was also a poll tax to be paid by everyone, later possibly replaced by a household, or hearth, tax.

Quite apart from putting the finances of the Empire on a solid footing (up to the eleventh century the state was never bankrupt), the chief result of the land tax was that it made possible the maintenance of a standing army and navy, so that pressure on enemies could be sustained. It was thus on the peasants of Asia Minor that the Byzantine Empire depended.[4]

Greece was restored to Byzantine control at the beginning of the ninth century, but the Bulgars remained a serious on-going problem. Several times Byzantine armies were defeated and the Emperor had to get tribes from the north, particularly the Magyars, to harass the Bulgarian rear. In 811 the Emperor Nicephorus himself was killed in battle and the Bulgar leader Khan Krum had his skull set in silver and used as a drinking cup. Shortly after, under Krum's successor, relations improved and in 845 the Bulgarians were christianised by monks from Constantinople. But trade disputes caused Byzantine-Bulgar relations to deteriorate again. Under the leadership of Tsar Simeon, the Bulgarian army twice in the early tenth century narrowly failed to capture

Constantinople and bring the Byzantine Empire to an end. Towards the end of the tenth century the Empire, finding a new surge of confidence after victories over the Arabs, decided to deal with the Bulgarians once and for all. After a number of campaigns the Emperor Basil II defeated the Bulgarian army at Clidion in 1014. 15 000 Bulgarians were captured after the battle, and Basil blinded ninety-nine out of every hundred in both eyes and the hundredth man in one eye, and had the one-eyed lead the rest back to their Tsar. The shock killed the unhappy man; his country disintegrated, and Bulgaria was restored to the Empire.[5]

The christianisation of Bulgaria was moving the frontiers of the eastern Church northwards and westwards but from the west Roman Church influences were moving southwards and eastwards. In between them lay their target, southern Slavs (Serbs, Croats and Slovenes) and western Slavs (Czechs, Slovaks and Poles) who, about 600 had moved into the areas they inhabit today.

After the beginning of the ninth century some of the western Slavs united to form the Kingdom of Moravia which soon became an object of competition between missionaries from east and west. Fearing Frankish aggression, Prince Ratislav proposed an alliance with the Byzantine Empire and asked for help to organise his church. The result was that in 863 two brothers, Cyril and Methodius, were sent to Moravia. They knew Slavonic, which at that time was only a spoken language, and translated into it biblical texts and the liturgy. Tradition has it that they also invented the Cyrillic script used today by Russians, Serbs and Bulgarians. The brothers thus not only made Christianity available throughout the Slavonic world, but provided much of it with an alphabet, thus laying the foundation for its literary development.[6]

In the event this Moravian kingdom did not last long, being overwhelmed by the Magyars in 906. Thereafter the christianisation of central Europe, today's Czech Lands, Slovakia, Hungary, Poland, Slovenia and Croatia would be undertaken by the Roman Catholic Italians and Germans, and the areas were lost to potential Byzantine control or influence.

Where the Byzantine Empire was successful was in Eastern Europe and the new power there – Kievan Russia.

The origins of the Kievan state were to be found in the Swedish Vikings who traded and plundered between the Baltic and the Black and Caspian Seas, using the swiftest form of transport, boats on the big eastern European rivers – Bug, Dniester,

Dnieper, Don, Dvina, Vistula, Volga and their many tributaries, as well as lakes such as Ilmen, Ladoga and Peipus and their access waters.

The area covered by these rivers contained many tribes, particularly eastern Slavs, Letts, Lithuanians, Finns and, between the Black and Caspian Seas, the Khazars.

The origin of the word '*Rus*' from which Russian is derived is a matter of some controversy. The larger body of opinion states that *Rus* comes from the Finnish word for Swedes, *Rhutsi*.[7]

In the middle of the ninth century, while many Norwegians and Danes were attacking the British Isles and France, their Swedish counterparts were invited by these east European tribes to come in, settle, and institute order among them and protect them against the Khazars. In 856 the Viking chief Rurik established a state around the town of Novgorod. Fifteen years later one of his followers, Oleg, reached Kiev and set up a state there controlling the Dnieper river.

Oleg's successors extended their control until the Kievan state included all the land between the Baltic and Black Seas and the Dnieper and Volga rivers, including Novgorod, Rostov, Smolensk and the small town of Moscow. Through intermarriage with Slavonic wives the Viking ruling class was gradually assimilated, a process confirmed by their assumption of Slavonic names.

For nearly a century Kiev alternately traded, warred or allied with the Byzantine Empire. Kiev sent furs, wax, honey and slaves to Constantinople, receiving luxury goods in exchange. Even before the establishment of Kiev Russian ships had appeared outside Constantinople with crews plundering the neighbouring towns and monasteries. As they settled down in Kiev the prestige of these Russians, known also as Varangians to the Byzantines, was very high. A century later the Byzantine Emperor was asking them for help against the Bulgars, and Varangians also fought for the Empire against Islam in the Mediterranean. At the beginning of the eleventh century Varangians were even organised as the Emperor's personal guard. One of the most famous Vikings of all time, Harald Hardraada, twice King of Norway, saw service in the Varangian Guard and action in the Mediterranean before falling at the hands of the English under King Harold Godwinson at Stamford Bridge in 1066.[8]

Kievan Russia, like Moravia, attracted religious missionaries, and in 957 the head of the Kievan state, Princess Olga, personally converted to the rites of the eastern Church, but it would be thirty years before the people as a whole were christianised.

For one was still very near Asia. Basil II had called on Olga's son Sviatoslav to help him against the Khazars, and he had obliged by destroying their state in 969 and then going on to help Basil against the Bulgars. But the destruction of the Khazars opened the gates to further waves of nomadic tribes from the steppes of western Asia. First came the Petchenegs who attacked Kiev in 972, killing Sviatoslav (his head too was turned into a drinking cup, this time in gold), and then sweeping on into the Balkans. And behind them came the equally ferocious Cumans.

Sviatoslav was succeeded by his son Vladimir, and as with Prince Ratislav, there was intense competition by religious missionaries to convert not only him but all his people. In addition to the representatives of the Eastern and Western churches there came Jews and representatives of Islam, which had reached the southern shores of the Black and Caspian Seas. In 988 Vladimir chose the Eastern Christian religion for himself and his people. Kiev became a diocese of the Patriarchate of Constantinople, and soon the Church was helping to stamp out paganism. Vladimir also ensured that the language of the Church should be Slavonic rather than Greek or Scandinavian, although almost all metropolitans of Kiev were Greeks, appointed by the Patriarch.[9]

Politically Kievan Russia did not remain a unit for long. By the middle of the eleventh century it had divided up into a number of principalities – besides Kiev the most prominent were Novgorod, Suzdal and Galicia – ruled by descendants of Vladimir, of the royal house of Rurik. However, there were frequent quarrels between the princes, who often did not hesitate to make alliances with outsiders – Hungarians, Poles, even Cumans.[10]

But the great point about society in Kievan Russia was that by and large the people in it were free. There were slaves, but these were of two types – permanent, such as captives in war awaiting ransom, and temporary, when a freeman, for whatever reason, sold himself into the service of another as an indentured labourer, but could later redeem himself.[11]

Otherwise, anyone could own land, so that there were small farms and large landed estates profiting from the rich agricultural soil, particularly the famous 'black earth' of today's Ukraine. And Kievan Russia was commercially thriving, with a large entrepreneurial merchant and artisan class. Textiles, metalwork and furs were produced, and Kiev and Novgorod became key centres on international trade routes – the north and south flowing rivers between the Baltic and Black Seas to Constantinople, and between Germany in the west and the caravan routes across the steppes to Asia in the east. Citizens of large towns paid no taxes and formed their own voluntary militia.[12]

And because society in Kievan Russia was free it was democratic in comparison with other societies in Europe. The princes themselves were not autocratic rulers but rather military leaders and providers of justice. Power was shared, to a greater or lesser extent, with the Council of the Boyars (notables or senior members of the Prince's court who were free to serve or not) and the *veche*, the city assembly, consisting of all adult males of the population.[13] Novgorod, indeed, where the prince was elected, was more or less a merchant oligarchy and the wealthiest of all the principalities.

By the end of the first quarter of the eleventh century the Byzantine Empire was at its height: the Arabs were being held, the Bulgarians had been subdued, and relations with Kiev, heavily penetrated by Byzantine religion, culture and art, were good. But the next fifty years would involve renewed strife with the West, economic and social decay, and ultimately shattering defeat.

Church and State in the Eastern Empire were still quarrelling with Papacy and Empire in the West on points of dogma and the issue of supremacy.

Byzantines considered the Eastern Emperor *the* Emperor. Since Constantine onwards an unbroken series of Emperors had ruled in the same city, exercising supremacy in ecclesiastical and civil affairs. To the Byzantines the Western emperors were German barbarians who had nothing to do with Rome. The Western emperors were recognised only grudgingly, if they had to be, for political reasons. Western emperors, on the other hand, felt it sufficient that their authority should derive from being crowned by the Pope in the city of the Caesars and St. Peter. Italians and Germans alike rejected Byzantine claims. And it was the same with the churches. There had been the Iconoclastic controversy, the long-standing question as to whether the Holy Spirit proceeded from the Father *and* the Son or from the Father alone, and the issues of priestly celibacy (allowed in Constantinople but increasingly being insisted on by Rome), and whether the bread used at Holy Communion should be leavened (as in the East) or unleavened (as in the West). And the Patriarchs of Constantinople, if accepting the senior standing of the Bishop of

Rome over other patriarchates as a result of the 451 Council of Chalcedon, did not recognise Papal rights to interfere in matters of church discipline while on questions of doctrine they would only accept decisions of an Ecumenical Council.[14]

What complicated matters further was the arrival, in increasing numbers, of Norman adventurers in southern Italy, Byzantine territory, in the second quarter of the eleventh century.

These Normans, the most fearsome warriors in the West, were taking advantage of the desire of the local Lombard notables to obtain independence from Constantinople to carve out territories for themselves. They were led, over a period of time, by the thirteen sons of Tancred de Hauteville, a knight with a small landholding in the Cotentin peninsula of Normandy. Regarded as brigands by the Papacy and the Emperors of both East and West, the Normans played off all sides against each other with great astuteness. Thus in 1053 a Papal army was defeated by the Normans, and the Papacy blamed Byzantine forces for not coming to its aid, an accusation which angered the Eastern Empire. The Normans then changed sides and Constantinople learnt that the Normans were imposing Latin customs on the Eastern churches in southern Italy, with Papal approval.[15]

In 1054 a Papal delegation was sent to Constantinople to discuss all these issues, but instead of reconciliation the claims and counter-claims between the Patriarch of Constantinople and the leader of the Papal delegation led to the latter, without any authority to do so, solemnly laying a Papal Bull of Excommunication on the High Altar of St. Sophia's Cathedral. The enraged Byzantines promptly burnt it in public. The Great Schism between the Eastern and Western Churches was thus inaugurated, and would last, except for a brief moment, until the end of the Eastern Empire four hundred years later.

Unfortunately Byzantine successes in the field in the tenth century brought with them the seeds of state decline. They strengthened the economic and military power of the military aristocracy of the generals commanding the *themes*, who began to enlarge their estates by appropriating the properties of their soldier-farmers and tax-paying free peasantry. These were reduced practically to the status of serfs. All this not only had adverse effects on state revenues but also on the number and quality of the soldiers at the generals' command. Basil II, a strong emperor, could keep the *theme* generals under control; his weaker successors could not. And soon the politics of the state were riven by the rivalry between the landed military aristocracy of the provinces and the bureaucratic aristocracy in the city of Constantinople. Attempts to make up for lost revenues by raising taxes led to revolt, and the decline in the quality of the army led to the recruitment of mercenaries, particularly the Varangians.[16]

This was critical, for in the very decade of the Great Schism, and while the Normans were taking control of southern Italy, another lot of very dangerous enemies had appeared in the East – the Seljuk Turks. These were nomads from central Asia who had been hired as mercenaries by the Abbasid Caliphate of Bagdad and converted to Islam. However, in 1055 they overthrew the Abbasids and their leader, Tughrul Bey, had himself proclaimed Sultan.

The Seljuks were also fanatical Sunni Moslems. One object of their hostility was the Shia Caliphate of Cairo, whose domains included Syria and Palestine; another was Christianity.

The Byzantine Empire might have been able to hold the Seljuks in check using forces from the distant province of Armenia. But the Armenians had been deeply demoralised by renewed persecution from Constantinople for their Monophysite beliefs as well as having taxes increased and their militia ordered to be disbanded. In 1063, after suffering several defeats and massacres, Armenia fell to the Seljuks.[17] Syria and Palestine followed, and, as hard-line Moslems, the Seljuks reversed the liberal policies of the Caliphs of Cairo and started to harass Christian pilgrims travelling to Jerusalem.

The year 1071 was a black one for the Byzantine Empire.

In April the Normans under Robert Guiscard captured Bari, the Byzantine capital of southern Italy, and snuffed out the last foothold of the Empire there. The new Emperor, Romanus IV Diogenes, could do little to help. A general and magnate from Cappadocia, raised to the purple as a result of palace intrigues, he had marched with the bulk of the imperial army to the eastern frontiers of the Empire to try and regain Armenia. Four months after the loss of Bari, in the August heat, the Byzantine army, weakened by desertions and treachery, was cut to pieces by the Seljuk Turks on the battlefield of Manzikert. The Emperor was captured but released on promises to surrender certain fortresses and pay a large sum in tribute. But on his return to Constantinople his promises were repudiated and he was dethroned and murdered, whereupon the Seljuks advanced on the Empire, seizing two-thirds of Asia Minor and pushing the frontier to today's Ankara.

The consequence of these events was that the new Emperor, Alexius I Comnenus, swallowed his pride and asked the West for help. The result was to be the Crusades, in which, astonishingly, the Western and Eastern Empires not only hardly ever combined against what one would expect to be their common foe, but the Western crusaders would even sack Constantinople itself.

6 The High Middle Ages: The Power of the Papacy 1000–1300AD

If the eleventh century was bad for Byzantium, by contrast for western Europe it inaugurated the period of the High Middle Ages, a period of three centuries of optimism and expansion. There were three reasons for this:

The first was psychological. The prophecies that the world would end at the year 1000 had not, to people's relief, been fulfilled.

The second was political. Violent incursions had ceased. The Avars had been simply eliminated; the Vikings had settled down in England and Normandy; the Magyars had not only settled down and created a state but had been christianised as well; and relations with the Arab world had become more orderly (or so it appeared). Travel and trade therefore simply became safer.

Third, agricultural techniques had improved. There was now a three-field system, with the field providing alternately a winter crop, a summer crop and lying fallow every third year, rather than the two-field system under which it lay fallow every other year. This led to an increase in production, which was also helped by ploughs now being made of iron and the horse replacing the ox as a draught animal. For individuals all this meant a better diet.

Thus in place of despondency and pessimism came a mood of confidence which acted as a spur to success in business, particularly in investment and the perception of opportunity, and affected social life through earlier marriages and larger families.

The chief consequences of this new situation was a rise in population. This had two knock-on effects: creation of a demand for goods, and land reclamation, especially in low-lying areas by the sea and rivers, and in forest areas, with the establishment of new villages and manor farms. Taking the lead in these developments were the monasteries. Land and river trade routes improved. Towns

75

started to come back into their own, often as centres for fairs, particularly those easily accessible by river transport or where travel conditions were not difficult, such as the Champagne area of northern France, the Low Countries and the Italian plain. And this confidence was reflected in an outward sign of the belief in the permanency of things – castles, churches, even private dwellings, were increasingly being built in stone.

The upturn in the western economy began in Italy. Italy was the most populated and urbanised part of the West. There had never been the often complete break with the past in terms of learning, skills and production techniques as occurred elsewhere.

Trade flourishes when two areas with different demands and different items of production come into contact. In the High Middle Ages Italy was the link between the Mediterranean world and the western European economies, in the first stage pushing economic power up the Rhône to northern France and the Low Countries, particularly Flanders. The two areas complemented each other well. Italy provided the varied items of the eastern trade. Flanders imported English wool and transformed it into cloth. Its many cities – Bruges, Ghent, Ypres, Arras, Douai, Lille – were the first centres of a European textile industry supplying the European market. As the Flemish economy developed it stimulated economic activity in Britain, the plains of northern Germany and the valley of the Rhine.[1]

As European trade expanded, so did its cities, bringing to the fore a new class of persons based on trade and commerce. In this period cities came to obtain a high degree of freedom and autonomy, usually paying a rent for their privileges to their local lord. The cities were thus not really part of the feudal system and one day their inhabitants would provide the challenge to it, although with differing effects depending on what part of Europe they found themselves.[2]

As in all medieval cities commercial life centred round guilds, associations of merchants only members of which could ply a trade. Guilds protected the quality of goods produced, fixed prices, purchased raw materials and trained apprentices to become Masters.

Of the institutions holding western Europe together the dominant one was the Papacy.

It has been said that the legacy of medieval Christianity to later ages was the problem of authority. 'Never in the whole history of the world did so many believe so firmly in so many things, the authority for which they could not test.' For educated and un-educated alike the Papacy satisfied the desire for guidance and certainty in a world where life was indeed nasty, brutish and short, wracked by tyranny, plague, famine and war.[3]

The main task of the Church was, of course, to provide reassur-ance through explanation of the divine mysteries, and there was no opposition from those who might base their views on 'reason'.[4] What is difficult to realise today was the pervasiveness of the Church in medieval society, for almost everything was couched in terms of one's relationship with God.

But there were other reasons for the dominant position of the Church.

Usually it was only the clergy who could read and write. If anyone wanted an education it was only the Church which could provide it. That was also because it had been the Church which had kept the flame of Roman civilisation going since the fall of the western Empire – the art of writing, illuminating manuscripts and interpreting law.

The Church was closely involved with law. Laws passed by territorial rulers had to be 'reasonable', and 'reasonable' was inter-preted as being in accord with church principles. It was canon law that regulated relations within the Church and between the clergy and the laity. It was church law that governed family life – mar-riage, legitimacy, adultery, separation. And it was church law that influenced trade, especially its hostility to usury (lending money at interest) on the grounds that one acquired money without risk, and its lack of enthusiasm for profit, especially gain resulting from chance. Unsurprisingly, therefore, with their mastery of writing and knowledge of the laws, clerics provided the embryo civil ser-vices of kings and other powerful territorial nobles.[5]

The Church had also grown to be a wealthy and expanding institution. The most striking example of this expansion was the founding of monastic orders and their development in the eleventh century. Two in particular were the Carthusians, founded by (Saint) Bruno of Cologne in 1084, and the Cistercians, founded by Abbot Robert of Molême in 1098 and then spectacularly developed by (Saint) Bernard of Citeaux, who became first Abbot of Clairvaux near Troyes in northern France in 1115. The Cistercian method was to get monks from one abbey to go and found another, and then get the new one to do the same. And these monasteries often spearheaded economic activity and development. The Church thus owned – and cultivated well – much land, and led the way in land improvement. As for money, the Church received tithes of agricultural production and fees for services or commutation of sin, whereas it only contributed to state revenue through taxation if the Pope so authorised.

Finally, the clergy continued to enjoy the immunity from the jurisdiction of secular courts introduced by Constantine, and was also exempt from labour duties and military service.

All in all the Church was as powerful as any state, to the extent that the word had much meaning in the Early and High Middle Ages. And when national states did begin to form, the Church, with its wealth and immunities, was indeed a very 'state within a state'. It thus had powerful means with which to play politics, whether at national or at European level.

By contrast, the Papacy's partner in the putative governance of western Europe, the Holy Roman Empire, was weak.

The main weakness was institutional. Because the Emperor was not a hereditary monarch but elected from a number of noble families, there was no fixed capital and therefore no fixed bureaucracy, no central treasury and no standing army. The Papacy may also have been elective, but because (except for a period in the fourteenth and fifteenth centuries) it had a fixed and recognised capital it was able to develop a very strong central bureaucracy and a full treasury.

Another problem was that theoretically in order to become Emperor the candidate had to be crowned by the Pope, or at least have his approval. This gave the Papacy enormous possibilities for intrigue. And it also gave the chance to demand special rights and privileges to those who actually elected the Emperor. Until the second half of the thirteenth century there were no rules formally laid down as to who was an Elector. In practice things were determined not by a majority of votes but by the personal, official and territorial power of the ecclesiastical and lay nobility participating and with the numbers of those participating liable to vary.[6] Not until the *interregnum* of 1254–73 was there a move to restrict the electoral college to seven: three ecclesiastical representatives, the Archbishops of Trier, Mainz and Cologne, and four lay members, the Duke of Saxony, the Margrave of Brandenburg, the Count Palatine of the Rhine (connected with the Dukedom of Bavaria and the by now extinct Dukedom of Lorraine), and the King of Bohemia. (Under Otto III Bohemia had been incorporated into the Empire under its own dynasty.)[7]

Until the *interregnum* the imperial crown was almost always worn by members of the great German dukedoms – Saxony (955–1024), Franconia (1024–1138), and Swabia, the famous family of the Hohenstaufen, (1138–1254). Most imperial rivals also usually came from these dynasties. But after the *interregnum* the Germans became less keen on electing strong vigorous Emperors who might become too powerful, and began electing weaker rulers. One, elected Emperor in 1273, was the owner of a small castle and land in the Swiss Canton of Argau. He was Rudolf of Habsburg, a family that as Holy Roman Emperors, Dukes, Archdukes and Emperors of Austria would become one of the most illustrious – and tragic – in European history over the next six hundred and fifty years.

But precisely because the Emperors had no standing bureaucracy, treasury or army, their ability to survive, let alone carry out their policies and ambitions depended on their own resources, the wealth of their lands, and the people who were personally loyal to them. Unsurprisingly, therefore, Emperors continually tried to build up their own family fortunes and increase the size of their territories, whether by marriages, alliances or war.

The alternative was to buy support. In 1220 and 1232 the Emperor Frederick II granted rights to bishops and the territorial princes which made them practically independent in their own domains: control of justice, rights to build castles and maintain troops, rights to legislate, to coin money and to tax.[8] But there would be a price to pay for all these concessions – the undermining of the unity of the German people.

The relative strengths of Papacy and Empire could be seen in the famous eleventh century conflict known as the Investitures Controversy, when Church reforms threatened the bases of Imperial power.

At the beginning of the tenth century the Monastery of Cluny in today's Burgundy began to press for reform in the Church. Its particular target was the growing secularisation of monastic life resulting from, on the one hand, the temporal powers exercised by senior clergy, and, on the other, control by secular princes of wealthy bishoprics and monasteries. Kings (and Emperors) preferred to give land to bishops because it was unlikely they would become hereditary. But the consequence was that bishops became increasingly involved in temporal rather than spiritual matters.

The first step in the conflict between Papacy and Empire was the attempt by Pope Nicolas II in 1059 to limit secular intervention in

Papal affairs. He declared that henceforward the Pope should be elected by the conclave of cardinals rather than, as hitherto, by the clergy and nobility of Rome following nomination by or consultation with the Emperor. Since this decision was a blatant rejection of an Emperor's rights the Pope had to look for secular defenders from his anger. And thus was ushered in the long period when the Papacy would begin to act like a state, developing foreign policies and even recruiting armies.

But the Emperor, Henry IV, was soon to face an even sterner opponent, Pope Gregory VII (1073–85).

It was he who put an abrupt end to the idea that priests could marry, and thus introduced priestly celibacy. True, there was nothing in the Bible forbidding priests to marry, but one object was to loosen links with the secular world. If the duty of the Church was to drive out sin it must separate itself from the sinful community. The other object was to end the danger of ecclesiastical offices becoming hereditary, with sons succeeding their fathers or fathers giving their sons Church property, the old charge made by Rome against the Celtic church.

The second target of the reformers was simony, purchase of an ecclesiastical office or its conferment for political reasons rather than the piety of the candidate. Secular rulers, including the Emperor, disposed of many bishoprics, giving them to friends and relatives or, as the phrase went, 'investing' them. 'Lay investiture' occurred when an ecclesiastic was invested not by his clerical superior but by a layman such as a King or Emperor.

However, in the case of Gregory more was to be involved than the issue of lay investiture.

Throughout his life he was guided by one ideal – the subjection of all Christendom, from the Emperors down, to the authority of the Church of Rome. But just as the Church had to be supreme on earth so too had the Pope to be supreme in the Church. The Pope was to be the judge of all men, responsible only to God. The Pope's word was therefore not only law, it was Divine Law. Disobedience to the Pope was practically a mortal sin.[9]

Gregory therefore declared in its starkest form the doctrine of Papal infallibility and supremacy that had been latent since the days of St. Ambrose: that the Pope was the supreme and absolute ruler of the Universal Roman Church founded by God; he alone could appoint bishops and, if necessary, dethrone them; that since Kings and Emperors were also representatives of God only he could approve them and he also had the right to depose them; that the Pope could absolve subjects of unjust rulers from their allegiance; that the Roman church had never erred and that no one could judge the Pope.[10]

In 1075 he started the Investitures crisis by forbidding any cleric to be invested by a layman and thus threatening the Emperor with loss of control over a considerable part of his land (and therefore wealth) in Germany and Italy.

The flashpoint was the vacancy of the bishopric of Milan, an important position since the bishop was also the lay ruler of the city. Control of the bishopric was vital for the Emperor if he wished to consolidate his power in northern Italy; for the Pope the bishopric was second only to Rome in importance. Pope and Emperor backed rival candidates.[11]

Referring to the precedent of the coronation of Charlemagne the Pope argued that Leo had placed the crown on Charlemagne's head and that as God's earthly Vicar it was the Pope's right to give the Imperial title to whom he wished. Thus the Pope, being able to choose the Emperor, was superior to him. For his part Henry argued that the Pope had crowned Charlemagne not because he, the Pope, was head of the Church but as a consequence of the power and authority Charlemagne actually had. And Henry claimed, correctly, that previous Popes had given Emperors the right to confirm the elected Pope.

However, the Pope had another weapon of terrifying power in the pervasive religious atmosphere of the Middle Ages – excommunication.

To gain acceptance of his candidate the Pope threatened the Emperor with excommunication and summoned him to Rome to be judged for his vices. Henry replied by calling a Synod of German bishops at Worms which in January 1076 declared the Pope deposed. Two months later Gregory declared Henry deposed and excommunicated, and freed all his subjects from their oaths of loyalty to him. Various German princes took the opportunity to revolt, and one appeared as a rival for Emperor. The result was one of the most astonishing spectacles of the Middle Ages. In order to get his deposition and excommunication lifted and the princes returned to their loyalty, Henry travelled to the castle of Canossa near Parma where he stood for three days in the January snow of 1077 in the courtyard of the castle doing penance, before Gregory had pity on him and lifted the sentences of deposition and excommunication.

But Gregory's triumph turned out to be short-lived. His continued support of rivals to Henry led to the Emperor acknowledging an anti-Pope, and Gregory was for a time imprisoned in Rome until freed by an army of Normans from the South under Robert Guiscard, the conqueror of Bari. And there were a number of long-term consequences of the crisis. Papal descent into the political arena and Imperial intervention in Italian affairs not only weakened the standing of both institutions (anti-Popes and anti-Emperors and the ensuing conflicts would dominate the politics of the Middle Ages) but set the scene for the continued disunity of Germany and Italy.

Not that the weakened standing of the Papacy was immediately apparent. Far from it. For the Papacy was now about to try and seize the leadership of the entire Christian world and give to it unity and direction. The opportunity to do this was provided by events in the Middle East.

The victorious advance of the Seljuk Turks after Manzikert had seen them seize much of Asia Minor and therefore much of the land from which the Byzantine Empire recruited its armies. For that reason in 1095 the Emperor Alexius I Comnenus appealed to Pope Urban II for help to replace the lost troops.

Obligingly, in 1095 Urban preached the First Crusade at Clermont, promising remission of sins to all participants. Quite apart from the opportunity to give Europe a lead, the Pope had also been concerned about the divisions within western Christianity caused by the many local feudal civil wars. What better way to channel that mis-spent energy than to send it against the Infidel? Indeed the Papacy had already been giving support to the Christian kingdoms in Spain against the Moors.

Three crusading armies marched overland to Constantinople and from thence through Asia Minor to Palestine where, on 15 July 1099 Jerusalem was stormed by the Crusaders and its Islamic garrison, as well as its Jewish inhabitants, put to the sword. A number of Christian statelets were set up: Jerusalem, Antioch, Tripoli and Edessa. But these were very vulnerable to Islamic counter-attacks and relations with their nearest putative back-up, the Byzantine Empire, were very bad. The reason was that in the West many held the view that the opportunity should be taken to unite the eastern and western churches by force, Pope Gregory among them. And indeed when the Byzantine Emperor failed to provide the money he had promised to the Fourth Crusade the Crusaders nearly achieved just that, sacking Constantinople in 1204 and briefly setting up Latin Kingdoms in parts of the Empire, particularly Greece. It would not be until 1261 that the Byzantines regained control.

Altogether six further Crusades were undertaken in desperate attempts to defend the Crusader states against Islamic counter-attacks. Closely involved in these events were religious orders of Knights promoted by the Papacy, particularly the Knights Templar and the Knights of St. John. Noble families in Europe were encouraged to have their sons join these Orders, which combined the ascetic vows of the monk to poverty, chastity and obedience with the ideals of chivalry.[12] But the failure to follow up conquest by extensive colonisation ensured that these isolated states failed to hold out.[13] Edessa went first in 1146. Jerusalem was lost in 1187, regained briefly in 1229 and lost definitively in 1244. Antioch succumbed in 1268 and Tripoli in 1289. The last Crusader outpost, Acre, fell in 1291.

But it was not only against Islam that Crusades were waged.

The rise in population in the eleventh and twelfth centuries in western and central Europe had led to a demand for living space. And, as it happened, the rulers of Poland also wanted to improve conditions in their country. The northern branch of the west Slavs had become a state and in the last half of the tenth century been christianised under Miezko I. Generally good relations were enjoyed with the Holy Roman Empire and it was therefore to the German world that these rulers appealed for settlers, urban and rural, to come in and clear the forest land. Large villages, even fortified towns, were established, which became centres of trade. Although the areas belonged to the Polish nobility these German trading centres were often able to obtain a degree of autonomy, benefiting from special laws and privileges.[14]

But as the Polish and German worlds began to expand and come together pressure was applied against the non-Christian Slavonic tribes between them, inhabiting the lands between the Elbe and Saale and the Oder. In 1147 the militant St. Bernard of Clairvaux, who the previous year had preached the Second Crusade, called for another crusade, this time against the Wends. Led by Henry the Lion, Duke of Saxony, what is now Mecklenburg and Pomerania became part of the German sphere of influence, and ultimately part of the Empire.[15]

Taking the lead in German settlement were the Cistercian monasteries, but they were not alone. The centres of Viking trade had by now disappeared to be replaced by Germans, and this led to the foundation of the Hanseatic League of trading German cities, spreading throughout northern Germany, Scandinavia, the Baltic and making contact with the Kievan principalities. In 1158 was founded the most famous of the Hansa towns, Lubeck. Other towns in the League were Hamburg, Stettin, Rostock, Kiel, Wismar, Danzig, Stralsund, Riga, Reval and Visby on the island of Gottland between Sweden and Latvia. At its height some seventy-seven cities were members of the League.

Then in 1225 another impetus to German colonisation of the east was given when Conrad of Masovia invited the crusading order of the Teutonic Knights (founded 1202) to help him against the heathen Lithuanian tribe of the Pruzzi (from which the word 'Prussian' is derived).[16] The Knights spread rapidly through today's Baltic states of Lithuania, Latvia and Estonia. Large amounts of territory were given to the Order which, until the fifteenth century, would function as a more or less independent community under its Grand Master. The latter was 'associated with the Empire', so that the Order and its territories were nominally part of the Empire.

With the defeat and conversion of the Pruzzi and Lithuanians systematic colonisation began, unlike in the Middle East. Towns were established, many of which joined the Hanseatic League. Knights needed to be merchants as well as warriors. But this expansion brought the Knights into often hostile relations with the Russian city-states of Pskov and Novgorod. In a famous encounter in 1242 an army of Teutonic Knights perished at the hands of Alexander Nevsky, Prince of Novgorod, when it fell through the ice of Lake Peipus.

This expansion of the Germans into the Baltic and eastern Europe brought these areas into the European trade system, so that the entire continent could, by the middle of the thirteenth century, be considered an economic whole.

Of all the areas of Europe, Italy was the one to benefit most from the main events of the High Middle Ages.

Because of the conflicts between the Papacy and the German Holy Roman Empire, Italian cities were able to develop complete political independence from secular feudal authority. Italian cities never became subordinate to other state structures as did the other main groups of European cities, Flanders, the Hansa League and the imperial cities of the Empire. Thus, in contrast to the rest of Europe, where the secular power would eventually create territorial states at the expense of cities, taxing them and limiting their privileges, in Italy it was the cities which created states.

Italian cities were generally three or four times the size of most other European cities but there was much less of a divorce between town and country, unlike elsewhere in feudal Europe. The élite of society, large landowners, were happy to live in the towns and use them as their headquarters. In Italy the political confrontation was between cities and the areas they controlled rather than between cities and feudal lords. This led to the eventual conquest of weaker cities by stronger ones seeking commercial assets, ending up with the latter controlling territories containing several cities and towns.[17]

And it was the Crusades – over nearly two centuries – that would provide those Italian cities with the opportunity to practice their commercial skills. Many Italian ports – Amalfi, Pisa, Genoa and Venice – grew in importance, transporting goods and soldiers to and from the Middle East, and were well rewarded. Genoa received warehousing and residential privileges in the Crusader states while Venice received trading concessions throughout the Byzantine Empire.[18] Genoa and Venice would become powerful independent states until swept away by Napoleon at the end of the eighteenth century.

It would be in this period too that Italy would take the lead in the development of commercial techniques, particularly in banking and double-entry book-keeping.

Towards the end of the thirteenth century merchants ceased to travel with their wares but remained at home, entrusting their goods to carriers. This led to the development of commercial partnerships, often between merchants in different cities. This led in turn to credit, bills of exchange, and eventually to institutionalised banking. The first bankers were money changers who dealt with the bewildering array of monies in use. Later they came to conduct credit transactions on their own account and on behalf of clients. The largest banking houses, like the Bardi in Florence, used a vast network of correspondents in Europe's busiest economic centres, and they would lend money to rulers and public authorities, particularly other Italian city states.

Florence, too, provided the earliest known practice of double-entry book-keeping, essential for the firm controlling, in this period of vibrant commercial expansion, of the multiplicity of operations involving labour, goods and capital that was rendering the market so complex compared to previous ages.[19]

But the period of the High Middle Ages would see two further developments, one in the West, the other in the East, that would have lasting effects on the future of the continent.

In 1066 William, Duke of Normandy, defeated King Harold Godwinson of England at Hastings and conquered England. Mindful that the Normans ruled over a basically hostile population William introduced – and most of his successors refined – a strong central authority. Among the ways this was expressed was the declaration by William that the first loyalty of every vassal was not to his superior but to the King, and the transfer of over one-third of the land of England into royal hands.[20]

It was the royal encroachment on unwritten customary feudal law that led the Barons of England in 1215 to force King John to accept a Charter of Rights, *Magna Carta*, described as a treaty between the King and his subjects.[21]

There were three significant features of the Charter:

The first was a limitation of royal power through restatement of the feudal principle of consent and therefore that only bilateral agreement could modify contractual arrangements. The importance of this lay in relation to money, for it admitted the right of the nation to be involved in decisions on new taxation. Whereas the king could use his own personal revenues as he wished, no taxes other than those already in existence could be levied 'except by the common counsel of the realm' and that counsel was to be taken by an assembly duly summoned.[22]

Second, the operation of royal justice should be on the basis of the common law following *stare decisis* rather than on the personal whim of the sovereign.[23]

Third, the Charter was to be enforced by a committee of barons who were empowered to wage war against the king, in conjunction with the community of the realm, should he refuse to provide justice on any claim laid before him.

The Charter thus established that the law was above the king and rebellion was justified if he broke it.[24]

It was from that committee of Barons that British Parliamentary democracy evolved, both earlier and very different from what would develop in the rest of Europe.

In the constitutional conflict between king Henry III and the Barons between 1258 and 1265, and in the frequent requests by the English kings for money to fight their wars with France and Scotland, the wealth and importance of the knights and the merchants was recognised. Increasingly both groups were invited not merely to approve but also discuss with the king and the barons the affairs of the Kingdom in Council. By the middle of the fourteenth century the divergence between the great baronial lords and the knights, as well as the growing sense of economic solidarity between the knights and the merchants saw the counsel of the realm divide into two chambers, with the lower one becoming known for the first time as the House of Commons.

Since landed elements belonged to both groups, so that anything affecting them had to be approved by both chambers, the convention developed that both chambers had to approve legislation. Two further consequences of this bicameralism were that Parliament ceased to be thought of as representing separate classes but rather the nation as a whole, and that statutes could only come from King, Lords and Commons acting together.[25]

By the end of the fourteenth century it was already being claimed that Parliament was the supreme authority of the land.[26] A few years later saw the beginning of legislation by Bill, a move designed to prevent the king or his officials drafting proclamations or administrative orders in terms different from those desired by Parliament by having measures prepared in their final form so that all that was required was the royal signature.[27]

But at the very time that representative democracy was about to rise in western Europe it began to decline in the East.

In the steppes of central Asia the various Mongol tribes had been united in 1206 by Temuchin, better known as Genghis Khan. Within a few decades the Mongols had broken out, overthrowing the Chinese and Persian empires and the sultanates of Bagdad. In the Middle East their intervention against Islam was greeted with joy by the beleaguered Crusaders, but Mongol defeat at the hand of Bibars, Sultan of Egypt, at Goliath Wells in 1260 more or less confirmed the Crusaders' impending doom.

It was in 1222–3 that a Mongol army appeared for the first time in Russia, routing at the Kalka river the forces of the Grand Duke of Vladimir. Because of Genghis Khan's death in 1227 the Mongol army returned to Asia, but in 1236 they came back again with a vengeance under the command of Genghis Khan's grandson, Batu.

The first to feel the Mongol fury were the steppe tribes of the Cumans and Volga Bulgars. Both were overwhelmed and forty thousand Cumans fled terrified to Hungary. Then came the turn of the Russians. Riazan, Moscow and Vladimir were burnt, and in December 1240 Kiev was put to the sword and the inhabitants massacred. In 1241 the Mongols advanced into central Europe, brushing aside a combined German–Polish army at Liegnitz and then invading Hungary and Croatia, forcing King Bela IV of Hungary to take refuge on an island in the Adriatic. Only the death of Genghis Khan's successor, Ugeday, in December 1241, obliged Batu to call off his attack on Europe and return to deal with the issue of the succession. That problem settled, Batu returned to Russia, setting up the Khanate of the Golden Horde at Saray near today's Volgagrad, from which the Mongols would dominate Russia for another two centuries, overthrowing the urban, commercial, democratic Kievan society and thereby decisively influencing the course of Russian history and society.

Economically, the sheer destruction dealt the Russians a staggering blow. Most cities were destroyed and artisans were requisitioned by the Mongols. The result was a disruption of industrial and commercial activity for nearly a century, to be replaced by an emphasis on agriculture and exploitation of other natural resources.

Because, apart from the Ukraine, which was under their direct control, the Khans of the Golden Horde ruled through the existing princes, politically the Mongol occupation marked a rise in the power of the princes at the expense of other institutions, beginning the process by which everyone became bound to the service of the state. The princes exercised their mandates in return for providing the Mongols with tribute and troops, although the organisation of this was in the hands of Mongol officials responsible only to the Khans. First to go was urban democracy. The Mongols disliked the '*veches*' and got the princes to abolish them. Citizens of towns were now subject to taxation and conscription. And as long as the princes retained the confidence of the Khan they could rely on him for support against internal opposition, *veche* or boyar. The only exceptions to these developments were Novgorod and Pskov, which had not been destroyed and were allowed to keep their autonomies throughout the Mongol period.[28] Whether, after Mongol rule had ended, these two city-states would enable the flame of democracy to continue, or whether what the Mongols had set in train in Russia would engulf them also would come to be the next question in Russian history.

7 The End of the Middle Ages and the Rise of States 1300–1500AD

In contrast to the glories and seeming certainties of the High Middle Ages the fourteenth century ushered in a period of doubt, pessimism and defeat. Disease, technology, even atrocious weather, struck at the roots of traditional institutions and marked the beginning of the end of the Age of Faith.

There had already been some signs of decline in the European economy, mainly due to overpopulation leading to surpluses of labour, but the continent was totally defenceless against the calamity which struck in the middle of the fourteenth century and would strike six more times before its end – the Black Death.

The Black Death, which would be responsible for the disappearance of anything up to one-third of the population of the continent, was a bubonic plague carried by black rats and transmitted from them to humans by fleas. Believed to have begun in China it had reached the Crimean port of Kaffa, where Genoa had important trading privileges, before appearing in Sicily in 1346. By 1350 the entire continent had been devastated.

Its first effect was to strike at the foundations of the feudal system's rigid control of society. The savage reductions in the numbers of the agricultural labour force hastened the process of economic and social instability. The survivors demanded higher wages, while those who had not achieved the status of wage earners sought to have their labour services commuted to paying rents and to share in the benefits of the higher wages, and if the landlord refused the labourer threatened to seek work elsewhere. On the other hand, with the fall in agricultural prices due to the fall in demand, many landlords let out parts of their estates for a cash rent. In many countries the authorities tried to curb the wage rises and the free movement of labour by introducing legislation forbidding wages higher than those existing before the Black Death, fixing prices, and compelling labourers to accept work at the rates offered. The resulting unrest led to a number of peasant revolts in France and England.[1]

Another institution adversely affected by the Black Death was the Church. The Church could offer no explanation of the phenomenon except that it was God's wrath on sinful Man. But 'good' clerics were hit just as hard by the plague as the 'sinful' laity. And priests who died were often replaced by those far less devoted or learned. Paradoxically, as Church prestige and authority declined, religious fervour increased. In the atmosphere of uncertainty, fear and ignorance, mass hysteria set in. Some tried to atone for their sins by forming groups and flogging themselves in public while wandering about the countryside. Others blamed the plague (or God's wrath) on the Jews, and a number of massacres occurred, particularly in Germany. People turned to quacks and miracle workers, or abandoned faith altogether, becoming sceptical and intolerant, with resentment at church wealth and complacency.[2]

For some however, things were not necessarily bad, as the Black Death led to wealth distribution with an improvement in one's economic and social standing. Since the amount of cash and capital remained the same, although the population had declined, inheritance ensured the survivors were wealthier. Others were able to take advantage of the increasing amount of land left empty. The increase in personal wealth benefited most the inhabitants of the towns who were well placed to take advantage of the increase in demand for manufactured or luxury goods. Faced with the recurrence of the Black Death an alternative reaction to embracing religious fervour or hysteria was individualistic self-indulgence, pursuing wealth and luxury or self-expression in regard to fashion and the creative arts, in an atmosphere of relaxed morals.[3]

But inability to explain the Black Death was not the only reason for the decline of the Church. The fourteenth century would provide two other reasons, one in the world of politics, the other in the world of ideas.

In the world of politics the Papacy began to face up for the first time to a new phenomenon: the national monarchy.

The struggle between the Papacy and these national monarchies began during the pontificate of Pope Boniface VIII (1294–1303). On the surface two issues were at stake. First, King Philip IV of France and King Edward I of England wanted to raise revenue and claimed the right to tax the clergy. Boniface, in his Papal Bull *Clericis Laicos* (1296) stated that the Pope's consent was required before the clergy of any state should pay taxes to a secular ruler. Second, the Kings wanted to be able to try clerics in the royal secular courts for certain crimes such as treason. The clergy claimed immunity from such courts. These two issues were, of course, secondary. The real issue was the continuing basic conflict between the claims of the Papacy to universal authority over both church and state, and the claims of the Kings that all subjects, including the clergy, were subject to the royal authority in regard to justice and taxation.

The Papacy was about to find out that strong Kings were a very different matter from weak Emperors. Philip and Edward threatened to remove royal protection from the clergy, and stirred up the powerful Roman family of the Colonnas to cause trouble for Boniface in Rome. Boniface at first agreed to disregard *Clericis Laicos* but in 1301 a bishop was arrested in France and charged with treason. Boniface failed to get him released whereupon he not only reactivated *Clericis Laicos* but also issued a series of Papal Bulls, the most important being *Unam Sanctam* (1302) which again claimed absolute Papal supremacy over secular rulers. And he then excommunicated Philip.

A century and a quarter earlier Gregory VII had made the Emperor Henry IV stand in the snow at Canossa. Less than a century earlier, in 1215, Innocent III had excommunicated King John of England and put the country under an Interdict. Philip's reaction was to get the French clergy to charge Boniface with heresy and to send a small force to seize Boniface and bring him back to France for trial. The Pope was captured at his summer residence in Agnani, a small town thirty-five miles from Rome, in September 1303. But although he was soon rescued by local Italian nobles the shock killed him a month later.

Philip's action had produced a clear victory for national monarchies. No later Popes would repeat Boniface's claims. And Philip then put tremendous pressure on the College of Cardinals to chose someone sympathetic to him. In 1305 the Cardinals obliged by choosing a Frenchman, the Archbishop of Bordeaux, as Pope Clement V. And what he did was to use the excuse of the turbulence in Rome to establish his residence at Avignon, on the east bank of the river Rhone. Avignon was in the Holy Roman Empire and not a French possession, nevertheless it lay just across the river from Philip's territories. One of Clement's first acts was to create 113 French cardinals out of 134 new appointments in order to balance the hitherto dominant Italian element.

Until 1378 Avignon was the seat of the Papacy, and its Popes supported France in the Hundred Years War against England. But their pursuit of wealth in order to transform Avignon into a splendid court, and the corruption, and the nepotism that followed, including the charging of fees for confirmation of clerics in office, investitures, and letters of absolution, the selling of indulgences and demands for annates did the Papacy no good in the eyes of the rest of western Europe.

However, in 1377, the then Pope, Gregory XI, decided to return to Rome. Avignon had become a symbol of abuses and there was a need to restore Papal prestige. In any case, the temporal power of the Papacy in Italy and Rome itself needed to be restored. However, the political results of this decision were unforeseen.

First, while at Avignon it had been much easier for the Papacy to maintain close relations with Europe north of the Alps. The return to Italy led, on the one hand, to a decline in its influence in northern Europe, and on the other, to increasing involvement in Italian politics.

Second, it led to the Great Schism of 1378–1415. In May 1378 Gregory died and the Cardinals elected an Italian as Pope Urban VI. This austere but tactless man railed against the luxurious lifestyle of the Cardinals. Angered not only with him but by being obliged to return to Rome, most of the Cardinals withdrew to Agnani and elected Robert of Geneva as Pope Clement VII, using the disorderly behaviour at Urban's election as an excuse. Clement at once returned to Avignon.

What sealed the Schism was national politics. Since the French supported Clement the English supported Urban. And since the English supported Urban the Scots supported Clement, who was also supported by the Spanish Kingdoms and Naples while the rest of Italy, the Empire, the Low Countries and Hungary supported Urban.

The effects of the Schism were serious. It was impossible for either Pope to maintain the former levels of wealth acquisition through taxation and appointment. There was therefore a sharp decline in Papal wealth. And the disrepute which the Schism brought to the Papacy led to a challenge to the accepted view that the Pope was the head who controlled absolutely the body of the Church and encouraged the development of an alternative concept of church authority.

The result was the Conciliar Movement, based on the idea of the Church as a corporation of which the Pope might be the temporary head but that authority lay in the hands of the Councils which could, if necessary, overrule the Pope.[4]

In 1409 a Council called at Pisa deposed both Popes and elected a new one. But those deposed refused to go, and had enough international support to ensure they stayed.

A second Council, at Constance (1414–18), deposed all three Popes and elected a Colonna as Martin V in 1417, and this ended the Schism. For a time the Conciliar Movement seemed very powerful. The Council of Basel (1431–49), not only resisted attempts by Pope Eugenius IV to dissolve it but threatened to depose him. But by the end of his life Eugenius obtained again acceptance of Papal Supremacy, and his successor Pius II declared in 1459 that Conciliar theory was heretical.[5] However, all this did was to engender the feeling that institutional reform of the Papacy from above would not be possible.[6]

But the election of Martin V led to the establishment of a Papacy that would henceforth be almost entirely Italian. He and his successors set about the establishment and control of a powerful temporal Papal State, with control over money, lay lords, and the institution of nepotism as a way of political life in the Church. The other side of the coin was the distancing of the non-Italian clergy from the Italian Papacy, hastening the idea of national churches, as exemplified by the 1438 Pragmatic Sanction of Bourges, when the French church, later to become known as the Gallican church, became less administratively dependent on Rome.[7]

The other area in which the Church came under attack was in the field of thought. The main issues were church wealth and temporal political power.

Already in the early thirteenth century two mendicant Orders had been founded – the Franciscans and the Dominicans. Their ideal was for their monks to live like Jesus, a life devoted to absolute poverty, chastity and preaching, based on begging and homelessness. The implication that the Church should renounce wealth and property was initially considered heretical, but even after the Papacy had composed its differences with the Orders the dispute on this point came to be involved in the struggle between Papacy and Empire, and even beyond.

Two persons who led the assault on Papal wealth and its temporal power were Marsilius of Padua (1274–1343) and William of Ockham (1285–1349). The latter not only defended the doctrine of the poverty of Christ but rejected the Papal doctrine of Supremacy in secular matters in favour of the Emperor. He it was who anticipated the Conciliar Movement by calling for a College of Popes to rule the Church, claiming that the true head of the Church was Christ.[8]

For his part, Marsilius argued that the Church had no claim to property and, just as Christ had accepted Roman government, the Church had no place in politics. Its work was to save souls, but like any private society within the state, the Church must be kept subject to the requirements of good order. The state could therefore regulate the Church, taxing it, appointing clergy, and rulers could even depose the Pope if he became too troublesome. His most famous book, *Defensor Pacis* (The Defender of Peace) was called by Pope Clement VI the most heretical work he had ever read.[9]

The arguments of both writers went down well with the Emperor Louis IV (the Bavarian) who had incurred the enmity of the Pope by insisting on rights of Imperial appointment in Italy, particularly in regard to Milan. They also were pleasing to the rulers of emergent states like France and England. And they also provided the inspiration for the Lollards in England. Led by John Wyclif (c.1329–1384) the Lollards opposed the doctrine of transubstantiation, held that people did not need a priest to mediate between them and God, and that only the Bible should be accepted as authority for Christian dogma. His views were condemned, but he had powerful friends who protected him.

Less fortunate was the Czech reformer Jan Hus (1369–1415), a priest who took up Wyclif's ideas on the Continent. He too insisted that Christ was the only head of the Church and that no doctrine could be established that was not based on the Bible. He condemned Church corruption, particularly the sale of indulgences and the worship of images. He also believed, as had the Celtic Church, in the laity being able to take communion in both kinds. Hus also wanted reform of the Church to be undertaken by the Bohemian state. He was summoned to the Council of Constance to defend his beliefs but although travelling under the Emperor's safe-conduct was seized, tried and condemned to death by being burnt at the stake in 1415. His martyrdom and the excommunication of the Hussites led to an uprising by his followers which rapidly took the form of Czech national resistance against the dominant Germans of the Empire. But the teachings of Wyclif and Hus would prepare the ground for Lutheranism a century later.[10]

If the condition of the Papacy was shaky, no less so was that of the Empire. Its history in the fourteenth and fifteenth centuries was one of the conflicting ambitions of three great families – Luxemburg (which included Bohemia), Wittelsbach (Bavaria and the Rhineland Palatinate) and the one destined to be the greatest of all, the Habsburg Dukes of Austria. Each house might have brothers, uncles and cousins ruling various parts of the Empire, loyal or otherwise to the putative head of the family. However, should there be a clash between family interests and those of the Empire all too often the former prevailed.

During the Early and High Middle Ages the Emperors had been heavily involved in fighting in Italy in fulfilment of the idea that the Emperor was also King of Italy. Although he had his supporters there Italy was generally hostile. The cities were independent, rich and republican and resented the destruction caused by German armies, and were therefore inclined to back the Papacy in its struggles with the Emperor. Louis IV of Bavaria was the last Emperor to invade Italy with an army. His successor Charles IV of Luxemburg (1346–1378) abandoned Italy as an area of political ambition for German Emperors.[11]

The Imperial withdrawal from Italy came at the same time as the Papal withdrawal to Italy, and the division between the German and Italian worlds became increasingly marked: hostility to Papal influence north of the Alps by an increasingly national clergy resentful of Papal attempts to control benefices being matched south of the Alps by fear of the German world and contempt for its civilisation.

But due to the concessions made by previous Emperors the return to German affairs by the Emperors of the Late Middle Ages did not halt the Empire's fragmentation.

The most important political divisions in Germany were called, as they are today, *Länder*. Germans were conscious of belonging to a 'Land', an area in which a particular set of laws and customs operate By the fourteenth century many of these *Länder* had their own Estates, assemblies of nobles and representatives of the peasantry (sometimes) and the towns, grouped in one or more colleges, with rights of taxation, control of expenditure, legislation, jurisdiction, and the appointment of councillors to the territorial prince.

But there were also over a hundred cities in the Empire, divided into three groups: territorial cities, founded by a territorial lord, usually for strategic rather than commercial reasons; free cities, mostly former ecclesiastical cities but now freed from their clerical overlords; and imperial cities, so called because they acknowledged no superior jurisdiction between them and the Emperor. The latter had usually gained their independence through being granted a charter by the Emperor in return for funding his wars. These cities were mostly to be found along the Rhine and the Danube.[12]

The problem for the last two categories was the feudal nobility.

In Italy cities dominated the countryside, integrating the rural and urban economy. In France and England the monarchy integrated the towns into the developing national economy. In all three countries and the Low Countries the merchant class participated in state and public life. But in Germany the countryside was feudal. The cities only controlled the fields beneath their walls. They were isolated, separate from the other sources of competing political power. And as in the thirteenth and fourteenth centuries the powers of the Emperors declined to the advantage of the territorial feudal nobility so the German cities were ever less able to prosper like their Italian, French, and English counterparts. To the German feudal prince towns were objects to be ruled and their privileges reduced rather than being seen as a source of strength.[13]

As for the peasantry of the Empire, conditions varied. Not all were downtrodden serfs. One area where traditional feudal control was weak and most of the peasants were free was central Switzerland. In 1291 the so-called 'forest cantons' of Uri, Schwyz and Unterwalden formed a confederation, the nucleus of the present Swiss Confederation, to protect their liberties against Habsburg encroachment. Twice in the fourteenth century the Swiss peasantry defeated Habsburg attempts to destroy them – at Morgarten in 1315, and in 1386 at Sempach. Soon other cantons joined, and then a number of cities like Lucerne, Zurich and St. Gall. By the middle of the fifteenth century the Swiss Confederation had become a large area, more or less independent, organised according to the interests of its peasantry and cities, and dominating the alpine passes. In 1499 the Emperor Maximilian I faced reality and by the Peace of Basel Switzerland received full political independence and separated from the Empire.

As the Holy Roman Empire entered the fifteenth century its state was parlous.

Quite apart from having no central treasury, no scheme for introducing direct taxation with the proceeds going to the crown and no unified legal system, there was also no centre for decision-making, apart from the Emperor himself. There was the Imperial Diet, or *Reichstag*, which consisted of three colleges – Electors, Princes and the Free cities. But all three and the Emperor had to agree in order for a law to be adopted, and these three orders were only concerned with pursuing their own interests. In addition there was the anger at their exclusion of the lesser nobility, the Imperial Knights, and the peasantry. Finally, not only were the *Reichstag* procedures cumbersome, it had no means of enforcing decisions other than those at the disposal of the Emperor.

Although there was wide agreement that this situation was un-satisfactory and constitutional changes were required, discussions on them did not begin until the last decade of the fifteenth century.[14]

The reformers wanted in particular a High Court, a Governing Council and a common tax system. The High Court was set up in 1495 and it adopted Roman law as its guide to the common law of the Empire. The courts of the *Länder*, Principalities and Cities soon followed suit.

Less successful was the introduction of a Governing Council in 1500. Composed of Electors and Princes its task was to enforce *Reichstag* and High Court decisions, but it fell foul of the Emperors Maximilian I and his grandson Charles V who did not want Imperial interests to interfere with dynastic Habsburg ones. Max-imilian indeed abolished the Council in 1502, and when it was reintroduced in 1521 it was only done on Charles' insistence that it have no powers other than those granted it by the Emperor.[15] Further efforts of reform were lost in the great religious crisis that would dominate the continent for the next one and a half centuries.

Since the days of Alexander the Great the prevailing view had been that mankind was one and, at least in Europe, this universality was postulated in the form of a universal church, a universal Empire (whether Roman or Holy Roman), and a universal lan-guage, Latin, used by clerics, scholars and diplomatists no matter in what part of Europe they lived. Below this universality feudalism ensured that authority was regionalised. If someone had been asked in the High Middle Ages what he was, his first answer would be a universalist one – that he was a Christian. He would then say that he was a subject of this or that King or Lord. And only then would he give, in third place, an answer based on language or culture. Yet by the end of the Middle Ages Europe would be well into its evolution into the division of numerous states that would shatter the universal concept of society that had dominated the previous centuries, and would begin a period in which, asked who he was, the responder would give a nationalist reply, first that he was the subject of this or that king or prince, second that he was of this or that culture, and third he would give his religion.[16]

The establishment of states thus required not only a decline in universal institutions and values but also a gathering of power into the hands of a lay ruler.

Since the Empire was so weak politically and institutionally it posed little threat to the rise of states. Far more formidable opponents of this process were the Church and the feudal aristocracy. The route to success would therefore lie in getting people to transfer their primary loyalty from the Church or local feudal lord to the King. This was done initially by increasing the level of involvement of people in public life but kings were also helped by the decline in the moral authority of the Church and the decline of the feudal aristocracy in face of technological advance, particularly the development of firearms.

Two of the outstanding examples of the establishment of states in the Middle Ages concerned the Kingdoms of France and England.

In each country the thirteenth century had seen a big expansion in the civil service at the disposal of the king, mainly due to the recruitment of persons from the laity rather than the Church. Indeed, the civil service soon become a rival to the Church for employment of the best and brightest in the land. One of the chief tasks of this civil service was to explain government policy to the people and challenge the Church for control of public opinion.[17]

The two key institutions were the Courts and the Treasury. The jurisdiction of church and feudal courts were gradually curtailed. In regard to revenue, mostly for war, it was essential to see that it came from the nation as a whole. Thus the role of parliaments, whether central as in England, or regional estates in France, was to approve the raising of national revenue.

With regard to the Church it was the civil servants round King Philip IV of France (1285–1314) who developed the theory that the Kingdom of France was an organic corporation with the King at its head. He had therefore the absolute right to pass laws, impose taxes, distribute property or take any steps he pleased for the good of the realm. Since France was a corporation everyone in France, including the clergy, was part of that corporation along with the aristocracy, towns and peasantry. Disobedience to the King's command was treason.[18] Philip thus arranged for the mobilisation of French society and resources.

Unsurprising, therefore, that Philip would try to kidnap the Pope, to brush off the sentence of excommunication, and that it was in his reign that the Avignon Papacy began. And it was he who destroyed not only something international but a real 'state within a state' in France, the Order of the Knights Templars founded during the First Crusade, trumping up false evidence and executing the members on the basis of that evidence, and seizing the property of a group of people perceived as owing primary allegiance to the Church. Burning at the stake, the Grand Master of the Order, Jacques de Molay, cursed the country and the King, prophesying that his line would die out. And indeed, within a year the King was dead; by 1328 his three sons had also died. Isabella, the daughter of the last, married King Edward II of England, and this would provide her son Edward III with a claim to France, instituting the Hundred Years War which would see France repeatedly laid waste from end to end.

In England, right from the beginning of William the Conqueror's reign, steps were taken to ensure that the Church never became a 'state within a state' Pope Alexander II had blessed William's banners prior to the invasion of England in 1066 under the belief that William would make England a fief of the Church. William did not oblige. English clergy were not allowed to recognise a Pope and no Papal ambassadors or decrees were accepted without prior royal approval. It was considered a crime to pursue in church courts cases recognised as falling within the sphere of English common law. And under Edward II the Order of the Templars in England was also dissolved.[19]

There were two other ways in which national cohesion was established, and again, particularly in France and England. One was war. The other was language.

The Kings of England, particularly the Plantagenets, were very good at getting military service from free men who had no obligation to fight. The wars of the first three Edwards against the Welsh, the Scots and the French saw troops raised from all classes of society. The numbers of knights were increased by getting wealthy freemen to assume the obligations of knighthood and equipping themselves accordingly. Commissioners of Array had the power to mobilise men for service, at the King's expense, particularly outside England. All this mobilisation broadened the feeling of responsibility for the realm and its defence. Common service made men aware they were part of something larger than their local community, stimulating loyalty to King and country.[20] On the other hand, in France reliance on the feudal chivalry, supplemented by foreign mercenaries, would linger on.

But the day of the feudal nobility was nearly over, and with it the regional strength that was an obstacle to national unity. The fifteenth century saw armoured knights and the castles they defended become obsolete in the face of firearms.

The writing had, however, long been on the wall. Already the cross bow and later the long bow had enabled the well armed, well born, wealthy knight to be struck down by a common soldier. Firearms completed the process. And thus the virtue of knighthood – personal valour – was destroyed by the impersonal nature of gunfire. The traditional élites thus lost their role in society as effective warriors in attack and defence. The most formidable person in society was no longer either the bravest or the one with the highest social status.

Since it implied that victory or defeat depended on naked (fire) power rather than the morality of the combatants and since it upset both the socially and the morally ordered hierarchy, the Church condemned the use of gunfire as being 'unchristian', just as in the twelfth century it had tried to ban the use of the crossbow (at least against other Christians).[21]

As the cost of waging war successfully got ever higher – forging artillery to blast enemy fortresses and equipping infantry to replace the now useless heavy cavalry which had dominated Europe since the days of Charlemagne, the successful King would be the one who could mobilise wealth to acquire firepower and organise war not only against external enemies but internally against the feudal aristocracy.

Thus the Kings of France used artillery to drive the English from their castles in Gascony, the last one, Castillon, falling in 1453 and bringing the Hundred Years War to an end. And the aristocracy would become much less of a problem with the disappearance of Burgundy. This Duchy, related to the French royal family, was a formidable and bitter rival, by far the most wealthy and cultured of the territorial nobility, owning the Low Countries, Luxemburg, Lorraine, some of Alsace, and Picardy as well as Burgundy itself. During the Hundred Years War it had usually sided with the English. Fortunately for the then King of France Louis XI (1461–93), Charles the Bold, Duke of Burgundy, was induced by the Habsburgs to make war on the Swiss Confederation, and in 1477 he perished with his army outside the walls of Nancy.

In England the feudal aristocracy fell out among themselves in recrimination over the defeat in France and rivalry over the government of the feeble-minded King Henry VI. The result was the Wars of the Roses (1455–85) in which three Kings, one Prince of Wales, eight royal dukes, one-third of the peerage and countless gentry were killed, enabling the victor in the war, Henry Tudor, to found one of the strongest monarchies in English history, under which England would begin its ascent to world power.

It is revealing to compare the French and English experience with that of Germany and Italy. The lack of cohesion of the Empire, the lack of a centralised bureaucracy, wealth-generating Treasury and Parliament deprived the knights of regular employment in an imperial civil service or as national political representatives. Left to their own devices the threat of impoverishment forced many of them to become robber-barons operating out of their local, often picturesque, castles, arousing the hostility of the towns and merchant class. They were not in a position to develop political leadership and therefore did not do so.[22] In Germany political leadership was assured not by the Emperor but by the most powerful of the feudal aristocracy, the territorial princes. They had the money. They could therefore pay for modern armies. And they would develop into states like Bavaria, Brandenburg and Saxony. But the cost was German unity. And the same applied to Italy, where the city states played the role of the German territorial princes Both areas would remain divided until the second half of the nineteenth century.

Today it is argued that wars are the result of excessive nationalism. In the Middle Ages one might consider whether nationalism developed as the result of excessive wars.[23]

A nation has been defined as a people who believed they were one.[24] The consciousness of being different from others would become a source of pride and attachment. Certainly in the Hundred Years War, which was fought for purely dynastic reasons, Frenchmen and Englishmen soon became very aware of the differences between them. And the most obvious difference was that of language.

One of the features of European unity in the Early and High Middle Ages was Latin, the language of the Church, bureaucracy and diplomacy. However, as ever more non-Latin speakers became involved in government the language used was increasingly the vernacular. The Italian Dante Alighieri (1265–1321) said that Latin might have been the most efficient vehicle for thought but was the mother-tongue of no one.[25] In the fourteenth century the vernacular took over from Latin in Italy and France and began to do so in England. But what gives an uplift to a language is its literature. The fourteenth century saw Dante's *Divine Comedy*, written in Italian in 1310–21; *The Canterbury Tales* written in English by Geoffrey Chaucer mainly in the 1380s; and Jean Froissart's *Chronicles of the Hundred Years War* written in French in the 1390s. All were the bases for indigenous development of the national languages. The many dialects of German would not be welded into a unified German written language until a century later when Martin Luther translated the Bible.[26]

Papacy and Holy Roman Empire may have been in decline in western Europe, but the problems they faced were as nothing compared to those of their rival, the Eastern Empire.

In 1202 the Byzantine Emperor Alexius IV had requested aid from the Pope Innocent III against the Turks, promising not only money but also the unification of the Greek and Latin churches. The Pope obligingly preached the Fourth Crusade, and thirty-five thousand French and Flemish crusaders agreed to sail for Egypt. The Republic of Venice agreed to transport them, but at a price: the conquest of Zara, a port on the Dalmatian coast. In 1204 the Crusaders took Zara and then went on to Constantinople. Unfortunately Alexius did not keep either of his promises, so the enraged Crusaders stormed the city and sacked it, deposing Alexius and establishing Baldwin of Flanders as the eastern Emperor.

The generally accepted view is that if Islam struck the final blow, it was the Crusaders who struck the fatal one from which the Empire never recovered.

The Crusaders divided up the European part of the Empire, giving Baldwin Thrace, and setting up petty political entities under western adventurers in Macedonia, Athens and Morea (Sparta). Venice obtained a large number of Greek islands, including Corfu, Crete, Rhodes and Naxos, and set up a chain of trading stations in the Adriatic. But the Byzantines rejected the idea of alien Latin rule and subordination of the Greek church to Rome. Rivals to Alexius before his deposition set up three Orthodox states, Nicaea and Trebizond in Asia Minor and Epirus in Greece. These states were very fragile.

It was the Nicaeans who, momentarily, did best. In 1261 they regained Constantinople and the Byzantine Empire was restored, but it was impoverished and decimated compared to the beginning of the century. It was also surrounded by enemies – ambitious and expansionist Serbia and Bulgaria in Europe, and the Osmanli or Ottoman Turks, who had replaced the Seljuk Turks as the main threat in Asia Minor.

By 1300 the Byzantine Empire had more or less abandoned Asia Minor in order to concentrate on Europe. The navy was put into the hands of the Genoese, who were also given the area of Galata, just outside Constantinople, as a trading port.

By 1337 the Turks had taken the southern shores of the Bosphorus. Only a small strip of land opposite Constantinople remained of Byzantine Asia Minor.

The middle of the century saw increasing anarchy as the Serbs seized northern Greece, and Venetians and Genoese indulged in their own private war. The Turks had been acting as mercenaries in these wars but in 1352 they crossed into Gallipoli in force, and the last act in the history of the Byzantine Empire began. In 1369 they captured Adrianople from the Emperor and advanced north. In 1385 Sofia was captured from the Bulgarians, and in 1389 at Kossovo, the Serbian army and state was utterly destroyed, not to rise again for nearly five hundred years.

Constantinople was now surrounded, with communication to the outside world dependent on the Venetian and Genoese fleets, and the Sultan, Bajazet, was determined to put an end to what was now merely an infidel enclave in his Empire. In 1394 the Turkish blockade of Constantinople began.[27]

These Turkish successes seriously alarmed the western powers, particularly the Hungarians, who saw themselves as next on the list. Their appeal to the West led the Pope to preach a Crusade and an international army of Hungarians, Burgundians, French, Poles and Bohemians marched into the Balkans. At Nicopolis in 1396 the Turks won a crushing victory, and it seemed as if the end was nigh.

But the end was unexpectedly delayed for over half a century. While the Turks had been marching triumphantly through the Balkans a new Mongol Empire had risen in Central Asia, led by Tamerlane, a descendant of Genghis Khan. By 1400 he controlled most of the Middle East and saw in Bajazet a rival who might exploit those disaffected with his rule.

Accordingly Tamerlane invaded the Ottoman lands with a massive army. His army and that of Bajazet met at Ankara in 1402 and the result was the utter destruction of the Ottomans.

Whether Tamerlane had any plans for an advance into Europe is not known. He turned back to Asia where, on his death in 1405, his empire collapsed. That of the Ottomans, on the other hand, recovered.

It was again clear that Constantinople now faced the starkest of choices: destruction and absorption into the Turkish Empire, or salvation by the West, the price of which would be church unity, probably on Western terms.[28]

In the past the West had always insisted on the supremacy of the Western church while the East wanted reconciliation achieved through a general council of both churches. Since this period also saw the zenith of the Conciliar Movement it was decided to hold a Council at Florence in 1439 to discuss the issue. The Pope attended, as did the Emperor of Byzantium, the Patriarch of Constantinople and Bishop Isidore, Metropolitan of Kiev, head of the Greek Church in Russia.

The result was a Decree of Union. The Byzantine delegation made a number of concessions, such as on the use of unleavened bread in the Eucharist and the celibacy of the clergy. On the question as to whether the Holy Spirit descended from the Father alone or from the Father and the Son, the compromise was that it proceeded from the Father through the Son. And on the key issue of supremacy, that of Rome was accepted.[29]

But when the Byzantine delegation returned home the Union was repudiated by almost everyone, clerical and lay, and thus hopes for unification were dashed. It also meant that the fate of Constantinople could not long be delayed. The Pope tried to help and another crusading army was raised by the Hungarians and Poles. It was overwhelmed at Varna in 1444.

In 1451 Mohammed II succeeded to the Sultanate of the Ottoman Turks and immediately began preparing to besiege Constantinople. The Turks massively outnumbered the defenders and had the largest and most modern artillery. On 29 May 1453 the city fell, the last Byzantine Emperor, Constantine XI Paleologus, was killed on the walls, and Mohammed rode his horse into the Cathedral of St. Sophia.

It was not so much the fall of Constantinople that would have such momentous effects on European history as the process of the

Byzantine Empire's death. The advance of the Ottomans would have four consequences:

The first was the Renaissance. Even before the end of the fourteenth century, as the grip of the Turks strengthened round Constantinople, scholars had been slipping away to Italy, and especially Florence, bringing with them Greek texts, and thus opening up the whole world of antiquity – its history, its philosophy and thought, literature, art and architecture. Plato and Aristotle were rediscovered and there was a renewed interest in the history of Rome, with some Italian city-states seeing themselves as the successors to the Roman Republic.

The result was the development of the Humanist movement which drew its inspiration from the ancient Greek spirit of free enquiry, the confidence in reason, the study of physical facts and the discovery of the laws of nature. A main target of the Humanists was the view that the Christian-based Middle Ages were better than the Age of Antiquity. Instead they came to be increasingly portrayed as a period of superstition and barbarity. The Humanists rejected the Church vision of the world as a vale of tears where pleasure was a sin, ignorance was proof of faith and in which the individual conscience had to be submitted passively to a rigid theological discipline, arguing that human beings should develop the gifts given to them by God, in other words, that they should have a more prominent place in the scheme of things. Whereas medieval learning had been the monopoly of the clergy, now the laity had a right to think.

A culture thus developed in Italy separate from the Church. Human existence was a joy to be accepted with thanksgiving, not a gloomy error to be rectified by suffering. The new emphasis was on personal merit and public service. Personal merit depended not on outmoded notions of chivalry (the Italians were contemptuous of the nobly born robber barons and knights practising brigandage in Germany or a nobility that looked down on trade) but, as Aristotle had said, on striving after good. And for that, again as Aristotle had said, one needed wealth. The Humanists attacked the concept of poverty as a Christian virtue, arguing that it stunted the personality whereas the creation of wealth enhanced human potential for achievement. And it was from Cicero that the Humanists re-learned the virtue of action and service for the community.

Unsurprisingly, therefore, it was Florence, with its republicanism, sense of public duty, material wealth, led by a popular and mercantile nobility based not on birth but on commerce, that would lead the Renaissance.

Humanism and the Renaissance were thus important steps in two ways. In the assault on the established thought of the Church, they prepared for the Reformation. And with the emphasis on reason and inquiry they prepared the end of the Age of Faith which had dominated Europe for a thousand years.[30]

Second, the Turks became a European power in their own right. During the eight years after the fall of Constantinople their expansion north and south was inexorable. The last Christian enclave of the Byzantine Empire, Trebizond, fell in 1461. To the north, the Crimea, southern Russia and Romania soon followed, so that the next barrier was the Kingdom of Hungary. On 29 August 1526 the Hungarians were destroyed at Mohacs and their king slain. An independent Hungary would not rise again until 1918. In 1529 the Turks appeared for the first time outside the gates of Vienna and were repulsed only with difficulty. To the south it was the same. Syria was conquered in 1517, Persia in 1534, and vassal states were established in North Africa – Tripoli, Tunis and Algiers.

This powerful Euro-Asian Turkish Empire became an immediate threat to much of the European world – to Russians and Poles in the east, to Germans on the Austrian front, to Venetians in the Adriatic and to the French, Genoese and Spaniards in the western Mediterranean. The Turks thus replaced the Moors, who had finally been evicted from their last stronghold in Spain, Granada, in 1492.

Third, the Turkish grip on the eastern Mediterranean and later the Black Sea, coupled with the uncertainties of the break up of the Mongol and Tamerlane empires, had the effect of hindering trade by land routes to India and China. This aroused interest in trying to reach these lands by sea, leading to voyages of trade exploration first to the south, then the east and finally to the west – the Atlantic world and beyond. In the fifteenth century Portuguese navigators had already explored the west coast of Africa, bringing back sugar, slaves and gold. The Azores and Canary Islands were settled. Improvements were made in boat building, and sailing and navigational techniques – use of the quadrant and astrolabe. In 1487 Bartholomew Diaz rounded the Cape of Good Hope; in 1492

Christopher Columbus made his first transatlantic voyage, discovering the West Indies; and in 1498 Vasco da Gama reached India. These voyages were to lead to European domination of the world for the next four and a half centuries.[31]

Fourth, the mantle of the Byzantine Empire was picked up by the new state that was emerging in eastern Europe – Russia.

At the beginning of the fourteenth century the Russian people were divided. Poland ruled the Ukraine, Lithuania controlled Bielorussia; and the Mongols ruled over Greater (eastern) Russia, which was divided into the five grand-duchies of Moscow, Vladimir, Susdal, Tver and Riazan. The next two centuries would see the rise to dominance of Moscow, around which the new Russian state would be formed.

Ivan I of Moscow (1325–41) is considered the originator of Moscow's ascendancy. His subservience to the Khan of the Golden Horde brought him two gains. One was as the Khan's collector of tribute, which gave him ample opportunity to further the interests of Moscow.[32] The other was the removal of the seat of the Russian church from Vladimir (where it had gone after the destruction of Kiev by the Mongols) to Moscow.

The Orthodox church in Russia had done well under the Mongols. In 1266 it had received a charter of immunity from interference by state authorities from the Khan. This enabled it to attract peasant settlers, expand the number of monasteries and be exempt from taxation, so that it became a wealthy and powerful institution. It also gave Russians a sense of unity and the Grand Dukes of Moscow strong support in their policy of overthrowing foreign rule and uniting Russians under their rule.[33]

The attractions of Moscow as the potential leader of the Russian people was enhanced by Ivan's grandson Dmitri Donskoy who, taking advantage of divisions in the Golden Horde, defeated a Mongol army at Kulikovo Pole in 1380.

Decisive steps in the unification of Russia were taken by Ivan III, the Great (1462–1505). As the Golden Horde disintegrated into separate Khanates, he brought under Muscovite control Tver, Riazan, Smolensk and the republic of Novgorod.

In 1472 Ivan married Sophia Paleologus, niece of the last Byzantine Emperor. Like the Byzantines, the Russian people and clergy had also rejected the Union of Florence, and Bishop Isidore had

had to flee to the West. When Constantinople fell the Russians claimed it was God's punishment for having accepted the heresy of the Union of Florence. The effect of these events was to intensify the independence and nationalism of the Russian church.

But Russians also claimed to be the political inheritors of the Byzantine Empire, indeed the Roman Empire. Ivan took the Byzantine double-headed eagle as the symbol of his power and introduced Byzantine court ceremony. Russian church theorists claimed that after the fall of Rome and Constantinople Moscow was now the second Jerusalem, the third Rome and its church the fount of the True Faith, Holy Russia.[34]

On the one hand, this would create a sense of mission for the Russian people and their leaders which would involve championship of the Orthodox Slavonic peoples in Europe and the beginning of the long duel with Turkey over the Balkans and the Black Sea which would last until nearly the end of the twentieth century.

On the other hand, Ivan was able to bring about the same relationship between church and state as existed in the Byzantine Empire into his state. He was the first to call himself 'Tsar' (i.e. Caesar), requiring acceptance of his authority not only in all temporal matters but, with some reservations, in religious matters also. And so it would remain until 1917.

And it was under Mongol rule in Russia that the process of regimentation and binding to service of the Russian people began.[35]

The boyars saw advantages to themselves in supporting the more likely Grand Dukes of Moscow in the race for Russian leadership. But they would find that the freedom of service enjoyed under Kievan Russia would end and that they would be bound to the Grand Duke's service.[36]

In the fourteenth and fifteenth centuries East Russian princes, descendants of Rurik, found it wise to surrender their hereditary rights to the Grand Duke. They entered his service to carry out the same high political and military functions as the boyars. It was the same, too, for the lesser gentry.[37]

After the victory of Dmitri Donskoy the Grand Dukes took over the internal administration of their areas, but since they still acknowledged themselves as the Khan's vassals they retained Mongol, rather than Kievan, patterns of taxation and army organisation.[38] Although technically free the townspeople and peasants had to pay taxes and supply labour, and the Mongol system of universal conscription ended the Kievan *veche* system of city militias. Mongol torture and capital and corporal punishment also came to influence Russian justice.[39]

But the Russians were not the only East Europeans to fall victim to despotism and serfdom.

The great significance of the expansion of trade into the Baltic in the thirteenth century was that it brought into the European economy food and raw materials in large quantities, at low prices, and easily transportable. The most important item of food was grain. Until the thirteenth century Middle Ages agriculture consisted of subsistence farming. Any surplus was used for feeding the growing urban populations. Now grain could be produced in enormous quantities in the vast flat plains of the Baltic states, eastern Germany and Poland, and shipped in by sea or river to reach anywhere in Europe.

Originally land was given to peasants as an inducement to get then to settle there, and they held that land as free men. But in these eastern frontier areas government depended from the very beginning on the land-owning aristocracy. These areas stood in need of military defence, yet both military and administrative resources were scarce because of the vastness of the territory and the comparatively thinly settled population. In the absence of a powerful and thriving middle class these aristocratic landowners were the only source of effective authority upon which rulers could rely, and therefore they had to have their loyalty.

And the only way to keep their loyalty was to pay for it through both grants of land and the means to exploit it. The problem was not land, of which there was plenty, but the people to work it. This became vital when the rate of migration fell as the Black Death and its subsequent visitations reduced sharply the continent's population, yet the demand for grain grew.

Since most of the good land was owned by the free peasantry and since this peasantry was the only available source of manpower, the aristocracy began to seize land and compel the peasants to work as common labourers. Their freedom of movement began to be restricted, as well as their status as free men.

Thus paradoxically trade, usually a liberating force, enhanced feudalism, and the peasantry in eastern Europe moved away from freedom towards serfdom just at a time when in most of western Europe the peasantry was throwing serfdom off, and the differences between the societies of eastern and western Europe began to widen.[40] The events of the next centuries would widen them even more.

8 The Expansion of Europe and the First Colonial Empires 1500–1650AD

As mentioned in the previous chapter, one of the consequences of the rise of the Ottoman Empire and the end of the Byzantine Empire was that traditional trade routes by land from Europe to India and China were blocked, leading to attempts to reach these areas by sea, and a period in world history was begun which would see Europe and Europeans come to dominate the globe. Leading the way were Portuguese, Spaniards and Italians, to be followed by Frenchmen, Englishmen and Dutchmen.

The route to India and beyond was opened by the Portuguese. In 1487 Bartholomew Diaz reached the Cape of Good Hope. In 1498 Vasco da Gama rounded the Cape and went on to India, arriving at the town of Calicut. From thence the Portuguese sailed on further east, reaching Malaya in 1509, the Moluccas (New Guinea, Borneo, Timor) in 1513 and at last China in 1514.

The search for a route to the east via the west was begun in 1492 by Christopher Columbus, a Genoese working for the King and Queen of Spain. In his first voyage he discovered only some Caribbean islands, but in later voyages he reached the central American mainland. For a long time Columbus was credited with having discovered the New World, although today it is generally believed that the Vikings were the first to do so, landing in Labrador, Newfoundland and even further south towards the end of the tenth century.[1] Newfoundland was re-discovered in 1497 by the Florentine Giovanni Caboto (John Cabot), working for Henry VII of England.

In the first half of the sixteenth century, the Portuguese Pedro Cabral discovered Brazil; the Florentine Amerigo Vespucci discovered the mouth of the Amazon and Uruguay, and the Spaniard Juan de Solis the River Plate.

In the years 1519–22 a Spanish expedition led by a Portuguese, Ferdinand Magellan, was the first to circumnavigate the world. In doing so it rounded Cape Horn, penetrating the Pacific from the west. Amongst its territorial discoveries was the Philippines (so named after the heir to the throne); its other importance was confirmation that the world was, indeed, round.

During the years of that voyage the Spaniard Hernando Cortez entered and, with a very small force of horse and firearms, overthrew the Aztec Empire of central Mexico, annexing it to Spain, and beginning the Spanish conquest of Central and the rest of South America. 1534 saw the conquest by the Spaniard Francisco Pizarro of the Inca Empire of Peru. In 1538 Gonzalo Quesada conquered Columbia, and in the 1540s Chile was discovered and explored.

These years also saw Europeans arrive in North America. Giovanni da Verrazano, a Florentine in the service of King Francis I of France discovered the Atlantic coast of today's United States. In 1534 the Breton Jacques Cartier sailed down the St. Lawrence river. In the 1540s Fernando de Soto penetrated Florida and Francisco Coronado New Mexico.

These voyages of discovery soon extended to trying to reach India and China by the north-east and north-west. The Englishman Richard Chancellor, searching for a north-east passage, reached Archangel in 1553, opening up a trade route with Muscovite Russia. In the 1590's the Dutchman Willem Barents discovered Spitzbergen and Novya Zemlya. Seeking a north-west passage John Frobisher reached Baffin Island in 1574 and Henry Hudson entered the bay that bears his name in 1610.

It was also in the 1540s that Europeans made contact for the first time with the legendary Zipangu, Japan, so that the only areas of the world not known to the Europeans by the end of the sixteenth century were Australia and New Zealand. They would be reached by the Dutchman Abel Tasman in the 1640s.

At the time that Europe began to expand overseas the most populous and advanced state in the world technologically was China. Chinese fleets had already penetrated the Indian Ocean. So why did Europe take over the world rather than China?

The reason was that China simply took the decision to turn its back on the world. Overseas trade was halted – indeed in 1521 it was made illegal for Chinese nationals – and the Chinese spirit of improvisation and enquiry was stunted by a static defence of the past, complacency about the superiority of Chinese culture, and rejection of the worth of anything foreign. Until 1840 European trade with China was restricted to Canton only, and only with licensed Chinese merchants.[2]

The Chinese government could take such a decision because the state was unified and centralised. By contrast Europe was divided into a number of states and this stimulated rivalry and competition, both military and entrepreneurial. Precisely because Europe was decentralised, economic development could not be suppressed and trade could not be forbidden. Thus what distinguished the captains, crews and explorers of Europe was that they came from an environment of competition, risk and entrepreneurship. Technological competivity would rapidly lead to improvements in map-making, navigational tables, and instruments such as telescopes, barometers and compasses. Advances in banking ensured that mercantile credit was plentiful and its availability not hampered by political divisions.[3]

There were four main developments arising from these discoveries. The first, a socio-cultural one, saw on the one hand a Europeanisation of the world through colonialisation. On the other hand, it was the beginning of a period of great shifting of peoples and a mixing of races. The most obvious example of this was the transportation of people for economic reasons – slavery when this migration was involuntary. Culturally, these discoveries led to the expansion of knowledge, particularly with regard to the natural sciences.

The first great movement of peoples was to the Americas from Europe and from Africa.

Those leaving Europe were varied: adventurers lured by prospects of gold, silver and precious stones; paupers, with nothing at home and everything to gain abroad; criminals, either sentenced as indentured labour to transportation, or volunteering for a new start; the landless sons of landowners; refugees fleeing religious persecution as a result of being on the wrong side in the series of European civil and national wars fought in the name of religion.

During the sixteenth century the chief areas for migration were Central America and the West Indies. Settlement of North America was very sparse. The big surge in migration there would come in the seventeenth century, at first establishing settlements along the coast. It would not be until the eighteenth century that attempts would be made to penetrate far inland, let alone go beyond the barrier of the Allegheny mountains.[4]

Two factors affecting the course of colonialisation were the weather and local labour supplies. In Central America, northern South America and the Caribbean the climate was unsuited for hard manual labour by Europeans. After the initial impetus, the rhythm of migration to these areas slackened off. In Central and northern South America the Spanish and Portuguese conquerors forced the local natives to work the gold and silver mines and plantations while they set up large landed estates and trading institutions.

The situation was different in the Caribbean.

Sugar had come to Europe via the Mediterranean from Persia in the thirteenth century, and it came to be grown in the eastern Mediterranean and North Africa. But when the Ottoman Turks conquered these areas they put a stop to production, and prices rose sharply.

By 1530 sugar plantations were being established in the West Indies but the local Carib populations were either dying from white man's diseases or were hostile to the idea of forced labour. It was therefore proposed to import black slaves from the west coast of Africa to work the sugar plantations. Not only were blacks believed to be docile and willing workers, they were resistant to one of the most fatal diseases of the tropics, malaria, because of sickle cells in the blood. The same applied to exploitation of a new product, tobacco, in the southern parts of North America.[5]

By contrast, further north, where the indigenous inhabitants were also few and often hostile, the climate was temperate like that of Europe, and therefore conducive to on-going immigration, and the immigrants were ready to work themselves. These were areas of British, Dutch and French settlement, small – usually Protestant – farmers, clearing and settling the land and establishing the commercial institutions to support such agricultural activity.[6]

Thus in Central and South America, the West Indies and southern North America one had the traditional colonial pattern of a dominant white society living off the work of local or imported labour, while in northern America society was much more egalitarian.

The second result of these discoveries was the expansion in world trade, and in the techniques of trade.

The former stemmed from the simple fact that new products such as tobacco, cocoa, and potatoes were coming onto the market, and old products such as fish, fur, coffee and sugar were now available in far larger quantities, while new areas of the world such as America and India were being opened for trade. Two patterns of triangular trade set in. In the early years the Atlantic sea-board countries exported firearms, cloth and salt to West Africa, which in turn exported slaves to the West Indies and the West Indies sent its rum and sugar back to Europe. Later the North American colonists wanted clothing, equipment and luxury goods which would be imported from Europe. At the same time, on the Caribbean islands where the land was almost entirely devoted to the production of crops, food (and particularly meat) had to be imported, and came to be so from North America. The Americans paid for their imports from Europe by exporting to the Caribbean which paid for its imports by exporting to Europe.[7]

The significant factor about this international trade was that of distance. The greater the distance the longer the time in transit of goods and the less frequent the ship from or to home. And that in turn meant the need to be able to hold large stocks of the goods in question. All these things required big capital outlays and extensions of credit since often goods had to be dispatched before receipt of payment either in cash or in kind.

Towards the end of the Middle Ages merchants were carrying on their business either alone or within the framework of the family. If they had partners they were in other towns or even other countries. What hindered trade expansion was debt. Every member of a partnership was legally liable for its debts without limit, and thus people went into business only if they controlled its management.

Now, however, the scale and risky nature of intercontinental commerce required more capital than one person could – or would – provide: money for ships, larger ships, even fleets of ships, and warehouses. This led to the formation of joint stock companies, associations of merchants pooling their capital, with or without state participation. Many of the great trading companies of the sixteenth and seventeenth centuries were indeed heavily backed by the state – the Dutch East India Company, the English Merchant Venturers, the Muscovy Company, the Honourable East India Company, the Spanish Carrera de Indias, the Portuguese Casa da India and the French East India Company.[8]

As with the later Middle Ages, payments were made by Bills of Exchange. These had applied to the two-way relationship between buyer and seller. During the seventeenth century, however, Bills came to be endorsed to authorise a third party to collect the money. This added to the supply of money available, sums which were increasing in any case because of the input into the European economy of Spanish gold and silver mined in the New World and used to promote Spanish political ambition. The money supply was also increased with the development of bank notes. Dealers in Bills and currency attracted deposits of these by offering to pay interest on them, and lending them out at higher rates of interest. In the sixteenth century, lending was mainly to kings, the aristocracy or municipalities, particularly the former since they could offer trading concessions and monopoly rights in return. It was in the seventeenth century, particularly in Holland and England, that banking houses began issuing deposit receipts which developed into issuing banknotes that were promises to pay, on demand, the stated sum of money.[9]

The third consequence of the voyages of discovery was the change in the balance of economic power from Baltic and Mediterranean Europe to Atlantic Europe.

In the late Middle Ages the leading commercial areas were Italy, the Low Countries and the Baltic. Europe's leading ports were Venice and Genoa, Antwerp and Lübeck, with Venice holding the monopoly of trade with the eastern Mediterranean, acting as middleman between the rest of Europe and Arab merchants trading with India and China for, particularly, silks and spices. But with direct contact now possible by sea round the Cape of Good Hope, this monopoly was challenged.

And since it was the Atlantic sea-board countries which had made the discoveries in the New World it was they who established and controlled the markets there. Unsurprisingly therefore, investors and bankers, particularly from Germany and Italy, switched their investments to these countries.

All this led to the rise of ports such as Seville (given the monopoly of the Spanish trade with the Americas, to the detriment of Mediterranean ones such as Barcelona), Lisbon, Amsterdam, Rotterdam, Bristol and London.

And with the shift in economic power to the Atlantic came, fourth, a corresponding expansion in the political power of these countries.

Whereas in central and eastern Europe where the political authorities had their hands full holding the line against further Turkish advance, in the west the sixteenth century saw the beginning of the colonial empires and the eventual division of large parts of the world between them. Indeed the process had begun before the end of the fifteenth century, and even before much had been discovered. Preferring alliance rather than conflict, Spain and

Portugal agreed to arbitration by the Pope, Alexander VI, in regard to ownership of the unexplored world. By the Treaty of Tordesillas (1494), everything east of a line drawn down the middle of the Atlantic at a point 370 leagues east of the Cape Verde Islands was assigned to Portugal, and everything west of that to Spain.

This enabled Portugal to establish itself in South America (Brazil), in Africa (Angola and Mozambique), in India (Goa), and beyond to the Indonesian archipelago and eventually Macao. Spain obtained the rest of Central and South America, much of the west and south of North America, the Philippines, and a number of important Caribbean islands, including Cuba, Jamaica and San Domingo.[10]

The Treaty did not, of course, prevent rivalry between the signatories, nor did the other Atlantic seaboard countries accept the exclusion implied by the Pope's ruling. France established itself in large parts of North America, notably Canada, and, in the seventeenth century, in the Caribbean island of Martinique. The Dutch established themselves in the Cape of Good Hope, Ceylon (today's Sri Lanka), the islands of today's Indonesia (ousting the Portuguese in doing so), and setting up trading posts in India, again to the detriment of the Portuguese. The English established colonies in Newfoundland and the eastern seaboard of North America before the East India Company, about 1600, began establishing trading posts in India to rival the Dutch and Portuguese.

The first country to profit from the discoveries was Spain. In the High Middle Ages the Iberian peninsular had been divided in two. In the North were six Christian states – Portugal, Leon, Navarre, Castile, Aragon and the County of Barcelona. In the South the Moors held sway. Over the next centuries two developments occurred. The first was the so-called *Reconquista*, under which the Moors were gradually pushed back until by 1450 only the deep South around Granada was left in their charge. The second was the emergence of powerful kingdoms. Portugal became a kingdom in 1139. Castile took over Leon in 1037 and spearheaded the *Reconquista*, capturing Cordoba in 1236. Aragon took over Barcelona in 1137 and expanded to become the leading power in the western Mediterranean, capturing the Balearic Islands in 1235, Valencia in 1238, Sicily in 1282, Sardinia in 1326, and eventually Naples in 1442. Navarre, however, remained a small independent state but was increasingly drawn into the politics of France on the other side of the Pyrenees.

Two events contributed to Spain becoming Europe's greatest power since the Roman Empire at its height. The first was the marriage in 1469 of Ferdinand of Aragon and Isabella of Castile. In 1479 the two states were united, although they both retained their original institutions. The war against the Moors was pursued energetically and in 1492, the year in which Columbus sailed for the Americas, Granada, their last foothold, fell.

The second was the wedding of Joanna, daughter of Ferdinand and Isabella to Philip, son of the Habsburg Archduke of Austria and Holy Roman Emperor Maximilian and Mary of Burgundy. Their son Charles thus inherited from his parents the Duchy of Burgundy (then in French hands), the Low Countries, and Austria, which included Bohemia, Silesia and Croatia, to add to the inheritance of his grandparents, a Spain that also controlled Naples, Sicily, Sardinia, Central and South America, and the Philippines. When in 1519 he was elected Holy Roman Emperor as Charles V in succession to his grandfather he could theoretically command the allegiance of Germany as well.

It was therefore perhaps not surprising that Charles should see as his task the restoration of the medieval universal and Catholic Empire. And the story of the next century and a half in Europe was the attempt of him and his successors to use the wealth obtained from the Americas to do that.

Nevertheless, the forces arrayed against this Spanish crusade for European and Catholic unity were formidable.

The Turks still controlled North Africa and would contest with Spain the western Mediterranean, while pressing against Habsburg possessions in eastern Europe.

France was particularly concerned at the rise of Spain. The English might have been driven out (with the exception of Calais that would not fall until 1558), but the Kingdom of France, which had more or less ended its internal feudal rivalries, was now surrounded on all its landward frontiers by territories owing their loyalties to Charles.

And then there was the rise of Protestantism – in the Low Countries, in northern Germany, in England, in Scotland, and even in France – which threatened to tear apart the religious unity of the continent far more ferociously than previous heresies.

Sixteenth century Spain possessed Europe's finest army and navy, and unparalleled financial resources. The army was based on a class of professional infantry and was the first to use firepower in the form of arquebuses as much as the pike. The arquebuses were used in combination with field fortifications and were decisive in defence. The strategy was to allow enemy cavalry and pikemen to attack fortified positions until, weakened or destroyed, the enemy would be open to Spanish infantry counter-attack.[11] But there were too many enemies, too many fronts to defend. Spain required intelligent mobilisation of the economy for the tasks in hand, but failure to do this would lead to overall failure and in the end relegation, by the second half of the seventeenth century, to second class status.

One reason for the failure to mobilise resources was, as with the Holy Roman Empire, that until 1700 Spain could not be said to exist as a politically integrated state. It was a collection of territories all of which retained their own privileges and institutional structures.[12] For a time it was believed that the bullion from the New World would be sufficient to support Spanish political ambitions, and for a start things seemed to go well.

The French Kings had sought to break the Spanish ring round them by attacking in Italy. Charles VIII of France had even seized Naples in 1495. Charles V would be involved in no less than four wars against France. In the first, 1521–26, the French King Francis I was defeated and captured at Pavia in 1525 and agreed to give up Burgundy and Naples as a condition for his release, as well as Milan. But he then repudiated the conditions and formed an alliance with the Pope, who was concerned at the apparently overwhelming strength of Spain, Milan and Florence. A second war resulted in which Rome was sacked in 1527 by the Spanish army, mutinous because it was unpaid, while the Pope took refuge in the castle of St. Angelo. This obliged Francis, a Christian King, to make an alliance with the Turks, and two further inconclusive wars were fought in the 1530s and 1540s, the main result of which was the devastation and decline, economic and political, of the Italian city states because in an era of large armies and heavy artillery they were simply too small.[13] There was success, too, in the Mediterranean. At Lepanto, off the west coast of Greece. Charles' illegitimate son Don John of Austria, at the head of a Spanish–Genoese–Venetian fleet, crushed the Turks in 1571.

Lepanto, coming on top of the failure of the Turks to capture Malta from the Knights of St. John in the Great Siege of 1565 heralded the end of the expansionary phase of the Ottoman Empire in the west. Henceforward the Turkish Empire would be on the decline. But Lepanto was also the high water mark in Spanish history.

The Low Countries consisted of well over a hundred prosperous cities with privileges and political liberties in seventeen autonomous provinces, under a royal governor. These provinces were by far the most thriving industrial and commercial part of Europe, handling over fifty per cent of world trade and providing in taxes a sum worth seven times the value of American silver to the Spanish Treasury. But Protestantism – particularly the Calvinist form – took hold in the 1560s, and Philip II, Charles' son, was determined to eradicate both it and the political liberties of the cities. A Spanish army was sent to the Low Countries on a mission of pacification, and war broke out in 1568.

Spain was able to retain hold of the southern Low Countries (today's Belgium) and stamp out Protestantism, but at considerable cost to the economy of the area as cities, notably Antwerp, were sacked. But the seven northern and overwhelmingly Protestant provinces continued to resist, coming together in 1584 under the leadership of the province of Holland to form the United Netherlands. The war for Dutch independence would continue in a particularly desperate fashion until the 1620s. Independence itself would not be formally agreed until 1648.

During much of the earlier phase of the war the United Provinces were supported by money and troops from England. And it was amongst other things, in order to end this aid, that Philip conceived the idea of sending a fleet to gain control of the English Channel and transport the Spanish army in the Netherlands to England. The fleet eventually sailed in 1588, but harassment by the English navy, which also used fireships, and bad weather, led to the destruction of the so-called Spanish Armada.

And with the lack of success in the Netherlands came economic decline. The destruction of the southern Low Countries in the campaigns of pacification led to a decline in Spanish revenue from that area. Nor was the bullion from the Americas enough, and sometimes fleets failed to arrive at all as they were attacked by the English and Dutch privateers or succumbed to bad weather.

In any case the bullion that did arrive was never used to develop the Spanish economy, but rather to pay the armed forces, and this meant that it was spent not in Spain but wherever Spanish forces were fighting, benefiting not Spaniards but other Europeans.

The costs of Empire obliged Philip II (1556–98) to increase existing taxes and set new ones. But the taxes were merely passed on in increased prices on manufactured goods, which rendered them uncompetitive in international markets, and led to revenue being used to pay for imports.

Another method of raising funds was to issue bonds, and the result was disastrous. The public debt increased six-fold. Funds were drawn in which might otherwise have been used to invigorate trade and industry. And the interest paid on bonds was so high that it often exceeded the total amount of ordinary fiscal receipts. Sometimes money was not paid out and the owners of bonds were asked to accept more bonds. Unsurprisingly, large sections of the entrepreneurial urban-commercial population of Spain abandoned trade to become '*rentiers*', and the once thriving cities of Spain became commercial graveyards.[14]

Nor did it help that one of the most entrepreneurial groups in Spanish society was persecuted.

Ferdinand and Isabella were determined to make Spain a Catholic state for a Catholic people. It was in their reign that the Inquisition was renewed, under the Dominican Tomas de Torquemada. Less than three months after the fall of Granada the Jews who did not convert to Christianity were expelled from Spain, thus depriving the state of a dynamic community whose capital and skill had enriched Castile. The effect was to weaken the economic foundation of the Spanish monarchy at the very outset of its imperial career.[15]

More than a century later came the turn of the Moriscos, Moors who had converted to Christianity. They were not as wealthy or as enterprising as the Jews but tended to be agricultural labourers and menial workers. Over ninety per cent of the 300 000 in Spain were expelled between 1608 and 1614, the practical consequences of which were soon realised.[16]

Spain in the period of its greatness, 1492–1659, was one of contrasts. On the one hand, for literature and the arts it was the 'Golden Age', with the *Don Quixote* of Cervantes and the dramas of Lope de Vega, and the paintings of El Greco, Murillo and Velazquez. In the field the Spanish army was still considered the best in Europe, and would be until defeat at the hands of the French at Rocroi in 1643 during the Thirty Years War. On the other hand, the way the economy had developed led to extremes of wealth and poverty, with no thriving middle class to bridge the gap.[17]

The unproductive nature of the Spanish state was further personified in the two areas to which Spaniards – at least in Castile – gravitated: the Church and the Court. There was a dramatic increase in the number of religious houses and religious orders, membership of which provided food and shelter to the poorer elements in society. For those with higher social pretensions, the Court in Madrid held out hope of employment in the households of the King and nobility, or an expanding bureaucracy.[18]

The Dutch did not make the mistakes made by Spain. Triumph in the War of Liberation against Spain led to Holland becoming, briefly, the world's foremost commercial power, and certainly the most prosperous. And even more remarkably the foundations of Dutch success were laid during that terrible war itself.

Dutch success can be ascribed to eight factors:

First, politics were dominated not by a warrior aristocracy that looked down on trade with contempt but a class of entrepreneurial merchants, experienced in mobilising resources.[19]

Second, the Dutch were excellent ship designers. They built ships with ample cargo space, and with relatively shallow draughts so as to enable them to operate in rivers as well as the sea. The costs of building ships were low and credit was easily available. Dutch shipping ranged across the whole world, from the Baltic and the North Sea to North America (New York was originally New Amsterdam), South Africa and the Far East. Freight rates were held down to win the international transport trade. The result was that goods, including raw materials, were available from all over the world.

Third, Amsterdam became the world's financial capital. Unlike Spain, Dutch society was essentially bourgeois middle class, based on centuries of entrepreneurship. Such a society facilitated savings, and savings were invested at home or abroad. Amsterdam hosted a stock market with stocks and shares in foreign as well as Dutch companies. The Bank of Amsterdam lent large sums of money at low rates of interest, also to foreigners. The Dutch guilder became a world reserve currency. The result was that capital was plentiful and cheap.

Fourth, Holland had a plentiful supply of skilled workers. This was partly because of the inflow of refugees fleeing religious persecution – Protestants from France and the Southern Low Countries, and Jews.

Fifth, Dutch commercial power was based on policies of lowering the unit costs of production, if necessary lowering the quality of production in order to increase the actual amount produced.

The above factors combined to make Holland commercially prosperous as the Dutch became Europe's middlemen. Raw materials were imported cheaply from all over the world in Dutch ships, to be transformed into finished products, and these would then be exported in Dutch ships.[20]

Sixth, this commercial prosperity was accompanied by the agricultural progress necessary to feed a population over half of which lived in cities.[21] Forty per cent of the United Provinces was below sea level. Large areas (*polders*) were reclaimed from the sea, and a new agricultural policy was developed. This involved introducing more vegetables, such as peas, beans and lentils, and also grasses, while reducing the area under corn, and even planting corn less regularly in crop rotations. This was made possible by the availability of plentiful supplies of grain from the Baltic, brought, of course, in Dutch ships. But the main object of planting these vegetables, besides providing a more varied diet for humans, was to increase animal feed and add nitrogen to the soil. The increase in animals led to an increase in manuring which actually led to improved output of corn per acre, so that the vicious circle that had dogged medieval agriculture – few animals meaning little manure, little manure leading to low corn yields, low corn yields meaning more land having to be ploughed for corn so that there was less winter feed for animals, and therefore fewer animals – was broken.[22]

Seventh, there was the behaviour of their enemies. The Spanish destruction of the southern Low Countries eliminated rival towns and markets – Antwerp (for banking and finance) and Bruges (for textiles). Spanish intolerance fuelled the flight of human capital in the form of skilled workers. And Spain was far too over-committed militarily to smash Holland once and for all.

Eighth, because they were wealthy, the Dutch were able to pay their forces regularly, and keep them in being throughout the year.

Like the Spaniards, the Dutch saw the importance of firepower on the battlefield and linked to defensive positions.[23] Dutch prosperity in the seventeenth century provided the basis for Dutch cultural civilisation, seen notably in the great era of Dutch painters – Hals, Rembrandt, Rubens, Rysdael, Van Dyke and Vermeer with their land and seascapes, but above all their portraits of the comfortable, well-fed, satisfied bourgeoisie.

Dutch independence was finally secured with the Peace of Munster in 1648, part of the overall settlement of the Thirty Years War, and for a few decades thereafter the Dutch were a power to be reckoned with in Europe. But their success had been based on their position as middlemen. Decline set in when faced with English rivalry. Their shipbuilding and banking techniques were copied; their role as middlemen was challenged by Navigation Acts which required goods to and from England and its American colonies to be transported in English ships; high tariffs made exporting difficult; and the almost continual wars with France and England from 1651–1713 forced increased taxation, leading in turn to higher unit costs and lower profits.

9 Reformation, Counter Reformation and Religious War 1500–1650AD

By the middle of the fifteenth century Germany was seething with dissatisfaction with the Church. Because of the weakness of German central political power the Papacy had a much stronger position than in England, France and Spain where the Church was much more 'national'. Thus the Papacy was still able to appoint French and Italians to German bishoprics and, since less money was coming from the countries with 'national' churches, it was demanding increased contributions from Germany.

A second source of resentment was the behaviour of the senior clergy, who considered their bishoprics as feudal fiefs and a means of maintaining standards of living commensurate with their social status rather than paying attention to their spiritual functions. These were left to the parish clergy, who were in many cases theologically ignorant or illiterate, and poorly paid.[1]

Third, at a time of intensification rather than decline in religious belief, there was resentment at the deterioration of ecclesiastical means of salvation into substitutes such as confessions and the sale of indulgences.

Martin Luther, a Saxon (1483–46) had studied law at Leipzig University, joined the Augustinian Order of Hermits in 1505 and was ordained in 1507. His Order sent him to Wittenberg University to teach moral philosophy, where by 1511 he was a Doctor of Theology and Professor of Biblical Studies.

And it was in Wittenberg on 31 October 1517 that Luther posted on the door of the castle church his ninety-five theses attacking the sale of indulgences, the Church's preoccupation with material possessions, and contrasting those material possessions with its true wealth, namely, the Gospel.

Crucial to an understanding of Lutheranism and its significance are Luther's interpretation of the relations between God and Man, and, linked to it, his views on politics and society, particularly the place of labour.

Luther accused the Church of lapsing into Pelagianism, that the individual was able to get into contact with God by his achievements and be accepted by Him on that account. But, following St. Augustine, who had argued that sinful persons could not reach God by their own resources, Luther believed that it was up to God, through His Grace, to reach out and find the individual. God's Grace was available to the penitent believer, but God's only communication with the individual was through His Word, as given in the Scriptures. God, through the Bible, spoke only to those who had Faith. Faith in God was the answer, not personal achievements such as good works. Thus a direct relationship with God was the only source of Grace.[2]

There were three consequences of these views:

First, because of the need for a direct relationship between God and the individual there was no need for intermediaries such as the Blessed Virgin Mary as mediator, the Saints as intercessors and the clergy as priests.

Second, the Bible was the only source of Faith, in contrast to the belief of the Church that not only the Bible but also tradition were sources (tradition being interpreted as the decrees of Popes and Councils, the infallible authorities on the scriptures).

Third, salvation was entirely in the hands of God. The individual could only know God, and be accepted by Him, if He so chose.

Accused, inevitably, of heresy, Luther defended himself in a public debate in 1519 in Leipzig with Johann Eck, Professor of Theology at Ingolstadt. And it was during this debate that Luther broke with Rome – denying the primacy of the Pope, the infallibility of Pope and Councils, and Church tradition.

The following year Luther called on the Holy Roman Emperor, Charles V, to take the lead in introducing reforms, and arguing that only two of the seven sacraments of the Church, baptism and communion, could be justified on a scriptural basis (the other five were confirmation, marriage, confession, ordination and extreme unction). When the Pope sent a Bull threatening excommunication, Luther publicly burnt it in Wittenberg. Nor did Luther get any help from Charles V, who placed him under the Ban of the Empire.

Nevertheless, Luther lived for another twenty-six years, developing the basis for Protestant forms of worship, catechisms, marriage ceremonies, baptismal booklets, communion services (including taking the Eucharist in both kinds), and the right of Lutheran clergy to marry. Luther himself married a former nun.

But why was Luther not burnt at the stake like so many heretics before him? Why did the threat of excommunication fall flat? The answer lay in the political situation at the time. In 1519 the Holy Roman Emperor Maximilian I died. The Pope did not want his heir, Charles, King of Spain, to succeed him, and sought the support of the German territorial princes. Similarly Charles wanted the support of the same princes. But the princes, and in particular the Humanist Frederick the Wise, Elector of Saxony, were very dissatisfied with the structures of the Empire and their roles in it, particularly the failure of the Emperors to use the Empire's institutions, and they showed it by their support for Luther. Several princes ignored Charles's ban on Luther after he became Emperor, and Frederick gave Luther shelter in his castle of Wartburg in Thuringia. Then in the 1520s and 1530s Charles was too preoccupied with his wars against the French and the Turks to give much heed to the new heresy. Crucially, Charles did not attend the Diet of Speyer in 1526 at which it was agreed that each German prince should decide his own policy on Lutheranism. This encouraged more rulers to adopt Lutheranism, with the result that Germany rapidly began to divide in two. When, at another Diet at Speyer in 1529 Charles proposed curbing Lutheranism by force, some of the princes 'stood up in protest' against the proposals, protesting also against the practices and beliefs of the Church of Rome. This resulted in those in the movement being given the title of 'Protestants'; prior to 1529 they had been called 'Evangelicals'.[3] Then, in 1531, eight Protestant princes and eleven cities formed the so-called Schmalkaldic League to resist threats against them by Charles, effectively ending German unity.[4]

What helped the division become rapidly wider was that during his four years in Wartburg Castle Luther translated the New Testament into German. Before then the Bible was hardly ever read except by theologians or experts who understood Latin. In 1445 Johann Gutenberg had invented printing with moveable metallic type. In 1455 came the first Bible to be printed. Printing spread rapidly throughout Europe. When Luther translated the entire Bible into German, which he did by 1532, he did so into a German vernacular that was intelligible to every German speaker. In doing so he laid the foundations of a uniform written German language.

Indeed, it has been claimed that Luther was the first to turn the Germans into one people by standardising the various linguistic dialects.[5] Translating the Bible into printed German ensured his doctrines became rapidly known.

During the years 1521–1555 Lutheranism established itself deeply in Germany, particularly in the north and east – in Saxony, Brandenburg and the Prussia of the Teutonic Knights. Protestant universities were established at Jena, Königsberg and Marburg. Big cities like Bremen, Magdeburg and Ulm adopted Protestantism. And beyond Germany Lutheranism spread to Scandinavia – Denmark, Norway and Sweden.

It was not until the 1540s that Charles was able to turn his attention against the Protestants. Although he defeated the Schmalkaldic League at Mühlberg in 1547 and captured some of its leaders, Lutheranism refused to die. Charles, caught up in another war with France, acknowledged that he, and the Empire, were war-weary. The result was the Religious Peace of Augsburg, 1555, which, following up the conclusions of the 1526 Diet of Speyer, basically recognised the *status quo* on the famous principle *Cuius Regio, Eius Religio*, that according to the religion of the Prince so should be the religion of his territory and his subjects. Should an Ecclesiastical Prince change his religion he would have to resign. Imperial cities were granted religious toleration.

The second important part of Lutheranism was its social philosophy, and in particular the point that Lutheranism was not about the righting of political and social wrongs. Far from it. Luther believed that the individual should accept his political and social environment and concentrate on his salvation. The political order were God's concern. Every government was ordained by God, and if rulers were evil or harsh this was Divine punishment for the sins of their subjects. People should therefore accept the existing order and obey princes and magistrates.[6]

The political significance of Lutheranism therefore was that it supported the existing order of the privileged classes. Thus, when peasants revolted in Germany in the 1520s against oppressive landlords, demanding the abolition of serfdom, Luther wrote and preached against them, urging the aristocracy to crush the revolt which, indeed, was bloodily suppressed.

And this same attitude of acceptance applied at the social level. God had placed the individual in an established station in life – Luther used the word 'calling' – and the moral obligation of the individual was to fulfil his duty in worldly affairs in that station. But it was also in this connection that lay the beginning of the so-called Protestant work ethic. Luther argued that monastic life was devoid of value. Labour was the 'outward expression of brotherly love' in that the division of labour forced every individual to work for others. Hence every legitimate calling had exactly the same worth in the eyes of God. It has been claimed that justification of this worldly activity was one of the most important results of the Reformation. Interestingly, Luther nevertheless held fairly traditional Catholic views about the work that one did, particularly that one should not work for gain beyond one's personal needs, and many sixteenth century Protestants therefore condemned usurers, monopolists, speculators and bankers, as well as the Jews. Finally, for Luther the differentiation of people into class and occupations was a result of Divine Will, and to persevere in one's allotted station in life was therefore a religious duty.[7]

Luther's contribution to German and European history was thus considerable. His gloomy view of human nature made him distrust the people as a whole. By preaching submissiveness to government, by encouraging German nationalism, by its hostility to liberal and democratic forces, Lutheranism's contribution to the development of the national character of important parts of Germany was very significant.

Protestantism had thus not only survived, it had a firm political base. And it was also acquiring others – notably in Switzerland.

In 1523 Ulrich Zwingli, a military chaplain in Zurich, got his city to adopt a programme of reform based on prohibition of all Catholic forms of worship – processions, relics, images. There was to be state control of church attendance, morality and care of the poor. Predestination was also emphasised. Zwingli's ideas were accepted in other Swiss towns such as Basel, Bern, St. Gall. and then in Strasbourg. Although he was killed in 1531 in a war between Zurich and the Catholic Swiss Cantons his views would influence one who would rival Luther as Protestant idealogue – John Calvin.

John Calvin (1509–64) was a Frenchman from Noyon in northern France who settled in Geneva in 1536. In 1541 he organised the first Calvinist church there, and Geneva soon gained the reputation of being the centre of a radical international movement that threatened to destabilise western Europe, inspiring the same fear in the sixteenth century as Moscow and communism in the twentieth century.[8]

In many important respects Calvin's doctrines were very different from those of Luther:

First, Calvin saw society as a religious community which should govern itself through the election of representatives to all spiritual offices – pastors, doctors, elders, deacons.

Second, the duty of the state was to help the religious community and see that its rules were obeyed, rather than the other way round. Among these rules were obligatory church attendance, prohibition of dancing and gambling, and the removal of all images, altars and candles.

Third, the sovereignty of the people was supreme, and because they had a covenant with God, prior and superior to that with any earthly rulers, they had a right to revolt against bad government or tyrants. Indeed, Calvin's successor in Geneva, Theodore Bèze, developed the theory of justifiable tyrannicide.

Fourth, the individual was predestined to salvation or damnation. God did not exist for individuals but they for Him. Only a small percentage of people could be chosen, the Elect, and for the damned to complain was simply like animals complaining that they were not born humans. Since God's decrees were immutable it was as impossible for those who had His Grace to lose it as it was for those who did not have it to obtain it.[9] But how did one know if one was one of the Elect? For Calvin, since communication with God was carried on in a deeply spiritual isolation, it was a matter of personal inner certainty. Indeed it was a duty to consider oneself chosen since doubt and lack of self-confidence were temptations of the Devil. Calvin's followers, notably Bèze, however, wanted a more concrete outward sign that one was of the Elect.[10]

Fifth, therefore, – and the fullest development of the Protestant ethic – worldly activity provided self-confidence, and success in trade, in one's 'calling' was the proof that one was indeed of the elect.

For the Calvinist, God worked through the Elect and the Elect were conscious of it. Their actions originated not from Luther's hopeful piety but from the militant certainty caused by God's Grace. For Luther the individual was a vessel of the Holy Spirit; for Calvin he was a tool of the Divine Will. For Luther, one's 'calling' was a fate to which the individual should submit and make the best of; for Calvin it was God's commandment to work for the Divine Glory, and indeed there was no reason why one should not have several 'callings' in one's life if this was useful to God, the community or the individual concerned. One laboured, therefore, for the Glory of God, and the better one worked and the more successful one was, God's Glory was correspondingly enhanced.

Whereas for Roman Catholics labour was necessary only for the maintenance of the individual in his station in life and the community, and desire for anything over and above what was needed was considered avarice, one of the seven deadly sins, for Calvinists profit was perfectly respectable. If God showed one a way lawfully to obtain more than in another way and one rejected it, one was rejecting one of the ends of one's 'calling' and refusing to be God's steward. One laboured to be rich for God. Wealth was thus not only morally permissible but to be encouraged, as in the parable of the Talents. What was *not* acceptable was enjoyment of wealth in circumstances leading to idleness, temptations of the flesh, and distraction from the pursuit of a righteous life. Waste of time was the deadliest of sins – every hour lost to labour was an hour lost to labour for the Glory of God.

Since the Glory of God was to be sought not only by prayer but by action, by labour, Calvinists scorned the idleness of mendicants, whether beggars or priests, as a sin against God and a social evil. They quoted St. Paul, 'He that does not work, neither shall he eat'. Calvinists condemned the army of beggars produced by monastic charity. Poverty, therefore, was *not* meritorious, as St Francis of Assisi had preached; and charity was condemned as a bribe by Popery to dissolutes and a cause of demoralisation.[11]

The basic principle of Calvinism, therefore, was that it was not an accumulation of riches that was wrong but their misuse in indulgence or ostentation. The 'elected' Christian was in the world only to increase the Glory of God by fulfilling His commands to the best of his ability. Work was not the cause of God's Grace but the means of knowing one's state of Grace.[12]

It has been claimed that since Lutheranism evolved essentially in rural Germany, it had little understanding of the economic forces beginning to transform Germany – and Europe – from feudal agriculture to urban capitalism, and that therefore it was not Protestantism in general which developed capitalism, it was Calvinism in particular because it challenged the religious barriers to capitalism.[13]

The radicalism of Calvinism lay in its appeal to the urban artisan class because it lent religious dignity to labour and productive activities. More important, social order, and particularly the position of the individual within that order, came to be seen as something which could be changed rather than being something laid down as inviolable. To the extent that the individual's position within the world was now declared to rest at least in part upon his or her own efforts, Calvinism was very appealing to those frustrated by their inability to make headway in a society dominated by tradition and hierarchy. And the theory of justifiable tyrannicide was a fundamental break with the medieval notion that existing power structures were somehow ordained by God. For the next two and a half centuries Europe would witness the conflict between those who believed in the Divine Right of Kings and those who believed in the right of peoples to overthrow their rulers.[14]

These Protestant onslaughts did not fail to have their effect on the Catholic Church, and the result was the Counter Reformation. Many in the Church readily acknowledged Luther's accusations of misused spiritual authority and institutional corruption. But another profound psychological shock was the 1527 sack of Rome by the troops of Charles V, seen as divine punishment for delay in tackling abuses. The Counter Reformation was designed both to rectify these and challenge Protestantism.[15]

The Roman Catholic reply came in the famous Council of Trento, 1545–1563. This Council clarified doctrine and dogma and dealt with the most flagrant abuses denounced by Protestants. Reforms included an end to simony, an end to the abuses of indulgences (but not their sale), far stricter clerical training, dress and duties of the clergy, including the requirement of celibacy.

However, in most other important aspects, medieval orthodoxy was confirmed: transubstantiation, justification by faith and works, confirmation of all seven sacraments, the existence of purgatory, and the supremacy of the Pope. The Inquisition was revived with the eradication of heretics and traitors to be achieved through terror and torture to obtain confessions and an Index of books prohibited by the Church drawn up (initially three-quarters of the books then published were on the list, and the Index was not abolished until 1966). Finally, the entire clergy was sworn to the provisions of the Council of Trento.

Protestants had begun by attending many of the earlier sessions of the Council, but hopes of reconciliation and unity were soon dispelled as the Roman Catholic Church insisted on acceptance of the provisions, with curses on those who did not agree. To the Protestants the Council merely confirmed their view that the Roman Catholic Church was unreformable.[16]

The sharp end of the Catholic counter-attack was seen not only in the revived Inquisition but in the tasks given the Jesuits. Founded in 1534 by a Basque nobleman, (later saint) Ignatius Loyola, 1491–1556, members of the Order of the Society of Jesus undertook to propagate the Faith by every means at the Order's disposal, the approach being that the end justified the means. Their three main tasks centred on education, counteracting Protestantism, and undertaking missionary work outside Europe.

The Jesuits provided a high quality education and training for Catholic believers. In France, the southern Low Countries, southern Germany and eastern Europe they won back large areas for the Church of Rome. And in America, Africa and Asia they sought converts among the native inhabitants and tried to counterbalance the greed of European adventurers and merchants.

The 1555 Religious Peace of Augsburg had involved only Catholics and Lutherans simply because the German princes were adherents of one or the other. The conversion in 1563 of the Elector Frederick III of the Palatinate to Calvinism rather than Lutheranism was widely regarded as a breach of the Peace of Augsburg.[17] But the Peace of Augsburg only concerned the territories of the Empire, and it was outside the Empire that Calvinism was spreading most rapidly. In the Low Countries it motivated the hostility to Spain and, as recounted in the previous chapter, the attempt by Spain to suppress it would lead to over forty years of war ending in Dutch independence.

In France, Calvinist missions had been particularly numerous, particularly in the south, because of the proximity of Geneva. In the years 1558–62 there had been massive conversions to Calvinism amongst the artisans and skilled craftsmen of the cities, and not only the new aristocracy of merchants who had acquired titles but also those descended from the feudal era. Their champion would be Henry de Bourbon, related by marriage to the ruling French Valois monarchy but also King of Navarre in his own right. The champion of the Catholics was Henry, Duc de Guise, of the House of Lorraine. Claiming descent from Charlemagne, the Guise family believed it had a greater claim to the throne of France than Valois or Bourbon.[18] In between the years 1559–74 two kings of France, brothers, Francis II and Charles IX, reigned but died without heirs and their third brother, Henry III, did not appear likely to provide an heir. Dynastic ambition was thus mixed with religious rivalry. Civil war broke out in 1562. In the fury of the struggle the Guises carried out a massacre in Paris of most of the leadership of the Huguenots, as the Calvinists were called,[19] on St Bartholomew's Day, 24 August 1572; the Duc de Guise was assassinated in 1588 on the orders of Henry III, fearful of the power of his family; Henry III himself was assassinated the following year, to be succeeded by Henry de Bourbon as Henry IV. During the war Spanish forces intervened on the side of the Catholics while the English, the Dutch and the Elector Palatine provided help for the Huguenots. Peace was only achieved when, with the famous phrase 'Paris is worth a Mass', Henry IV converted to Catholicism, and procured toleration for the Huguenots (temporarily) with the 1598 Edict of Nantes.

In the British Isles events took a rather different course.

In England King Henry VIII, 1509–47, had begun by denouncing Luther and, as a reward was given by the Pope for himself and his successors the title Defender of the Faith.[20] But the Pope was soon to be disappointed. To secure the Tudor dynasty by having a male heir Henry sought to divorce his wife Catherine of Aragon, daughter of King Ferdinand and aunt to the Emperor Charles V. After a large number of miscarriages she had only been able to give birth to a daughter, Mary, and Henry wanted instead to marry one of her ladies-in-waiting, Anne Boleyn, whom he was soon to make pregnant.

The Pope had already granted a number of divorces to European rulers but hesitated to grant one to Henry, the reason being that since its sack in 1527 Rome had been under the control of Charles V. Remembering his previous services to the Papacy Henry's attitude became increasingly hostile.[21] Since the Pope would not grant the divorce, Henry would divorce the Church of Rome.

Under his minister Thomas Cromwell, an avid reader of Marsilius of Padua,[22] legislation was passed in the years 1532–40 which amounted to the break of the Church in England with Rome. Under the 1532 Act for the Submission of the Clergy the King was given control of the Church's law-giving functions; in 1533 the Act in Restraint of Appeals designated England as a sovereign state with a King who owed no submission to any other ruler and who had full powers to give his people justice in all causes; the Dispensations

Act stopped all payments to Rome; the Act of Supremacy, 1534, recognised the King as Head of the Church, and gave the Crown rights in regard to clerical appointment, the reform of canon law, and supervision of the formulation of doctrine; the Act for First Fruits and Tenths dealt with taxation of the Church; the 1536 Treason Act made it treasonable to declare the King a heretic, tyrant or usurper, or for any official to refuse an Oath renouncing the jurisdiction of Rome; later in 1539 the Six Articles Act gave the King sole authority over doctrine.

Under these circumstances the English Church soon agreed to declare Henry's marriage to Catherine as null and void (on the grounds that the Pope had had no right to permit the marriage, when asked, because she had consummated her former marriage with Henry's brother Arthur, something Catherine denied). And an Act of Succession vested the royal succession in the heirs of Henry and Anne Boleyn.[23] Considered as important as the Dissolution of the Monasteries was the appearance of the first complete translation of the Bible in English by Miles Coverdale in 1535, based on Luther's German translations and some in English by William Tyndale. It was promoted by Thomas Cromwell who, in the Lutheran tradition, wanted to establish a religion based on the Bible. It has been claimed that the influence of this Bible was immense, providing the foundations of Anglicanism and Nonconformity, and even English constitutionalism and imperial expansion, as well as inspiring in the following century Bunyan's 'Pilgrim's Progress', the pioneers of New England, and Oliver Cromwell.[24]

The break with the Church of Rome was accompanied by another measure with far-reaching consequences – the dissolution of the Monasteries. Their land and wealth went to the Crown, and then the lands, after a few gifts to royal supporters, were sold off, principally to the gentry and yeoman farmers, substantially enlarging their numbers as well as enriching them. This growth in numbers reduced the hitherto dependence of this class on noble families and pushed them into local government, the professions, farming and trade. On the one hand, the traders in this new middle class would be able to take advantage of the expansion in world trade due to the voyages of discovery; on the other hand, the emergence of this class in politics and particularly the House of Commons, would soon lead to demands for political and constitutional change that would bear fruit in the next century.[25] Henry's break with Rome was far more personal and administrative than ideological. He still encouraged consent for the – by now – Church of England. It was in the reign of his son, Edward VI, 1547–53, under the growing influence of continental Protestantism, particularly Calvinism, that the Reformation in England became zealous. 'Superstitious ceremonies and customs' were proscribed; relics and images were swept away. The English liturgy alone was ordered for public worship. Royal decrees replaced consent. In 1549 an Act of Uniformity required use of the new Protestant prayer book, with severe penalties for non-compliance.[26]

Edward died young, and was succeeded by his half-sister Mary, a fervid Catholic. In her equally short reign (1553–58) Catholicism was restored to favour and English Protestantism found its first martyrs – some two hundred and seventy-five were burnt at the stake.[27] Much of the blame for this was put on Spanish influence: Mary had married King Philip II of Spain in 1554, a step which provoked numerous small uprisings in view of the fear in England of possible Spanish domination. A sign of this was Mary's decision to help Spain in its war with France, one result of which was the loss of Calais, the last English possession on the mainland of Europe.

Mary was succeeded by her half-sister Elizabeth, daughter of Anne Boleyn, and it was in her reign that Protestantism was decisively established in England.

A new Act of Supremacy in 1559 provided the Queen with the title of Supreme Governor of the Church of England, and all clergy and persons holding offices of state had to take an oath thereto. Mary's Statutes restoring the jurisdiction of Rome and her heresy laws were repealed. This situation would cause a crisis of conscience for those English Catholics, happy to be nationalist on the one hand but not ready to forswear their religion on the other, when the foreign policy of Spain came to threaten England directly.[28]

For the first ten years of her reign Philip attempted to woo Elizabeth (marriage was even considered), as a useful ally against France. But English sympathies with the Dutch and French Protestantism gradually earned Philip's enmity. In 1570 the Pope at last excommunicated Elizabeth, and Catholic priests were sent to England to stir up the Catholic population; there was even a small Catholic uprising. But what caused concern to Protestant England was that as long as Elizabeth was unmarried her heir was the Queen of Scots, Mary Stuart.

Mary was the daughter of King James V of Scotland and Mary of Guise. She had married Francis II, King of France, but he had died in 1560 after reigning only a year. A fervid Catholic, Mary claimed the throne of England, on the grounds that Anne Boleyn's marriage was invalid and Elizabeth therefore illegitimate, whereas she was the great-granddaughter of Henry VII. The consequences of Elizabeth's death, perhaps through assassination, would be incalculable.

Unfortunately for Mary the situation in Scotland was not good. John Knox, a pupil of Calvin, had established the Scottish National Church in 1560, to which the nobility had massively converted. Mary's efforts to reinstate Catholicism on her return to Scotland, coupled with unwise choices of husbands, led to her being forced to flee the country in 1568, leaving her son James to be brought up in the Church of Scotland.

Mary, however, chose to take refuge in England. Her tragedy was that as long as she was alive Elizabeth could not be safe. After nearly twenty years of house arrest Mary was executed in 1587 on the grounds that she was privy to Catholic plots to murder Elizabeth. Ironically, Elizabeth's heir was now Mary's son James.

It was partly Mary's execution that roused Philip to send the Armada against England. For Europe its failure was significant but not decisive: the Counter Reformation looked less likely to succeed; religious unity did not look as if it could be reimposed by force. But Protestants everywhere were encouraged to believe that God was, as they had always supposed, on their side, while French, German and Italian Catholics were secretly relieved that Spain could not, after all, claim to be God's champion and use that as an excuse to dominate them too.[29] Where the effects of the dispatch of the Armada was decisive was Ireland. In the sixteenth century English control of the island was patchy, particularly in the northern province of Ulster where the allegiance of the Irish chiefs was especially doubtful. The Reformation had led to the establishment of the Church of Ireland which, however, had looked for its inspiration not to Luther but to the old Celtic church of St Patrick, and in any case was having difficulty in making headway against the fervent Roman Catholicism of the population. When in the 1590's the Ulster chieftains took up arms against the London government and the Irish received Spanish support, the government of King James (since 1603 King James I of England and VI of Scotland) arranged in 1610 for the dispatch of thousands of Lowland Scots, mainly Calvinists, and supported by English money, to 'plant' Ulster with colonists and make it secure for the Crown. A third

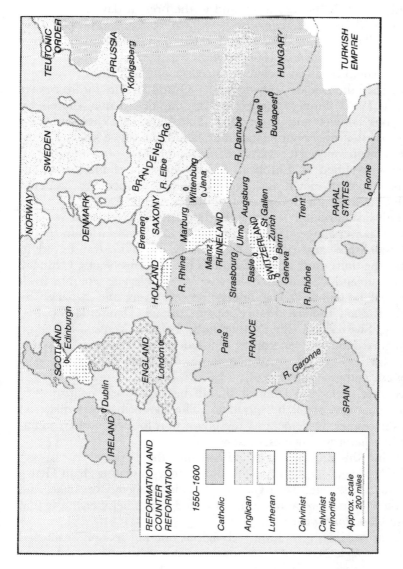

6 Reformation and Counter Reformation 1550–1600AD

religion would thus come to be encamped on Irish soil to contend for the allegiance of the population, but its concentration in Ulster would affect the politics of Ireland to the present day.[30]

In 1618 the final religious showdown of the catastrophic and bloody Thirty Years War would begin. But before then, with a 12-year truce agreed in 1609 between Spain and the Dutch, Europeans would be given a chance to reflect on their future.

In 1610 the Duc de Sully devised a 'Grand Design' for his master Henry IV of France. Concerned at the destruction caused by religious conflict and alarmed at Habsburg encirclement, Sully believed that only continental unity could guarantee safety against one's neighbours. He therefore made the first of a number of proposals aimed at European unity, generally similar proposals being repeated down the ages, particularly after big conflicts, including those for European integration after 1945.

The first proposal was that Europe should be divided up into fifteen 'powers' in such a way that a balance between them should be established and preserved. Territory could be transferred to make the units more equal. Frontiers for religious blocks, Catholic, Lutheran and Calvinist, could also be established separate from national boundaries. The fifteen 'powers' were the Papacy, the Holy Roman Empire, France, Spain, Britain, Denmark, Sweden, Savoy, Switzerland, the Netherlands, Poland, Venice, Bohemia, Hungary and 'Italy' (to consist of a federation of regions). 'Asiatic' Moscow was excluded. All boundaries, once fixed, would be permanent and guaranteed.

Second, a federal Council should be established consisting of representatives of all fifteen states. The Council would make all laws necessary for cementing the union thus formed, and for maintaining the order once established.

Third, this Europe would unite against the Turks.

Sully's ideas came to nought. Soon after presenting them Henry IV was assassinated by a Catholic fanatic, François Ravaillac, and in a few years Europe would be engulfed in a general civil war that would last thirty years.[31]

In its origins the war was a religious one but it soon developed into a struggle between the leading powers of Europe. It took place in four phases, the first of which involved Bohemia.

In 1575 the Emperor Rudolf II, a Habsburg, had been elected King of Bohemia on the understanding that he extended toleration to the country's Protestants – Hussite Utraquists, Lutherans and

Calvinists. Catholicism was nevertheless re-established as the official religion.

In 1609 Rudolf tried to withdraw this toleration but the fierce reaction led to his issuing the so-called Letter of Majesty by which Protestant worship was guaranteed. He was succeeded in 1612 by his brother Matthias, as both King and Emperor. The problem was that he had no heir, and the Habsburg family favoured the candidature, when Matthias should die, of Ferdinand of Styria, a fervent Catholic who had extirpated the Protestants in his lands. However, the King of Bohemia was also an Elector of the Empire.

In 1617 the Bohemian Estates elected Ferdinand King, and he formally guaranteed the Letter of Majesty, but violation of Protestant privileges led, the following year, to a Protestant *coup d'état*, and the beginning of the war.

As the armies manoeuvred, in March 1619 the Emperor-King Matthias died. The Bohemian government declared Ferdinand deposed and offered the throne instead to the Calvinist Frederick V of the Palatinate. In the meantime in Frankfurt Ferdinand was elected Holy Roman Emperor, the second of that name.

The Protestant princes of Germany, grouped into the Evangelical Union, did not want Frederick to take the throne of Bohemia. He would be leaving his Palatinate, a key area on the route taken by Spanish armies against the Dutch, just when the twelve-year truce was ending. Promises of support in what would inevitably be a long war were few, and shortly afterwards the Union declared its neutrality. The only troops Frederick had available were those of a mercenary, Count Mansfeld, and in November 1620 these were routed by the forces of the Catholic League under Count Tilly at the Battle of the White Mountain just outside Prague, and Frederick had to flee. At the same time Spanish troops took Frederick's home base, the Palatinate. Bohemia was the subject of savage reprisals, with enforced catholicisation and germanisation which cemented the existing Czech hatred of Germans. Frederick was deprived of his Electorship, which was given to the new German power on the rise, Bavaria, under its Duke Maximilian.

But the victory of the Habsburgs caused general Protestant alarm. With the end of the Spanish truce the Dutch had their hands full, but they, together with England, provided money for the Lutheran King Christian IV of Denmark to take up the Protestant cause.

But in this second phase of the war, 1625–29, the Protestant cause fared no better. Ferdinand's new general, Count Albrecht von Wallenstein, a wealthy and ambitious Bohemian nobleman, defeated Mansfeld at Dessau in 1626 and shortly afterwards Tilly routed the Danes at Lutter. All north Germany to the Baltic came under Ferdinand's control and the Danes were forced out of the war. The triumphant Emperor then adopted the 1629 Edict of Restitution under which all church property acquired by Protestants since 1552 had to be returned to the Catholic Church and Calvinists were to lose all political rights, decisions which would be enforced by the Imperial armies. What was particularly shocking about the Edict was that its property clauses applied to Lutheran German States which, hitherto, had generally remained loyal to the Emperor.[32]

The triumph of the Habsburgs, Spanish and Austrian, gave everyone in Europe food for thought. Two powers particularly concerned were France and Lutheran Sweden.

In France the government of Louis XIII, under Cardinal Richelieu, had been involved with domestic problems, reducing the political privileges of the Protestants obtained under Henry IV and particularly the right granted under the Edict of Nantes to have fortified strongholds. The last of these, La Rochelle, had been taken in 1628 and the French government could now consider a foreign policy in terms of extending the state to its natural frontiers of the Rhine, the Alps and the Pyrenees. But France was still weak and Habsburg encirclement seemed imminent. Protestant armies had everywhere been defeated, where was another one to be found? The answer was Sweden.

The decline of Poland as a military power in the first quarter of the seventeenth century, with defeats at the hands of Russians and Turks, whetted the appetite of the Swedes under their King Gustavus Adolphus. Under his leadership the administration of the state had been modernised and resources maximised. Conscription already existed but the King also developed a light and mobile field artillery, and adopted Dutch weaponry and tactics; a fleet of warships and transports was created.[33] Poland was invaded, and by 1626 its Baltic territories were all in Swedish hands. Gustavus was too busy just then to answer the despairing cries of the Protestants in Germany except to send a small force to relieve Stralsund, but he was alarmed at the arrival of the Habsburgs on the Baltic. Wallenstein's troops were already helping the Poles and Gustavus knew that if the Habsburgs obtained control of the Baltic Dutch commerce there would be reduced and might induce the United Provinces to make peace, and the ports on the southern shore could be used to launch attacks on Sweden itself.

In 1630, therefore, Gustavus Adolphus landed in Pomerania both to help Protestantism and to ensure the security of Swedish possessions on the mainland of Europe, and this third phase of the war saw a dramatic swing against the Habsburgs.

In January 1631 Gustavus concluded the Treaty of Bärwalde with France under which the latter agreed to finance his armies for five years. In May the city of Magdeburg on the Elbe, strategically important and Protestant was taken but so savagely destroyed by Tilly that the Lutheran States of Brandenburg and Saxony abandoned their neutrality and joined Gustavus. In September the combined Swedish–Saxon army caught up with Tilly at Breitenfeld outside Leipzig and the Imperial army was driven from the field. The Swedes then marched across Germany and liberated the Palatinate. Protestants all over Germany rejoiced and re-emerged to lend Gustavus their support.

In 1632 the Swedes invaded the hitherto untouched lands of Maximilian of Bavaria, laying the land waste. Another Imperial army under Tilly was destroyed at Rain on the Lech, and that meant that Wallenstein's army in Bohemia was now the only large one left for the Emperor. In November his army and that of King Gustavus met at Lützen in Saxony. After a long, bitter and confused battle Wallenstein withdrew and the Swedes claimed the victory, but the price was high: their King was among the fallen.

For the next two years the war continued as fiercely as before. Swedish armies continued in the field, led politically by the Swedish Chancellor Axel Oxenstierna. Bavaria was again ravaged. But suddenly things changed again. A Spanish army was sent to southern Germany to reinforce the Imperial cause and at Nordlingen in September 1634 the Swedes were, for the first time, defeated. The following year Saxony made peace with the Emperor.

These events hastened the intervention of France. In the fourth and final phase of the war (1635–48) further French subsidies kept Swedish armies going (and winning victories) while France seized Alsace and control of the left bank of the Rhine, defeating the Spanish army at Rocroi in 1643.

But the pressures for peace were relentlessly building up. For Spain, defeat on land at the hands of the French was complemented by defeat at sea at the hands of the Dutch, while Catalonia, Portugal and Spanish possessions in Italy were in revolt over the taxation for the war, and there was an outbreak of the Plague. In France, too, taxation caused local revolts as the burden of paying for the war and Swedish subsidies continually increased. Nor were the Dutch too happy to see a strong France replace a weakened Spain on their borders.

Peace negotiations began in 1644 at Munster and Osnabruck, and would last four years. Under the terms of the so-called Treaty of Westphalia, the 1555 Religious Peace of Augsburg was confirmed, but this time the Calvinists were included, with 1624 as the date for determinating ecclesiastical possessions. In terms of territory France received most of Upper Alsace. Pomerania was divided between Brandenburg and Sweden, and the latter also received Stettin, Bremen, Wismar and Rügen.

The political changes were, however, profound:

First, it marked the replacement of Spain by France as the leading power on the continent of Europe. War between the two would, in fact, re-open and an end to the Franco-Spanish rivalry begun in the days of Charles V would only be brought with the 1659 Treaty of the Pyrenees, under which France extended its territory further to include Artois and Roussillon.

Second, it was the end, for all practical purposes, of the Holy Roman Empire of the German Nation as an effective state, and the confirmation of German disunity. Territorially there was the loss of Upper Alsace and Swedish Pomerania, and the confirmation of the independence of the Netherlands and Switzerland. But the proof of its disintegration was the power given to the territorial princes to make foreign alliances as long as these were not directed against the Emperor, and the provision that the Emperor would now have to have the permission of the princes to declare war, impose taxes or raise troops.

Out of the ruins would rise four large states – Austria, Bavaria, Brandenburg and Saxony – as well as a myriad of small ones. Theoretically the Empire would continue to exist with its Supreme Court and Imperial Diet but for most of its remaining one hundred and fifty-eight years the Emperor would be an Austrian Habsburg Archduke for whom Austrian interests rather than those of the German people would be paramount.

Third, there was the economic and social decline of Germany. Germany itself had been a battlefield over which French, Spanish, Danish, Swedish armies, those of the Empire, and marauding mercenaries had marched, bringing with them destruction, famine and plague. Large areas had been laid waste. It is generally agreed that the loss of population cannot be gauged accurately, but some estimates are of over a third. From the point of view of the economy the decline in German trade and commerce in the sixteenth century was accelerated by the war and the aftermath. There was an economic vacuum in the heart of central Europe as normal trade routes were disrupted, and control of many German rivers were in non-German hands – the Swedes held the mouths of the Weser, the Elbe and the Oder; France and the Netherlands dominated the Rhine. As it was fragmented politically, so the level of development of the German economy would come to depend on the support given by the rulers of the emerging states rather than the free enterprise of the cities, and this too was confirmation of a trend that had set in early in the previous century.

The effect of the war on the peasantry was to accentuate northern and eastern as opposed to southern and western differences already marked by religion. In the Catholic and Calvinist south and west the war was akin to the Black Death, and therefore the peasantry was able to use the factor of labour shortages to gain concessions. The reaction of the landowners in the Lutheran north and east to such shortages was to clamp down feudal obligations even more severely than before.

The war also marked the decline of much of the lesser nobility, the robber-baron class of previous centuries. They too would be obliged to enter the service of the state rulers, either as bureaucrats or army officers.[34]

It has been claimed that after such a catastrophic conflict that owed its origins to religious strife, to make war in the name of religion would be seen as anachronistic, and the wars of the next century and a half would be mostly dynastic.[35] Yet religion would be a factor in the wars of Louis XIV of France against the Dutch and Britain.[36] In the meantime the terms of Westphalia prepared the ground for new conflicts – not only France versus Holland, but Brandenburg versus Sweden over Pomerania. For Brandenburg at least the lessons of the Thirty Years War and the Swedish War would result in developments that would seriously affect the course of European history.

10 Continental Absolutism and English Political Liberty 1650–1789AD

For a century and a half Europe's religious-inspired civil and international wars had plunged Europe into anarchy so there was a need for order, a craving for strong rulers.

The justification for absolutism was provided by philosophers such as Jean Bodin (1530–96) and Thomas Hobbes (1588–1679). For Hobbes, writing after the Civil War in England, in a state of nature it was 'all against all'. The only guarantee of a person's self-preservation was his own defence. The only way to end this anarchy and have peace and security would be if individuals agreed in a 'social contract' to surrender their rights of self-defence definitively to a sovereign authority (one man or an assembly) which would ensure obedience to a code of rules, if necessary by force. In the Commonwealth thus created the sovereign authority was not accountable to its subjects but only to God and his laws. The power of the authority was absolute and indivisible. Having surrendered his or her rights to it the only rights the subject now had (apart from that of self-defence) would be those re-granted by that authority. The authority was above the civil laws because if these were over it there would be a confusion in the exercise of power, an end to the Commonwealth and a return to the state of nature. Power could not be divided because any quarrel between the holders would lead to the destruction of the Commonwealth. To oppose the sovereign authority would mean civil war and an end to the Commonwealth since a subject could not obey two masters. The idea that the private judgement of individuals was the ultimate arbiter of what was true and proper was seditious since it implied that they could still possess in the Commonwealth what they held in the state of nature.[1]

To begin with the tendency was to associate the strong ruler with the King, in terms of Divine Right, although Hobbes' theory of consent could – and was – used to justify the rule of Oliver Cromwell. Bodin believed that the King was the image of God on earth.[2] But during the eighteenth century, as religion declined in the

144

face of the philosophical challenge of the Enlightenment, rulers such as Frederick II (the Great) of Prussia, Joseph II of Austria and Catherine the Great of Russia, would justify their position and powers less in terms of Divine Right and more in being the first servant of their state, dedicated to efficient rule.[3]

But as with the creation of the nation, so the exercise of royal absolutism required continued domination of alternative sources of power, notably the aristocracy and the church. How this was done on the continent depended on the way society in the individual countries had developed, but the technique was the same, holding out the poisoned chalice of privilege in order to obtain compliance in the organisation of the state. But for all the countries concerned there would be a high price to pay.

In France that price was bankruptcy and inefficiency that would lead to defeat and revolution.

As a young king, Louis XIV (1643–1715) had had to flee his capital when some of the nobility joined with the *Parlement* of Paris (*parlements* promulgated royal decrees) at the raising of taxes. He was determined that a like humiliation would not happen again, and that the royal power must be absolute.[4]

Accordingly the nobility was emasculated, and became almost parasitic – Louis moved his court to the palace of Versailles, fifteen miles outside Paris, and it was there, amid rigid social ceremony and etiquette, that the high nobility intrigued for positions of influence decided by the King. These positions might be in the church or the army; they might be meaningless posts or sinecures; but they were very rarely in government, whether national or provincial. Government itself was by royal decree, implemented by departmental ministers appointed by the King. Instead of the old feudal provinces France was divided into some thirty *généralités* controlled by royal *Intendants*. Ministers and '*Intendants*' were men of talent, usually commoners. Away from their traditional power bases the senior nobility could not provoke anti-government unrest, and without them the provincial nobility had no leadership. In return, and in addition to their appointment to offices in and around the court, the nobility were exempt from almost all royal taxation, and their sinecures and pensions were paid by state revenue.[5]

The clergy too was exempt from royal taxation, paying only a *don gratuit*. Yet its properties yielded an income of between forty and fifty per cent of landed wealth.[6] In Catholic countries like France the Church's corporate wealth in land, tithes, precious metals and art treasures made it a rival to noble or royal splendour. Indeed, it has been calculated that up to two percent of the population of the Catholic States of Europe were clerics, and the Church owned anything from seven to twenty per cent of the territory of these states. However, the revenues of the Church were devoted to maintaining the lifestyle of the senior clergy or embellishing Church property rather than to the needs of the parish priests, many of whom were desperately poor.[7]

The will of the King was everything. Justice was royal and the King could always override any decision by the courts. He delegated his powers to individuals, and in this way 'the principle of absolutism passed down through the administrative hierarchy.' Anyone in the land could be appointed or dismissed.[8] And the French Church generally supported this view. The French ecclesiastical orator Jacques Bossuet argued that Louis depended on the Grace of God. As God's deputy he was accountable neither to the Church nor to the people.[9]

But the France of Louis XIV was also politically ambitious. The King particularly wanted to extend his territories to the natural frontier of the Rhine, and that meant war with the Dutch. The French army became the largest and best in Europe, but fear of French aggrandisement only provoked coalitions against Louis, the Dutch being helped first by England and then later Austria and Prussia.

Unfortunately for France the absolutism of its monarch was not matched by administrative efficiency and the ability to mobilise the resources of what was Europe's richest nation.

Exempting the Church and aristocracy from tax meant the loss of a major source of revenue. Direct taxation, the *taille*, was the main tax, and the total sum to be raised annually was decided by the Council of Finances. But the provinces and towns were not assessed on an equal basis, the nobility and clergy did not pay and thus the burden fell on the rural population. Of the indirect taxes, the *gabelle*, or salt tax, was the most widely resented. It was consistently increased but imposed throughout the country with such diversity that it led to smuggling and an inevitable diversion of resources to suppress it. Revenue was also received from customs duties levied at the many internal frontiers of France but the amount could hardly compensate for the disincentive to the national economy that these frontiers invoked.[10] Nor did it help that Louis XIV, encouraged by Bossuet, whose formula was 'One King, one faith, one law', revoked the Edict of Nantes in 1685 and instituted a persecution of the Huguenots.[11] Some half a million from France's commercial and artisanal classes fled abroad, particularly to England, Holland and Prussia, with incalculable harm to the economic fabric of the nation.

It was unsurprising, therefore, that for all the architectural and artistic splendours of the reign of the 'Sun King', France at the time of his death was bankrupt. War, almost continual since 1667, had ruined the finances; the poor and the Protestants had been driven to revolt. Nor had Louis' political aims had been achieved. In the War of the Spanish Succession (1701–13), the French armies were decisively beaten by the English general John Churchill, later Duke of Marlborough. France gained neither the Spanish Netherlands nor the frontier of the Rhine.

Under Louis XIV's successor, his great-grandson Louis XV, several attempts were made to reform the state finances, including in the middle of the eighteenth century a proposal to apply a five per cent tax to all incomes without exception. But the opposition of the nobility, the clergy, the *parlements* and the provincial estates ensured that it failed.[12]

Although most people in the French administration knew that the country's financial situation would make it difficult to wage war, France did so twice in the reign of Louis XV. In the first, the War of the Austrian Succession, fought in Europe, 1740–48, France gained nothing. In the second, the Seven Years War, 1757–63, France lost most of its colonial empire.

Throughout the century colonial rivalry had been developing with Britain. The West Indies provided France with twenty per cent of its total external trade; in North America English colonies with a population of one and a half million on the eastern seaboard were seeking to open up the continent but found themselves blocked by thinly-populated French colonies in the interior stretching from Quebec to Louisiana; in India the *Compagnie des Indes* competed with the East India Company, both sides taking advantage of the rivalry of local princes.[13]

Under the circumstances it was unwise of France to get involved in a European war in 1757 with Austria and Russia against Prussia in which it had no vital interest, while facing the challenge of the English in the Colonies.

In 1757 East India Company forces under Robert Clive captured the French base in India at Chandenagore, and then defeated

France's ally, the Nabob of Bengal, at Plassey. Bengal was taken over and provided the base for the future control of India by Britain. French influence in India was ended. In the Atlantic and Caribbean the British Navy ensured control of the sea. One by one most of France's West Indian islands fell to Britain. In 1759, Britain's '*annus mirabilis*', the French navy was defeated at Quiberon Bay and Lagos and British forces captured Quebec, thus ending French rule in Canada.

In 1763 at the Treaty of Paris Britain obtained from France all the latter's possessions in North America, including Canada and Louisiana, Florida (from Spain which had unwisely joined France in 1761), Senegal in Africa, and the West Indian islands of Grenada, St. Vincent, Tobago and the Windward Islands. Apart from Guadeloupe and Martinique the first French colonial empire was over. Nor were there any gains in Europe.

But the defeats, the losses, the waste of resources, and the taxation to pay for these only increased the level of discontent rife throughout the country with the French absolute monarchy. Louis XV's successor would reap the harvest.

In Brandenburg (Prussia after 1701) absolutism created a spirit of slavish obedience – even reliance – on authority.

In 1640 Frederick William became Elector of Brandenburg. He inherited a number of disparate territories, Brandenburg itself and the East Prussia of the Teutonic Knights in the east of Germany and the smaller Cleves and Mark in the Rhineland and Ravensberg between the Ems and the Weser in the west. The population of these territories was Lutheran but the Hohenzollern dynasty, which originated in Swabia in the twelfth Century, was Calvinist.

During the Thirty Years War the Elector's army had been mainly composed of mercenaries, and proved itself useless in defending a country that was generally flat and had few natural obstacles to invasion. Frederick William was resolved that this situation should not happen again. The result was the militarisation of Prussia.

Unlike in France, the nobility was not emasculated, it was incorporated. In 1653 the Elector made a deal with the landowning aristocracy, the *Junkers*. In return for a large sum of money the Elector ended the system by which the *Junkers* held their estates under the crown in exchange for military service. The *Junkers* got their land outright. They also got exemption from taxation and, unlike the aristocracy in France, recognition as the governing class in all state matters. On the other hand, they were designated as the natural officer class. They had to send their sons to military academies from the age of twelve. And unlike the custom elsewhere in Europe, they were forbidden to enter foreign service. All officers had to take an oath of loyalty to the Electors – and later Kings – of Prussia as Head of State and Commander-in-Chief of the army. And thus at an early stage the *Junkers* and the army were intimately connected. The army officer became an important person in the Prussian state. Promotion was by merit and seniority rather than birth or purchase. With the money from the *Junkers* a regular army was built up and the mercenaries dismissed. State posts were found for senior officers, and discharged soldiers were set up as farmers on the royal domains, thus creating a strong reserve. When Frederick William – now known as the Great Elector – died in 1688, the miserable mob of incompetent mercenaries he inherited in 1640 had been replaced by an army of thirty thousand men. In 1675, to Europe's astonishment, this army defeated an invading force of the much-feared Swedes at Fehrbellin, and chased it back to Riga. By 1713 the army numbered forty thousand reliable, well-trained and disciplined men.[14]

A great leap forward was made by King Frederick William I, 1713–40. He was known as the Sergeant King because he always wore uniform. His advice was, 'Always keep a large efficient army; you cannot have a better friend and without that friend you will not be able to survive.'[15]

Frederick William's arrival on the throne coincided with the Peace of Utrecht that ended the War of the Spanish Succession. One result of the Peace was the ending of subsidies, and the realisation that the way the state was organised did not provide adequate funds for the army. Accordingly, in 1722 he combined the Directorates of War and Finance (which involved the administration of his crown lands) into one General Directory. This body came, in the end, to direct the whole economic life of the Prussian state, shaping its economic growth and development entirely to the needs of the military.[16] On Frederick William's death the army had doubled to over eighty thousand men out of a population of less than two and a half million. Eighty per cent of all revenue was devoted to the army, which had become the fourth largest in Europe. A quasi-universal system of military service was introduced and regiments were assigned specific recruiting areas. The result was that since most of the peasantry were still bound to the land but were compelled to serve in the army, the peasant might find himself obeying the same officer in the army as he did at home. This feudal bond reinforced the discipline of the army.[17]

The military spirit even extended to the state bureaucracy. Not only were military affairs its chief sphere of activity but it actually behaved in a military fashion, with orders being carried out with military precision and punctuality.[18]

Under Frederick William's successor, his son Frederick II, the Great (1740–86), the Prussian army held its own against almost all Europe, winning an astonishing series of victories. In the War of the Austrian Succession Frederick defeated the Austrians and Saxons, and took Silesia, with its valuable resources in coal, from Austria. In the Seven Years War, with help from British subsidies, the Prussians held off a coalition of France, Austria, Russia and Saxony.

The Lutheran ethic of obedience had now been married to Prussian military discipline. Prussia had become a regime of service and servants, but the price would be high.

The bureaucracy was subservient and officials with ideas of their own were dismissed, so that self-reliance, the mainstay of civil service efficiency, was sapped away. To develop the latent energies of the urban middle class and the peasantry would have required fundamental reforms, not only in the state administration but also in the organisation of the Prussian people. But as long as Prussia was a military state the prestige of the army made reform impossible. It was difficult to argue that discipline was bad for the civil service of the Prussian people when the discipline of Prussian troops had won such splendid victories in the field. It was difficult to press for social reform when the loyalty of the officer corps depended on the protection of the feudal rights of the *Junkers* and hereditary serfdom remained the basis of the recruiting system.[19]

Similarly for Russia, emerging from the Mongol yoke and surrounded by Swedes, Poles, Lithuanians, the Teutonic Knights in Livonia and Tartars (beyond whom were the Turks) there was a need for order. But was the Russia of the Grand Dukes of Moscow to be Europe's most eastern state, or Asia's most western? Would Russia return to the comity of European nations as it had been under Kievan Russia or would it take the place of the Golden Horde? Would Kievan democracy, European absolutism or Asiatic despotism be the model?

During the last half of the fifteenth century and the first half of the sixteenth Russia, under Ivan III and his son Vassili III, looked as if it

was going to 'return' to Europe and make up for the separation of the centuries. A capitalist economy started up, cities expanded, there was even the beginnings of a middle class. The government introduced local self-government, and even set up something like a national parliament, the Assembly of the Land. Nor did it try to destroy the boyars.[20] Russia's decisive turn towards despotism was begun in the reign of Ivan IV, the Terrible (1547–84), with the establishment of a parallel state, the *Oprichnina*. The price of this despotism was:

> ...a political revolution which doomed Russia to a strange cyclical reproduction of its history, and an economic revolution which condemned it to the alternation of periods of feverish modernisation with long periods of stagnation [repeated attempts to 'overtake and pass Europe' always ending in dependence on Europe].[21]

More than that, it provided the basis for the 'command economy'.

The origin of the *Oprichnina* lay in the hostility of the boyars to Ivan's foreign policy. To begin with, all had gone well, with Ivan attacking the Tartars and capturing their capital Kazan on the Volga and then subduing Astrakhan. The boyars were less happy when Ivan called off his campaign against the Crimean Tartars and turned against Livonia, a war which soon involved Poland, Lithuania and Sweden, and would drag on for almost all the rest of the Tsar's reign, during which the Crimean Tartars would even counter attack and capture Moscow.

The *Oprichnina* was that part of Russian territory which in 1565 came under the direct and absolute control of the Tsar without any limitations, almost his own private estate, with its own government, treasury, army and police. The rest of Russia, the *Zemshtshina*, was administered by a Council of Boyars, which, however, had no political power. It was in the territory of the *Oprichnina* that were to be found the wealthier towns and cultivated areas, and also the lands of the old boyaralty.

Ivan used the security forces of the *Oprichnina* not only to destroy the Boyars, but to eradicate any form of opposition, including the wholesale frenzied extermination of villages and towns, the most notable Novgorod. The lands of the dispossessed and murdered were given to Ivan's *Oprichniki*.[22]

Ivan's actions aimed at eliminating completely the high nobility and substituting it with a service élite of persons devoted to him and

the state alone with no ulterior motives or personal calculations.[23] These *dvoryanin* were now the new nobility, but they held their land on condition of state service, usually of a military nature. Since it might be only for a short time there was little interest in the peasants working on the land except to get the most out of them. Legal limitations on a peasant's freedom of movement had existed since 1497. But if peasants were increasingly being forced to work the land of the *dvoryane* theoretically they could leave the land. However, as a result of Ivan's wars, and the thirty years political instability which followed his death (the 'Time of Troubles'), including some years of famine, many peasants simply fled. Gradually, over the next century and a half, even if only to ensure settled taxpayers, the right to leave was curtailed and periods after which peasants who had fled did not have to be returned by their new landlords were reduced. Eventually in 1649 in the reign of Alexis Mikhailovitch, second Tsar of the Romanov dynasty, founded in 1613, a law established that a landowner had a legal, unlimited right to the peasants on his estate registered in the census, with penalties for landowners who took in runaways. Serfdom was thus formally established, and it applied not only to agricultural labour but to labour employed in commercial and industrial concerns as well.[24]

With regard to business activity the state asserted a proprietary right to all natural resources. It also controlled all industrial and commercial activities through monopolies. The aim of the state was to obtain tax revenue, and therefore economic policy was subordinated to fiscal interests. The result was that merchants and tradespeople also became servants of the state.

Because Russia had long stood outside the main currents of European economic and commercial development, its merchants had not experienced the commercial revolution and technical advances of the Middle Ages. In the sixteenth and seventeenth centuries Russian merchants, faced with the dynamism of their western counterparts, felt unable to compete, so that much control of foreign trade was surrendered to foreigners. In any case, since most of the Russian population were serfs with little disposable income, demand was weak and the possibilities of market expansion limited. It therefore fell to the state to take over.

And it was Tsar Alexis Mikhailovitch who was the largest single producer and trader in his realm. Thus even as the revenue from the crown lands of the Electors and Kings of Prussia had led to the

militarisation of their country, so the lands of the Tsar became the foundation for the 'command economy' of Russia, which would last until the fall of communism.

Faced with the power of the state, Russian merchants never organised themselves as a coherent group pressing for a political role in the running of the state, but preferred to manoeuvre between established institutions, traditions and forces. They had no conception of the western experience of collective action by individuals to establish companies or banks, or develop fleets. There were no guilds. If organisations were set up, it was at government initiative and for governmental reasons. Since banks did not exist loans could only be obtained from the government, or the church, or foreign merchants.[25] When Peter the Great acceded to the Russian throne in 1689 his country was far behind its European neighbours in almost all respects.

His aim was to make Russia a great power, and that meant making a great leap forward economically and militarily. The key aspect of Peter's modernisation programme was the use made of European foreigners. The Tsar toured Europe in 1697, during which time he arranged for large numbers of Europeans – army and naval officers, scientists, civil servants, craftsmen and business-men – to set up in Russia and even participate in the running of the state. The army was reorganised; the artillery developed; the latest tactics learnt; conscription was introduced. A navy was built to challenge the Swedes in the Baltic and the Turks in the Black Sea. And Europeans were put in charge of much of the foreign trade.

For most of Peter's reign Russia was at war. His greatest success was the defeat of Sweden in the Great Northern War of 1700–21. Swedish ambitions outstripped their means, and the Swedes were to become the first Europeans to experience the hazards of penetrat-ing deeply a country of such vast distances, inexhaustible human resources and inclement weather. The end of the war saw Russia gain the Baltic coast and hinterland up to and including Riga. But freeing the Crimea and southern Ukraine from the Turks would have to await the reign of Catherine the Great, 1762–96, and the two Turkish wars of 1770–74 and 1787–92.

At home, however, the grip of the state on society was tightened further as Peter spared neither the nobility, nor the church, nor the peasantry.

The *dvoryanin* were obliged to choose at the age of fifteen whether to serve in the army, navy or bureaucracy. Peter then produced a

Table of Ranks, fourteen in all, laying down the qualifications for service in the army, navy or state, with ennoblement as one advanced up the scale. Promotion depended on merit rather than lineage, and thus the nobility of service replaced the nobility of birth.[26]

Income from the estates of the church was taken over. The numbers entering the church were reduced and the number of monasteries limited. In 1721 the Patriarchate was abolished and replaced by the Holy Synod, a state agency with control exercised through the office of the Procurator, appointed by the Tsar. However, Peter did not interfere with dogma so religion did not become a cause of unrest as in the west.[27]

The serfs, ninety per cent of the population, were subjected to a poll tax, which actually increased budgetary income by fifty per cent, as well as being made liable for military service and forced labour in mines and factories. And the introduction of an internal passport system obliged every serf to have his owner's written permission before being able to leave his village – a system whose principle would even survive the communist revolution.[28]

In Russia, therefore, as in Prussia, the regime was one of service and servants. The activities of all were decided by the state in its own interests. Nobles, clergy, merchants, soldiers, civil servants, all did as they were told. There was no 'noble' class or 'merchant' class to the extent that they had their own 'class' interests.[29] Nevertheless, if Russian rulers could order the aristocracy around they still needed their support, and that meant maintaining serfdom.

There had been a moment when the Russian monarchy might have taken a more liberal turn. In 1613 Mikhail Romanov was elected first Tsar of a dynasty that would last for another three hundred years. But the election came after Russia had suffered a disastrous thirty-year 'Time of Troubles' following the disintegration of the regime after the death of Ivan the Terrible. Russia suffered internal strife, famine, and Polish invasion. Moscow was burnt and the country became practically a Polish province. What held Russia together was the Orthodox Church. It was the son of its Patriarch who was elected Tsar, but the memory of the past would ensure that future government would be strong and that the autocratic prerogatives of its ruler would be maintained. Thereafter, it would be difficult to change.

In one other way unique to Russia was that country affected. There was much resentment at foreign influence. It was in

Peter's reign that was seen for the first time the mixture of fascina-
tion of Russians for westerners and their superior knowledge,
coupled with fear of how this knowledge could be used militarily
or to undermine traditional Russian spiritual values, that has lasted
until today.

Prussia and Russia were successful in the seventeenth and eighteenth centuries. With a few exceptions their leaders were efficient.
They knew what they wanted, and why. They controlled the
machinery of government and crushed internal opposition. They
were ready to appreciate and learn from technical advances, to
promote people in terms of merit, and they possessed the energy
to mobilise resources available to a maximum. Their ethos, as
leaders, was that they were the first servants of their state.

In contrast, Turkish despotism in the seventeenth and eighteenth
centuries was inefficient, and the Ottoman Empire would go into
irreversible decline in the absence of able and energetic leaders.
One problem was that no Turkish Sultan would consider himself a
servant – the state belonged to him as a toy. This was an invitation
to indolence. Another problem was that the offices of state were
purchasable, including military commands, or favourites could be
appointed. But if posts could be purchased, not only was the system
open to bribery, but there was no way to ensure that competent
persons were appointed, so the quality of military command and
the civil service was adversely affected.

Much worse, there was no systematic revenue service for organis-
ing resources. Money had been obtained as victorious campaigns
expanded areas under Turkish control, and these sent tribute to
Constantinople. But as the Turkish Empire began to decline after
Lepanto frontiers were pushed back and correspondingly less
revenue was received. Nor did it help that the volume of trade in
the eastern Mediterranean dried up as Europeans increasingly
traded directly with Asia after the voyages of discovery. And the
failure to control resources began to be reflected in the failure to
keep up with military technology – Turkey's enemies were becoming much more professional militarily, better organised and better
equipped.

In 1683 the Turks launched a new campaign to seize Vienna. But
on 12 September a European army led by King Jan Sobieski of
Poland routed them and the long decline of Turkey to its present-
day frontiers began. By the end of the seventeenth century Austria
had taken Hungary, Transylvania and Croatia, and replaced

Turkey as the major political power in the northern Balkans. By the end of the eighteenth century the Turks had lost the northern shores of the Black Sea to Russia as well.[30]

But undoubtedly the greatest victims in eastern Europe in the seventeenth and eighteenth centuries were the Poles.

Living in a country without natural defences and surrounded by enemies made it essential to have strong leadership with the ability to mobilise resources for defence. Unfortunately the Kings of Poland were elected, and the Parliament, which was filled by nobility and gentry, required all decisions to be taken by unanimity. This provided unlimited opportunities for foreign powers to intervene in order to get someone favourable to them elected. Power in the provinces lay with the nobility and gentry, and since they controlled the wealth and were reluctant to pay taxes (and could not be forced to) the crown failed to build up a tax and revenue system, relying on levies on merchants, Jews and minorities. It thus failed to create a system for marshalling the nation's resources, and thus failed, unlike Prussia and Russia, to raise an effective national army. There was no centralised bureaucracy, the nobility and gentry merely carrying out what was required in the provinces. Poland was hardly better than a collection of aristocratic estates which might or might not co-operate with the crown or each other. Three quarters of the population were serfs.

What kept Poland together was not state institutions but the Roman Catholic Church. Poland had been a particular target of the Jesuits, who had wrenched it out of the jaws of Lutheranism. Catholicism was the main feature of a national identity which distinguished Poland from Lutheran Sweden and Prussia, Orthodox Russia and the Ukraine, and Moslem Turkey.

Between 1772 and 1795 Poland was gradually dismembered through three partitions, with the south going to Austria, the west to Prussia, and the east (and Lithuania) to Russia, which thus gained all today's Baltic states. Poland as a state would not emerge again until 1918.[31]

*   *   *

The world of absolutism and the privileges of the nobility and clergy that accompanied it came under attack from two sources in the seventeenth and eighteenth centuries.

The first was from the movement known as the Enlightenment.

Since the dawn of time, Gods, or God, had provided an explanation for the unexplainable. Things were so because God had ordered them so. The interpreters of God's word, and thus the cement of society, was organised religion. However, in the previous centuries religion had fallen into disrepute. That did not mean that God had fallen into disrepute. But as scientific discoveries began stripping away ignorance, and providing explanations that did not appear to have so much to do with God, the attitude to God began to change, and society began to change.

The seventeenth and eighteenth centuries saw extraordinary advances, particularly in the fields of mathematics and astronomy. For example, in 1590 Jansen invented the microscope; in 1605 Kepler discovered the principles of the telescope; in 1609 Galileo constructed his own telescope with which he made a number of discoveries relating to the planets and astronomy (for the interpretations of which he was condemned by the Inquisition); in 1614 Napier discovered logarithms; in 1615 Kepler developed the laws of planetary motion; in 1618 Harvey discovered the properties of blood circulation and Snellius the laws on the refraction of light; in 1637 Descartes discovered analytical geometry; in 1642 Pascal invented the adding machine; in 1662 Boyle discovered the physical properties of gases; between 1665 and 1669 Newton developed differential calculus, the law of gravitation, and the reflecting telescope; in 1673 Leibnitz invented the calculating machine; in 1675 Romer calculated the speed of light; in 1711 three-colour printing was invented; in 1718 Fahrenheit invented the mercury thermometer and in 1742 Celsius invented the centigrade thermometer.

These discoveries by individuals were not made in isolation. Interested researchers from widely differing disciplines corresponded with or even visited each other. And an important role in the advance of science was played by the Learned Societies – groups of people who wanted to push back the frontiers of knowledge but found the universities did not provide the answer either because they did not teach science or education at all, or because of the claustrophobic effect of religious restrictions. Thus in the 1660's were founded the Royal Society in London and the *Académie des Sciences* in Paris. Similar institutions were founded in Berlin in 1700 and in Moscow in 1754. Under their auspices observatories were built, botanical gardens created, encyclopaedias written. Expeditions were sent out to acquire fauna and floral specimens and test hypotheses about the shape of the earth and the earth's relation to the rest of the universe.

There were five results of these developments:

First, from believing that the universe was a mystery, that nature was the abode of terrifying and evil forces, that the world was a place where a punishing God alone protected humanity, humanity was finding that God and nature were losing their terrors.

Second, it was argued that the universe was being run by natural laws, laws that governed nature without being beholden to divine purposes, and that these laws – and the principles behind them – could be deduced by reason. And thus reason, rather than faith, would henceforth increasingly be the guide to action.

Third, people began to demand freedom of thought, action and expression in the search for the truth needed to comprehend the universe, and this led to attacks not only on religious dogmatism, with the ideas of hell, original sin and predestination, but on governmental absolutism and all its trappings, particularly press censorship.

Fourth, with universal principles of behaviour able to be deduced and valid everywhere, came the idea of continual progress within a perfectible world; that human beings, not God, could be responsible for improving themselves; that they should be responsible for the institutions that shaped their lives; that indeed the perfect society could be created.

Fifth, that not only social but economic barriers should be removed – unequal taxation, guild regulations, tolls – in the belief that if the economic environment improved so would the individual's standard of living. In particular the group known as the Physiocrats believed that the aim of government should be to increase the happiness of all. They attacked the sixteenth and seventeenth century policies of mercantilism by which nations sought to get a favourable trade balance by means of state intervention in the form of monopolies, embargoes and tariffs, and called for restrictions on economic activity to be lifted, free trade encouraged, and serfs emancipated.[32]

A different atmosphere thus set in: one of optimism, that things could and would naturally improve, and that what one needed to do was overthrow the remaining obstacles to this infinite progress – arbitrary power, intolerance, superstition, social status ordained by accident of birth.

The Enlightenment's greatest weakness was that few people were involved, only those coming from the ranks of the wealthy and educated. And it was therefore difficult to make much impression on Europe's autocratic rulers. Scientific and even some social progress might be very desirable, even acceptable, if the power of the state was enhanced but all too often the support of the aristocracy, forced or otherwise, required by the autocrats, was enough to block reform. The only 'Enlightened Despot' to abolish serfdom was Joseph II of Austria in 1781.[33]

But what about the position of God in all this? Many of the leading intellectuals of the Enlightenment such as Diderot were atheists, but not all were. The Deists, which included Voltaire, perhaps the most famous Enlightenment philosopher of all, postulated that the world was indeed governed by God's laws. But God was not a despot acting according to whim. He, too, was bound by the very laws of nature he had created and which humanity had to learn. God was therefore a kind of constitutional monarch, and the question asked therefore was that if God was bound in this way how could kings on earth continue to want to be absolute monarchs, ruling arbitrarily, by whim, making irrational laws? Politically, European society in the seventeenth and eighteenth centuries would be engrossed with this question, the period stretching between two revolutions, the English revolution in the middle of the seventeenth century and the French revolution at the end of the eighteenth.

For it was the example of England that gave comfort to the Enlightenment by providing an alternative vision of the acquisition and exercise of political power.

The decline of the old English feudal aristocracy after the Wars of the Roses and the gradual increase in the powers of the English Parliament as well as the broader social composition of that Parliament had created a better balance of power *vis-à-vis* the Crown than existed on the European mainland.

Under the Tudors the Crown had had to seek parliamentary support for the sake of national cohesion following the separation from Rome and because of the need for money for defence and foreign policy issues. The money from the sale to the gentry of the lands of the monasteries had all gone, and could only be raised through the sale of monopolies and taxation, particularly of the middle class.

And this was the class that was on the rise, as the Stuarts found when they succeeded the Tudor dynasty in 1603. The economy was flourishing externally and would do so increasingly as English merchants expanded to the Baltic, the East and West Indies and North America. But it was flourishing internally as well since first, unlike on the Continent, there were few internal barriers to trade; second, the ban on interest on capital had been lifted and money could be borrowed at rates only matched by the Dutch and this stimulated the landed classes to provide the necessary liquidity for expansion.

The great beneficiary of this wealth was the city of London. Its population grew sevenfold in the years from 1500 to 1640, to nigh on half a million, eight per cent of that of England and Wales. No other town had more than twenty-five thousand inhabitants. It was the principal overseas trading centre of the country, and the seat of most of the monopolist trading companies. During the seventeenth century London was handling eighty to ninety per cent of the nation's exports and seventy per cent of imports. The concentration of economic and political power and professional expertise ensured that as a capital London was more dominant than any other European city.

And an added feature of English social life in the seventeenth century was that the poor were not taxed, as abroad; and the old, sick and unemployed received poor relief.

Thus in the two centuries between the reign of Henry VIII to the outbreak of the Civil War the social composition of England changed. Although the population had doubled, the landed classes had trebled (as had their income and wealth), and there was also a striking expansion in the numbers and the wealth of the merchants and the professional classes, particularly lawyers. The result was a massive shift of relative wealth away from the Church and Crown and away from both the very rich and very poor towards the upper middle and middle classes.[34]

Adding to the woes of Church and Crown was the challenge of Puritanism, with its Calvinist roots and zeal to bring about moral improvement in every aspect of individual and national daily life. In particular the Puritans believed in the superiority of individual conscience and biblical interpretation over the law, and a reduction in the authority of the Anglican church. An important issue was that of bishops. Puritans wanted to do away with them, whereas the

Crown saw their abolition as the prelude to abolition of hierarchy in society.[35]

In class terms the main source of Puritan strength was, as on the Continent, with the artisan and trade sectors, but there was also support amongst the gentry, the nobility and the universities for a number of reasons – the idea of public service as a calling, anti-popery, anti-clericalism and the postulation of lay control over the Church.

But it was the position of the Crown itself that was critical. It was the centre of patronage, the great dispenser of pensions, monopolies and appointments. Under James I and Charles I patronage was unwisely dispensed to a few favourites, engendering a ferocious corruption and alienating the remaining nobility and gentry.[36] The Crown still made foreign policy, which, whether pro-Spanish or pro-French, was too pro-Catholic and aroused concern. And the Crown still had powers of arbitrary arrest.

The focus of hostility to the Crown was Parliament. It was Parliament which retaliated against Crown patronage by refusing taxation. And it was the Puritans who provided the opposition leadership. By the 1620s dissatisfaction with the Crown led to pressure not only to discuss matters but to initiate discussion and influence policy in regard to such issues as the right to impeach ministers, freedom of speech, consent to taxation and freedom from arbitrary arrest.[37]

The long-term causes of the English Civil War were three:

First, there was the decision of Charles I in 1629 to rule without Parliament. Basically the Stuarts still believed in the Divine Right of Kings and accountability only to God. The King was angered by Parliament's refusal to vote him money, and rejected demands for its consent to taxation and freedom of its members from arbitrary arrest. He would be further angered by rejection of his request for money to increase and strengthen the navy in 1635.

Second, Church and Crown instituted a policy of religious uniformity, reviving and insisting on High Church forms of worship, persecuting religious opponents and particularly condemning Calvinist predestination. One result was a massive emigration of Puritans to North America.

Third, the economic life of the country was hampered by the imposition of a multitude of petty and irritating regulations designed to provide the Crown with money.

The short-term causes of the war were two:

First there was the attempt to impose Anglican uniformity on Presbyterian Scotland. The result was an uprising, and the swift defeat of the unenthusiastic English troops sent to quell it. With no money to pay the costs of the war, including reparations to the Scots, the only recourse was to summon Parliament. But the 1640 election saw a massive defeat for supporters of the Crown. Within a year the future 'Long Parliament' had secured consent for taxation, and that there should be no arrest without trial. It also forced the execution of the Earl of Strafford, one of Charles' strongest advisers.

The second event was a rebellion by Irish Catholics in 1641 which saw the massacres of the Scottish and English Protestants who had been encouraged to settle in Ulster and make the area safe for Britain and Protestantism in 1610. Clearly an army would have to be raised to defeat the uprising, but who should control it? And for what other purpose might it be used? Parliament feared it would become an instrument of the King's revenge and the annulment of the constitutional gains that had been achieved. Both King and Parliament issued ordinances to raise troops and all over the country local authorities had to decide whom to obey.[38]

War broke out in 1642 and for a time the King, who had withdrawn to Oxford, seemed to have the upper hand. What weighed the scales against him were the massive financial resources of the city of London and the development by the Parliament's General Oliver Cromwell of a disciplined and religiously zealous élite force.

Charles was finally defeated at Naseby in 1645 and next year surrendered to Parliament. Even during the war the aim of the Parliament had been constitutional reform rather than the deposition, let alone execution, of the King. But his intrigues, even under arrest, to have the Scots or even the Irish reopen the war, made the Parliamentary leaders feel there would never be peace or, indeed, reform, as long as he was alive.

On 30 January 1649 the King was led out of his palace at Whitehall and publicly executed. The groan that rose from the crowd was echoed all over Europe. An annointed King had been put on trial for treason against his own subjects. But for those of the

Calvinist persuasion it was right that a tyrant, a 'man of blood', could and should be struck down.

For the next eleven years, nine of them under Oliver Cromwell as Lord Protector, England was a republican Commonwealth dominated by Puritanism, and for the first time vent was given to the idea that the English were God's Chosen People.

The first to feel the brunt of this triumphalism were the Irish and Scots. In order to eliminate all hopes of a Royalist revival in Ireland, but also to avenge the Catholic uprising and massacres, Cromwell crossed to Ireland in 1649. Royalist garrisons and Catholic populations of some towns were massacred, Irish Catholics were deprived of their land which was given to Cromwell's soldiers, and the harshest anti-Catholic measures were imposed on the island. The Scots, who had intervened in support of Charles' son and heir, Charles II, were crushed in turn.

Cromwell then turned to foreign affairs. The Dutch might also have been Protestant but that did not prevent England from passing the Navigation Act which required all goods to and from England to be transported in English ships. The result was a war in which the English navy defeated the Dutch. War was also engaged with Catholic Spain, as a result of which Jamaica was captured.

But for all its military triumphs the Commonwealth was unloved. When Parliament refused to accept Cromwell's wishes, like King Charles he dissolved it. England was divided up into twelve regions ruled by Major-Generals. Puritan ethics prohibiting most forms of social amusements were imposed, as were requirements for strict religious worship. When Cromwell died in 1658 the country was ready for change.

It was the army which engineered the restoration of the monarchy. Charles II was wise enough to accept the gains made by the revolution. It was in his reign that the *Habeus Corpus* Act was passed protecting the citizen from arbitrary arrest. But despite the King's Catholic sympathies non-Anglicans, whether Catholics or Puritans, were excluded from all governmental posts.

Charles died in 1685 and was succeeded by his brother James II, an avowed Catholic. Fatally, James was not only a fervid believer in Divine Right but also wanted to reverse the results of the past fifty years. He attempted to restore the Catholic religion. He also attempted to establish a standing army. With the birth of a male heir there was a general fear that England would have a Catholic dynasty and military rule would be substituted for that of Parliament.

The result was the so-called 'Glorious Revolution' of 1688. Parliament invited William of Orange, Stadtholder of the Netherlands, who had married James II's daughter Mary, to become King. At war with France, William was only too delighted at the prospect of having the resources of England at his disposal. On William's arrival in England James fled to France. He tried later to return with French troops via Ireland but defeat at the battle of the Boyne in 1690 ended his hopes.

The 'Glorious Revolution' was significant in that for the first time in European history arbitrary royal rule based on Divine Right was replaced by a constitutional monarchy with a massive transfer of power to Parliament.

Before becoming King, William had to accept a number of drastic limitations on the royal power. These were that the King should no longer be able to suspend Parliament or its laws; that parliamentary approval was needed to make war and to raise a standing army; that all taxes had to be authorised by Parliament; that MP's should be freely elected and there should be immunity for parliamentary proceedings; that the King should not be able to pardon persons impeached by Parliament; that judges should be appointed for life and be only removable by both Houses of Parliament. In addition, Roman Catholics should be barred from succession to the throne. Finally, in order to remove the temptation to raise funds for himself, the King would be voted an annual sum of money for his needs (the so-called civil list).

The philosophy underlying the Glorious Revolution was that of John Locke. In contrast to the pessimism of Hobbes who argued that government was there to control man's evil warring nature, and that therefore rights could only be created by the government, Locke was much more optimistic. In his *Two Treatises of Government* Locke maintained that government was based not on Divine Right but the consent of the governed. He agreed with Hobbes that in a state of nature it was right for people to give one or more of their fellows authority over them for their own preservation, but argued instead that that authority was not arbitrary but limited to exercise for the public good of society by known laws. Individuals might well convey to society as a whole their right to exercise certain functions which were best exercised collectively but other rights they retained, particularly the preservation of their property, property being interpreted as being not only material possessions but lives and liberties. Government was thus a trust, and people had a right to remove the government if it betrayed its trust. And if the government was removed that did not mean a return to the state of nature; the community merely took power back into its own hands before re-issuing it.[39]

In the following decades constitutional government developed further in four ways:

First, the 1694 Triennial Act provided that each Parliament should not last for more than three years.

Second, the Cabinet evolved as the link between Crown and Parliament. Because of William's frequent absences fighting against France in the Netherlands there was need for a body to advise Queen Mary and to co-ordinate wartime planning, England inevitably being drawn into the war against Louis XIV, his Catholic ambitions and support for the exiled Stuarts.

Third, the principle of separation of powers in government between the Crown (the executive), the House of Commons (the legislature) and the House of Lords (the judiciary) was established, with the object of ensuring that none of the three institutions became too powerful but would hold each other in check.

Fourth, the concept of a 'loyal opposition' was established. The problem was that since the Crown was used to identifying its interests with those of the nation, and the King also chose the Ministers how could one attack corruption or incompetence without also attacking the King and thus being guilty of treason? Henry St. John, Viscount Bolingbroke, argued that one had a right to try and rid the government of the corrupt and incompetent and replace it with a new group because it was in the interests of the nation. The Crown should recognise that such opposition was not an attack on the constitution or the dynasty, and therefore should not automatically be considered treason.[40]

British parliamentary democracy had thus been established. True, it was limited. One had to have a certain annual income to vote in elections, and women did not have the vote at all. Powerful magnates and landowners would often choose the parliamentary candidates in their areas. And with population shifts the voting population of constituencies varied considerably. But the brake on absolutism, the development of a political party system with Whigs and Tories, as well as the personal and political liberties of at least the propertied class made Britain the envy of eighteenth century Europe, and the ideas behind them became part of the intellectual property of the nation, providing the foundation for their extension at a later date.[41]

In 1707 the Parliaments of England and Scotland united and 'Great Britain' as such rapidly became a world power. International trade brought prosperity, and the distribution of wealth ensured that it did not remain in only a few hands. With this wealth English subsidies kept continental coalitions going against its enemies in the wars of the century. The navy was strengthened and soon became the best in the world, ensuring the colonial gains in North America, the Caribbean and India. But more important, unlike continental armies, a navy could be no threat to society. This factor, coupled with English distaste, because of the Cromwellian experience, for a standing army, ensured that the English developed their economic, social and political institutions without foreign interference, and thus very differently from the rest of Europe.

The ethos of this new confident nation was unashamedly anti-Catholic and anti-French. In 1701 the Act of Settlement provided that should Queen Anne, James II's daughter and William III's sister-in-law, die childless the succession would devolve on the House of Hanover (the Protestant Elector of Hanover being des-cended on the female side from James I), to the exclusion of James II's Catholic son. And twice in the first half of the century, in 1715, with James's son, and in 1745 with his grandson Charles (Bonnie Prince Charlie) risings in Scotland in favour of the Stuarts received little support because of their association with France and, in particular in 1745, the belief of the English that if Charles won he would be beholden to France which would demand large parts of their colonial empire as a reward for its help.[42] Defeat of the Jacobite army at at Culloden in 1746 ended Stuart pretensions to the British throne.

Indeed, the only reverse for Britain during the century came in the loss of their North American colonies in the 1775–1783 War of Independence, and the reason for the war was that the British departed from their own political principles.

With the removal of the threat of the French after the Seven Years War the American Colonies had become a thriving commer-cial society. However they were not represented in Parliament in London, which imposed a number of taxes and insisted that goods to and from the colonies be transported in British ships. Demands for representation in Parliament were rejected, whereupon the colonies declared martial law and suspended trade with Britain. Independence was declared on 4 July 1776 and the colonial militias defeated the British forces sent against them. France and Spain sided with America, and the French sent volunteers. Despite some naval victories British forces eventually surrendered at Yorktown in 1781, and in the Peace of Paris two years later Britain recognised American independence.

The eighteenth century may have been one of absolutism and dynastic wars, but the idea of European Union was not dead.

In 1713 the Abbé de St. Pierre, Secretary to the French delegation at Utrecht negotiating to bring an end to the War of the Spanish Succession, produced the first version of a work entitled 'Project for Settling an Everlasting Peace in Europe'. He proposed a permanent union between twenty-four Christian sovereigns, including the Tsar of Russia. (By the time of the last version, in 1738, the number had been reduced to nineteen.) In the final version these nineteen states would form a congress which would rationally rearrange boundaries after which no changes would be allowed; settle all disputes within the Union; guarantee Member states against invasion or rebellion; use the troops of the Union against recalcitrant Members; mobilise the troops of the Union against the Turks; and ensure religious toleration. Secession from the Union would not be allowed. Although inspirational for later generations, St. Pierre's proposal at the time was ridiculed.[43]

In 1789 another 'Plan for a Universal and Perpetual Peace' was proposed by Jeremy Bentham. His plan was based on the need to settle Anglo-French rivalry, and he saw trade as a cause of war. His proposal was that Britain and France should not have any colonies, nor make treaties of alliance, nor make treaties that gave them commercial advantage. If Britain and France agreed the plan could be extended to the eventual permanent pacification of all Europe including limiting the size of armies. Bentham also proposed that disputes would be settled by a European international court because the honour of Kings was an important motive for war. A decision by a court would save the face of the losing party. The court would not, however, have any coercive powers.[44] Bentham's observations on Anglo-French relations would take on much urgency in the next twenty-five years.

11 The Industrial and French Revolutions 1750–1850AD

The industrial revolution has been described as one of those rare occasions in world history when the human species altered the framework of its existence, comparable to the Neolithic revolution when agriculture replaced hunting and gathering as the basic form of production, and thus instituting settled communities instead of migratory bands and increasing the number of people who could be supported around the world.[1] It was a revolution in technology and the organisation of production. The revolution in technology provided power; the revolution in organisation brought about profound social changes.[2]

The industrial revolution began in Britain in the second half of the eighteenth century. But why should it begin there, and why should it have begun when it did? The answer lies in a number of other developments – an agricultural revolution, a population explosion, technological invention, an entrepreneurial environment, an inflow of capital and a good infrastructure. Some of these factors existed in Europe, but others applied to Britain alone.

The agricultural revolution was also due to a number of factors, amongst them land reclamation, advances in the breeding of livestock and enclosures increasing the size of farms and thus productivity per unit of labour. But more important was the introduction in Norfolk of four-course field rotation based on wheat, turnips, barley and clover. This also increased animal fodder, allowing more livestock to be kept, and increasing the supply of manure. Yields of grain doubled. Elsewhere in Europe agricultural output was also increasing, but not as substantially as in Britain.[3] But the result was a population better fed and with higher incomes. With people better fed they were more resistant to disease; with more income there was an increased demand for consumer goods.

Resistance to disease coupled with advances in medicine (inoculation, eradication of smallpox) led to a fall in the death rate and longer life spans. The population of Britain would treble from an estimated 7.4 million in 1750 to 20.8 million by 1850.[4] The increase in population would lead to an increase in demand, and the provision of a labour force to take advantage of the new technologies.

Among these were Hargreaves' Spinning Jenny, Cartright's Power Loom and Crompton's Mule. They had the effect of multiplying the amount of yarn that could be produced by one person, producing cotton strong enough not only to be mass-produced but of a quality smooth enough to compete with silk and linen. The weight of cotton spun in England in 1765 was less than 500 000 lbs, and was spun by hand; by 1784 the total was 16 million lbs, all spun by machine. With the invention in the United States by Eli Whitney of the saw gin in 1793, the acreage under cotton increased massively. In 1784 Britain was importing cotton to the value of £20 million, none of it from the United States; by 1850 the total was £1.5 billion, 82 per cent from the United States. But these machines required a factory organisation. Workers had to be brought from their homes to the machines, and that spelt the end of the small cottage industry production based on the home and the family.[5] In the meantime steam power was being harnessed by such engineers as James Watt and Richard Trevithick. Blast furnaces were improved by the use of coking coal instead of wood and charcoal, and the result was the development of wrought iron, superior to the traditional cast iron. And later, with this improved iron, railways would be built so that steam engines could run on them, thus revolutionising transport.

But industrial development needs capital and an entrepreneurial spirit, and Britain had both. With the defeat of the French at Plassey in 1757 Britain became the dominant power in India, and the subcontinent provided an abundance of precious metals. Together with the rest of a thriving commercial empire there was no lack of money to be invested. And that investment brought about in turn a whole infrastructure of banking and credit. In 1750 there were hardly a dozen banks outside London; by 1800 they were to be found in every market town.[6]

And the leadership was there. Unlike on the Continent the British aristocracy did not look down on trade and commerce or estate management with disdain. There were also the religious minorities – Quakers, Methodists, Dissenters and Non-Conformists. Still excluded from government employment they provided a disproportionate number of early manufacturers imbued with the Calvinist ethic that disciplined work, frugality and economic drive were pleasing to God.[7] And they were stimulated by the ideas of Adam Smith who rejected mercantilism, arguing that the price of goods in a market was determined by the natural law of supply and demand, and therefore a free economy and free trade was the right solution to society's economic problems. His *Wealth of Nations* published in 1776, has been called the Bible of Capitalism.

It was Britain's accumulation of wealth through international trade, however, rather than the technological inventions of the industrial revolution that enabled Britain to withstand the great challenge of the French Revolution and the subsequent quarter of a century of war that would shake the continent of Europe.

The immediate cause of the French Revolution of 1789 was that after involvement in the American War of Independence the country was bankrupt and government credit exhausted.

Clearly the only way the government could get money was to end the fiscal privileges of the nobility and clergy, particularly their exemption from taxation. Equally clearly most of the nobility and certainly the Church hierarchy would oppose such a step. It was felt that only a true national assembly could authorise such a step, and it was therefore decided to summon a meeting of the States General, the French parliament, consisting of the three traditional estates of the realm, clergy, nobility and middle class in equal numbers so that the first two could outvote the third, for May 1789. The last time it had met was in 1614. Some of the nobility, however, hoped that as a result the absolutism of the monarchy would be limited and they would be able to get back some of their powers. And some of the clergy had more sympathy with the Third Estate than with the views of the hierarchy.

But because of the expansion of the numbers of the middle class during the eighteenth century it was agreed to double the representation of the Third Estate even before the States General met, and when it did meet the Third Estate immediately demanded that voting should be by head rather than by Estate.[8] This might well give it a majority and the opportunity to introduce reforms. When it seemed unlikely to get its way the group declared itself to be the National Assembly, implicitly claiming all the powers of the States General, and making clear its determination to regenerate the state.[9]

It was when fears arose that the King, Louis XVI, under pressure from an increasingly frightened nobility, would dissolve the Assembly that the latter turned to the Paris mob for support.[10] On 14 July 1789 the mob stormed the fortress-prison of the Bastille, symbol of Royal tyranny, an event that stimulated peasant risings elsewhere in France.

With the fall of the Bastille a new era of optimism set in. In England, America and liberal circles all over Europe the event was well received. Wordsworth wrote of that time that: 'Bliss was it in that dawn to be alive, but to be young was very Heaven.'[11] And the National Assembly went to work with a will.

The feudal order was abolished and the peasantry freed from its obligations, and a Declaration of the Rights of Man proclaimed equality before the law and in access to jobs, putting the emphasis on personal liberty and the worth of the individual. A new three-tier system of local government was introduced, whereby *départements*, districts and *communes* replaced the existing medieval system. Church land was expropriated and put up for sale; monasteries and orders dissolved; the Church lost the right of self-taxation. On the other hand, the clergy would be paid, and all clergy had to take an oath of loyalty to the state. The judicial system of the *ancien régime* was abolished. Henceforward judges and jurors would be elected, and all criminal cases tried by jury.

The French Revolution had its intellectual origins in the ideas of the Enlightenment that Man was perfectable; that even without God a better world, through reason, could be created. Far from society requiring tyrannical rulers to coerce sinful men, scientific knowledge would provide society with the means to an inevitably better existence. Reason and will-power were enough to regenerate human nature and reform society. In his *Social Contract* the Swiss, Jean-Jacques Rousseau (1712–78) had argued that corrupt social organisation was the chief cause of evil and therefore if society's institutions could be reformed all would inevitably be well. The triumph of the revolution in the years 1789–91 seemed to be proof that tyrannical society could indeed be destroyed and then reformed for the benefit of mankind. But not everyone was convinced. In Britain Rousseau's views were challenged by Edmund Burke, founder of modern Conservatism, in his book *Reflections on the Revolution in France*, written in 1790. For Burke tradition was preferable to reason because it was the progressive experience of mankind. The France of the *ancien régime* was reforming but, warned Burke, revolution led via anarchy to tyranny.[12] To rebut the Revolution conservatives needed to show that the world was not so easily changed and that pain and evil behaviour were not temporary phenomena originating in an unjust society and capable of elimination by the elimination of existing institutions. Rather, because of free will, human beings are – and always will be – imperfect creatures; that there were limits on what the individual and the state could achieve, and if these limits were not respected the fabric of society would be destroyed; that nothing was inevitable, and certainly not inevitably good, because the future was unknowable.[13]

Burke – and conservatives – were soon vindicated.

In September 1791 the new constitution was proclaimed, and elections were held to a new Legislative Assembly. The aim of the Assembly was to create a constitutional monarchy, not overthrow it. However, fatally, one of the last acts of the National Assembly was to pass a self denying ordinance under which its members disqualified themselves from membership of the new Assembly. Almost all the moderates were thus eliminated.[14] The new Assembly was much more republican, a sentiment that had two sources. Three months previously the King had become increasingly reluctant to cooperate in the constitutional experiment. In June 1791 he had tried to flee the country but had been ignominiously captured and returned to Paris where he was placed under house arrest and had all his political powers removed. Most of the clergy had refused to take the oath of loyalty. And many nobles had fled abroad from where they urged foreign governments to wage war on what they portrayed as a godless society at the mercy of mob rule.

Their wishes seemed to be granted when in August, at Pilnitz, the Emperor of Austria (whose sister was Queen Marie Antoinette of France) and the King of Prussia declared themselves ready, with other sovereigns, to restore Louis. Fear of invasion and the restoration of the *ancient régime*, as well as to create unity at home led the French government to declare war on Austria in April 1792.

In the meantime in France itself the threat of foreign invasion together with economic catastrophe (high inflation and failure of the harvest for the fourth successive year) led to vicious infighting among the groups in the Assembly. Most of the deputies were individual independents with little political experience; the largest group, the *Girondins*, was composed of republicans who wanted a regional decentralised structure for France; while the *Jacobins*, fanatical, radical republicans with great influence with the Paris mob sought a unified and centralised system of government. The Republic was proclaimed in September 1792 but the government soon degenerated into a dictatorship of the Jacobins ruling through a Committee of Public Safety and a Revolutionary Tribunal. For two years there was a period of terror – denunciations, spy hysteria and executions of perceived enemies – aristocrats and clergy, the King and Queen, and eventually the Girondins. Troops were sent into the Provinces under Commissioners with full powers to quell mercilessly disturbances whether caused by loyalists to the monarchy in Brittany and the Vendée or simply protests at food shortages, inflation and the collapse of the currency.

The terror only ended when so many persons felt threatened that the only way to save themselves was to unite to overthrow the Jacobins. In July 1794, the Jacobin leaders were overthrown and summarily executed. Soon after France was governed by a Directory of five persons at the head of a two-chamber legislature. But the pressure from abroad on the one hand, and resurgent royalists and the remnant of the Jacobins at home on the other, meant heavy reliance on the army.

And that was not surprising. The revolution may have turned sour in France; abroad its universally powerful ideals – Liberty, Equality, Fraternity – were enjoying greater success.

Faced with invasion the revolutionary French government responded first by the *Levée en masse*, total mobilisation of the country, including conscription. This new revolutionary army of over one million men was officered by persons chosen for their enthusiasm, courage and skill rather than their noble birth. Tactics were now based on the offensive through massed columns of attacking troops. Second, the philosophy of the government was that the only way to secure the revolution was to export its ideals in order to undermine reactionary and absolutist rulers of the continent, at the same time extending France to the natural frontiers of the Rhine and the Pyrenees.

The aggression and idealistic enthusiasm displayed by the revolutionary French armies enabled it to win startling victories over the more experienced professional forces of its opponents. In the north Prussian and Austrian armies were defeated, the Austrian Netherlands (Belgium) and Holland captured. In the south the Austrian domination of Italy was challenged by the brilliant generalship of a Corsican artillery officer, Napoleon Bonaparte. Satellite states were set up in Milan, Genoa, the Papal States and Naples. Switzerland too was invaded and transformed into the Helvetian Republic. Stressing the democratic aspect of the revolution, plebiscites on their future were organised in a number of French-speaking areas when the French armies arrived. In this way Avignon (which still belonged to the Pope), Savoy and Nice (which belonged to the

Kingdom of Piedmont-Sardinia), and some enclaves in Alsace, the Rhineland and Liège were added to France.

In 1799 Napoleon overthrew the Directory and for the next sixteen years France and Europe would have to face up to his attempts to impose a new order on the Continent based on French ideals and with France at its head.

At home Napoleon first had himself elected First Consul, with sole rights to initiate legislation and appoint government officials, and then in 1804 had himself declared – and crowned – Emperor of the French. France itself was consolidated through administrative, social and educational reforms, many of which still provide the foundation of the French state.

During the twenty-five years of the Revolution and Napoleonic eras France was profoundly changed. Monarchy by Divine Right was ended – nearly a century and a half after the English experience.

The aristocracy lost its monopoly of high office in Church, state and the army, its feudal dues, rights of jurisdiction and hereditary privileges. But the aristocracy did not disappear. Most returning emigrés kept their land, and Napoleon expanded the aristocracy by creating titles for supporters of his régime, titles maintained after the fall of his régime. After 1815 the enlarged aristocracy would own substantial property, and become much more open to business.

If the Church never regained its old status and authority because its economic power had been destroyed by the Revolution, Napoleon recognised religion as a stabilising force in society. In 1801 he signed a treaty with the Pope under which Catholicism was recognised as the religion of most Frenchmen and obstacles to its practice removed. But the reinstatement of religion and particularly Catholicism as, more or less, the state religion, met with the antagonism of republicans – an antagonism which affected French society, particularly in regard to education, until well into the twentieth century.

The feudal obligations binding the peasantry to the soil were ended. Many – and certainly the richer peasantry – had been able to purchase lands confiscated from the Church and emigré aristocracy. The peasantry thus gained a new social status and a measure of economic security that would henceforth account for the conservatism of rural France.

With the elimination of impediments to trade and industry such as reactionary guilds, restrictions on the movement of labour, seigneurial dues and internal tolls and the acceptance of social mobility, the middle class would be able to profit when the Industrial Revolution came to France after 1815.

France was consolidated through centralisation. Administrative centralisation was achieved through *départements* headed by prefects responsible to the Minister of the Interior. A new administrative class of civil servants with careers open to all and promotion based on merit was created by Napoleon to run the country on the basis of his Civil Code, which provided for personal liberty, equality before the law, civil marriage, right to divorce, and guaranteed private property. Educational centralisation was achieved through the *Lycée* system. This would all mark France as a country of centralisation and uniformity.

The strength of the French Revolution was its postulation of universal values. Paradoxically, the Revolution also gave birth to their opposite, modern nationalism. From the *levée en masse* when Frenchmen mobilised as a nation in 1792 to resist foreign invasion through twenty-three years of war against almost every country of Europe, the French became aware of themselves as an organic whole. Until 1789 French people had been inclined to consider themselves as coming from this or that region, speaking French or regional languages as the case might be, and owing loyalty to the King. Revolution and Empire led to a transfer of loyalty from the crown to the people, called a *nation*, endowed with sovereignty and identified with the state.[15]

These experiences were not happy ones for all. On the eve of the Revolution thirty per cent of the people in France still spoke regional languages – Breton, Basque, Catalan, Occitan.[16] The new France, however, adopted a cultural arrogance. On the one hand, to speak French seemed proof of rational enlightenment. People enjoying the freedom of the French Republic – and later Empire – should be proud to speak the language of the Declaration of the Rights of Man.[17] On the other hand, the French language was seen as an important instrument for promoting the cohesion of the French state and its solidarity vis-à-vis the threats from abroad. But if a language is either a symbol of prestige or an outward sign of solidarity other languages stand out as threats to that solidarity, arousing hostility or contempt. Thus revolutionary and Napoleonic France sought to ridicule and eliminate regional languages and cultures, seeing them as threats to '*La Nation une et indivisible*', an attitude barely changed even by the last decades of the twentieth century.

It was the same story in Europe.

Between the years 1792–1809 the maps of the Low Countries, Germany and Italy were redrawn. Belgium was annexed; Napoleon's brother Louis was placed on the throne of Holland; Northern Italy became a Kingdom ostensibly under Napoleon himself but in fact ruled by his step-son Eugène de Beauharnais. In Germany Napoleon aimed to create from the myriad of small states a counterweight to Prussia and Austria. As a first stage a number of small principalities, counties and free cities were dissolved and their lands added to make larger states, including Bavaria, Württemburg, Baden and Hesse-Darmstadt, the first two becoming Kingdoms and the other two Grand-Duchies.

1806 was a critical year for Germany. Sixteen southern and western German states formed the Confederation of the Rhine, declaring themselves under French protection and seceding from the Holy Roman Empire. Shortly after, the Emperor himself, Francis II, under pressure from Napoleon, brought the Empire to an end, becoming instead Emperor Francis I of Austria. When Prussia, together with Russia and Saxony demanded the withdrawal of all French troops east of the Rhine and the dissolution of the Confederation, the French invaded Prussia and the Prussian army was crushed at Jena, leading to French occupation of the country, and the obligation of Saxony to join the Confederation.

When the Russians were defeated the following year in East Prussia, Napoleon was able to impose the Peace of Tilsit on the two powers. Prussia was shorn of its territories west of the Elbe which were used in the creation of a new Kingdom of Westphalia (on the throne of which Napoleon put his brother Jerome); its former Polish territories were taken by Napoleon to create a new Grand Duchy of Warsaw; the army was limited to forty-two thousand men.

In 1809 it was Austria's turn. Angered at appeals to the Germans to rise against the French, Napoleon invaded Austria. The Austrian army was defeated at Wagram. Salzburg and North Tyrol were given to Bavaria; South Tyrol was added to the new Kingdom of Italy; Carinthia and Slovenia (Illyria) were actually taken over by France; Austria's Polish territories, like those of Prussia, were given to the Grand Duchy of Warsaw; and the Austrian army was limited to one hundred and fifty thousand men.

And wherever the French armies marched they brought with them the principles and values of the Revolution. Feudalism was overthrown and aristocratic privilege ended. The French Civil Code was introduced. Equality of rights was given to Jews and religious minorities. Church and seigneurial justice was uprooted and systems of law courts and juries established. Cheaper and more efficient administration replaced the myriad of competing and overlapping authorities surviving from the feudal past.

With the sweeping away of feudalism and privilege careers were opened to men of talent, internal markets were liberated from restrictive barriers and all this combined to expand trade and create opportunities for the middle class.

However, the same cultural arrogance was expressed.

To begin with, France's revolutionary rulers announced that they were waging war on kings not peoples. Men of all countries were brothers who should aid each other. French armies should not impose French laws or systems of government on the newly liberated. But things soon changed to war not only against kings but those who supported these kings and the traditional institutions of their country, and that meant all who did not enthusiastically adopt French institutions. People had to be taught to be free.[18]

Also, French imperialism had to be paid for, and was paid for by plunder. The occupying French armies seized national treasuries; French armies were quartered on the satellite states, and these states were required to provide and pay for troops to further the Emperor's ambitions.

What was particularly disliked was the distortion of trade arising from Napoleon's attempt to defeat Britain.

Traditional British foreign policy since the days of William III had been to ensure a balance of power, to prevent any one country dominating the Continent and certainly to oppose any Great Power establishing itself in the Low Countries from which an invasion of England could most easily be attempted. Britain's hostility to developments in France meant that whereas in the eighteenth century the French had looked to it as an example of liberalism, it now became for them the leader of world reaction.[19] Between 1793 and 1815 Britain alone, with its navy and gold promoted no less than six anti-French coalitions, and Napoleon knew that it was Britain that had to be defeated if he was to achieve the mastery of Europe. In 1798 he had hoped to defeat Britain in the Mediterranean where its navy was supporting anti-republican forces in Toulon and Naples. But it was the French fleet that was sunk by Nelson at the Battle of the Nile. In 1805 hopes of gaining control of the Channel so as to transport a French army to England were ended by Nelson's victory at Trafalgar.

The British navy was also mounting a blockade of coasts belonging to France and its allies, so in 1806, under the Berlin decrees, Napoleon retaliated with the Continental system closing all ports in French or allied territory to British shipping and goods. The British replied by threatening to confiscate all neutral shipping using ports denied to British ships.

The result was abacklash of nationalism, but a different kind of nationalism. French, and before it English, nationalism had originated in the struggle for individual rights against authoritarian government. Nationalism elsewhere in Europe originated in the struggle against foreign domination, with a rejection of not only French cultural values, but by implication, the assertion of individual rights against those of the larger collectivity, however that collectivity might be expressed.

Nationalism in Britain and France had been based on the middle class and had thus looked to the future. In Germany, Italy and eastern Europe where the middle class enjoyed neither initiative nor experience in government, the nationalism that was aroused looked to the past, and nowhere more so than in Germany where it was linked to the Romantic movement of the eighteenth century.[20]

German Romanticism was an interpretation of life, nature and history that was opposed to the rationalism of the Enlightenment. It was rooted in sentiment and emotion rather than reason.

Romanticists believed the nationality of a people was based not on forms of government but upon traditional customs which develop organically and must not be interfered with from outside. One of the foremost German Romanticists was Friedrich Schlegel (1772–1829) who argued that a nation was a closely knit family held together by ties of blood, language and a common past – in this case the Germany of the Middle Ages, the Knights, the Guilds, the *minnesänger*. The nation was the source of all aesthetic, political and ethical creativity; an object of love and devotion; a great family; and the individual therefore should submit himself to it, and indeed could only fulfil himself within it and was nothing outside it.[21] Heinrich Luden, Professor of History at Jena, believed in the uniqueness of each nation, that nations should compete. And he believed that only a state built on the principle of ethnicity could be a true fatherland, that state and nation must coincide.[22] Above all, the language was stressed – symbol of the spiritual and intellectual independence of the nation, the only bond linking the past to the present, the only bond linking Germans wherever they were after the dissolution of the Holy Roman Empire, uniting them for a common effort.[23]

Henceforward German nationalists would maintain that the reason for the pitiable state of Germany was that it tried to imitate 'foreign' (i.e. French) culture. They would call for the creation of one fatherland out of all lands where German was spoken. For some, like Friedrich Jahn (1778–1852), this would mean a 'Greater Germany' to include Switzerland, the Netherlands, Denmark and Alsace-Lorraine as well.[24]

In the end it was the Continental system which would lead to Napoleon's downfall.

In 1807 Napoleon attacked Portugal on the grounds that it was trading with Britain. But the need to cross Spanish territory involved France in Spanish domestic politics in which liberals were struggling against the reactionary Bourbon monarchy. But French intervention, which included deposing the King and replacing him with Napoleon's brother Joseph, only roused Spanish nationalist resistance. The British were able to land forces under Arthur Wellesley, later Duke of Wellington, in Lisbon and keep them supplied. Harassed by guerillas, and rarely reinforced because of commitments elsewhere, the French were gradually pushed out of Spain until in 1814 Wellington's army crossed the Pyrenees into France itself.

And then there was Russia. At Tilsit Tsar Alexander I had been obliged to participate in the Continental System. By 1812 Russia was facing such economic difficulties that the Tsar wanted to abandon that participation. To enforce his will Napoleon invaded Russia with nearly 700 000 men, the largest army ever seen, which included Germans, Italians, Poles, Swiss and Dutch. After several costly victories Napoleon entered Moscow. But the Russians refused to make peace, and when Moscow was burnt (probably deliberately by the Russians) in October there was little option, with winter coming, but to retreat. The result was a catastrophe. There was little food; the army was harassed by Cossacks; cold and hunger did the rest. Only 30 000 survived.

This defeat, coupled with the news from Spain, emboldened resistance to French domination throughout Europe. In October 1813 Prussia, Austria and Sweden threw off their neutrality and joined Russia against Napoleon as the French armies retreated, inflicting a heavy defeat on the Emperor at Leipzig. Six months later, the allies entered Paris. Napoleon abdicated and was given the island of Elba as a place to retire, while the Bourbon dynasty in the shape of Louis XVIII, a brother of Louis XVI, was restored.

Less than a year later Napoleon tried to return, taking advantage of the unpopularity of the restored monarchy and rivalry amongst the allies meeting in Vienna to decide the peace settlement. On 18 June 1815 the French army was decisively defeated at Waterloo by a British-Dutch army under Wellington which held out against superior numbers until the Prussians could come to their aid. This time Napoleon was exiled to the small island of St. Helena in the South Atlantic, where he remained until his death in 1821.

Twenty-five years of war might have consolidated the French nation but part of the price to be paid by the French was a catastrophic decline in the birthrate. Whereas the nineteenth century saw quantum leaps forward in all European countries because of falling death rates and higher living standards, in France the increase in population was much slower. Whereas in the seventeenth and eighteenth centuries French armies tended to be larger than those of their opponents, this would not be the case in the nineteenth century, especially when faced with the rise in population and power of Germany. This would come to affect French European politics.

Inevitable also, perhaps, was the idea that Europe should organise things better. In 1814, as the statesmen were assembling in Vienna to decide the map of Europe after Napoleon's abdication, Claude-Henri, Duc de St. Simon, saw the rivalry between Britain and France as the chief cause of war in Europe. He wanted the two to unite, and together to restore the medieval federal community of Europe united by common institutions. But why Britain and France? The answers were two. First, Britain and France together would be stronger than anyone else in Europe, or indeed stronger than the rest of Europe, and second, because these two countries possessed liberal forms of government. Having united, with a common parliament, the two should bring about the reorganisation of Germany and introduce throughout the continent parliamentary government in order to ensure compatible social and political systems.

St. Simon particularly admired the British Constitution and the balance of internal power between the King, Lords and Commons, and he hoped a supranational parliament independent of national

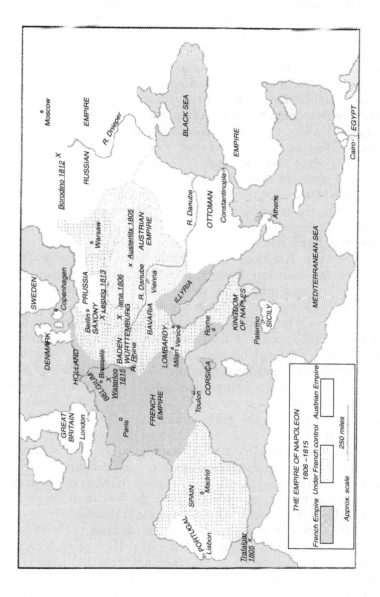

7 The Empire of Napoleon

parliaments could be created that would concern itself with the general interest. It would be given the power to judge disputes and to raise whatever taxes it thought necessary. But, more significantly, it would control European public instruction, one of the objectives of which would be to develop a European patriotism to compete with existing thinking in terms of national patriotisms. Because of the need to see things in the terms of the general interest the parliament should consist of businessmen, magistrates, intellectuals and administrators only. There would be an Upper House composed of peers nominated by a hereditary King, but St. Simon did not reveal whom he thought should be King.[25]

However, few of those present at Vienna were interested in sentiments of unity and liberalism. The other part of the price to be paid by France for the previous twenty-five years was that that country would be seen as the source of future unrest, and for those, mostly reactionary, meeting in Vienna, it was vital to ensure that the forces of liberalism and nationalism remained bottled up.

Under the Final Act of the Congress of Vienna France was hemmed in by a Kingdom of the Netherlands enlarged by the addition of the Austrian Netherlands (Belgium); a Switzerland whose territory and neutrality were guaranteed by the Great Powers; and a Kingdom of Piedmont-Sardinia enlarged by the return of Savoy. The map of Germany was again redrawn, this time into a Confederation of thirty-nine states including German-Austria, Prussia, enlarged by the addition of part of Saxony (the price the latter had to pay for supporting Napoleon) and Westphalia (which would mean that a future industrially rich and Catholic area would be added to a state essentially agricultural and Lutheran), Hanover (ruled over by the King of England), Holstein (ruled by Denmark), and Luxemburg (whose Grand Duke was King of the Netherlands). The Diet of the Confederation was situated in Frankfurt under the chairmanship of Austria, but decisions usually required unanimity. The forces of reaction in Italy were strengthened when Austria was compensated for the loss of Belgium by obtaining Milan and Venice. Austria also got Dalmatia.

The key figure in European politics in the period 1815–48 was the Chancellor of Austria, Prince Metternich. He was well aware that the Austrian Empire was no cohesive state but merely a collection of areas and peoples acknowledging the Emperor as their head. Austria was thus particularly vulnerable to nationalism – indeed, if all the nationalities in the Empire (and it included

Germans, Italians, Czechs, Slovaks, Poles, Hungarians, Romanians, Serbs, Croats and Slovenes) were to become independent Austria would cease to exist. But Metternich saw another threat – that if Germany and Italy were each to become united Austria would not only lose the territories it had gained at Vienna but would be caught between a new Great Power to the south, Italy, and a Germany which would certainly be dominated by Prussia, a German state that from the point of view of its emerging industrial and military might would be the most powerful of all on the European mainland.

His policy, therefore, was to prevent nationalism destroying Austria and uniting Italy and Germany. And he was able to do this by playing on the fears of the rulers of the Germanic and Italian princely states, as well as the Tsar of Russia, that if the liberalism and nationalism of the French Revolution broke out again and triumphed they would all lose their thrones and privileges in the new democratic states that would emerge.

Horrified by the destruction, internal as well as international, caused by the French Revolution, Metternich sought to establish order through a just balance in society. He believed there was an equilibrium inside each state, and that one therefore had to defend the existing social order against destructive forces. But he also believed that there should be an equilibrium between states, for if one was to have order states could not be left to their own devices but should be part of the international community and responsible to it. Metternich thus believed in a balance of power, that the political strength of states be so distributed that aggression by any one single power would become a hazardous business. And the balance in Europe would be upset if some countries should grow larger (i.e. if Prussia should take over Germany) or if a vacuum should appear because a country should grow weaker (i.e. Austria).

Metternich's idea was that the five Christian powers of Britain, France, Austria, Russia and Prussia should 'concert together' to decide what to do should there happen a particular event likely to upset the peace in Europe. But Metternich also wanted the Five to have the right to intervene in the affairs of other states – including those of the Great Powers – if political stability should be threatened by liberalism or nationalism.[26]

His ideas were warmly supported by the autocratic rulers of what became known as the Holy Alliance – Austria, Russia and Prussia. But Britain, a constitutional monarchy, was not in favour. And

France may have had the Bourbons restored but only on condition that the gains of the revolution were maintained.

In the 1820s the representatives of the Five met in Congresses in various European towns as the forces of liberalism and nationalism frequently raised their heads – in Spain, Portugal, Piedmont and Naples in 1820 and Greece in 1821. And in Central and South America, inspired by the examples of the American and French Revolutions and taking advantage of the Napoleonic wars in their founding countries, the colonists rose to obtain their independence from Spain and Portugal – in Venezuela (1811), Argentina (1816), Chile (1818), Greater Colombia (1819), Mexico and Peru (1821), Brazil (1822), Bolivia (1825) and Uruguay (1828).

Britain was hostile to intervention and protested against decisions which enabled a French army to go to Spain and restore its reactionary monarch and an Austrian army to go to Piedmont and Naples in order to crush liberalism there. And Britain recognised the new Latin American states, supporting the United States President James Monroe whose 1823 Doctrine warned against intervention by European states to suppress revolts in the Americas.

When in 1821 the Greeks rose against the Ottoman Empire Metternich wanted to let the Turks crush the revolt. But when it looked as if the Greeks would indeed be crushed, a wave of pro-Greek feeling swept not only Britain and France but also Russia, which saw itself as the champion of Christianity in the Balkans and hoped to destroy Turkey and capture Constantinople. A combined Anglo-French-Russian fleet sank that of Turkey at Navarino Bay in 1827 and a few years later Greece became independent. These events struck a big blow against Metternich's principles – disunity among the Great Powers and victories for nationalism. And another blow was struck to the Congress map of Europe in 1830 when Catholic Belgium broke away from Dutch and Protestant domination in the United Netherlands. The Congress system was slowly unravelling, and as it did the Industrial Revolution would exacerbate the differences in the economic and political strengths of the Great Powers and intensify their rivalry.

Europe 'took off' economically after 1815. Despite prohibiting the export of machinery and migration of skilled workers, the techniques developed in Britain were passed on to the Continent. Capital was available as international banking expanded during and after the Napoleonic Wars through transfers of funds, loans to allies and reparation and occupation payments. Initially the European areas where industrialisation started were the ones with traditional experience in trade and commerce, banking and entrepreneurship – the Low Countries, the Rhine Valley, the Paris Basin, the Rhone Valley, Saxony, Silesia and Bohemia.

As in Britain, the first industrial revolution on the Continent was based on textiles, coal and steam. The 1820s saw the development and expansion of steam railways; the 1830s that of steamships. This first industrial revolution had four effects, two social, one economic, one political.

The first social effect was the growth of towns. These were expanding in a usually uncontrolled fashion around factories, creating immense problems of housing and sanitation. The result was that towns had to start planning and receive powers of local government in order to raise money and spend it on housing, streets, transport, lighting, water and sewage.

The second social effect was migration. In Europe itself this took three forms: from the countryside to the towns to provide the labour force for the factories; from poor countries to rich countries to find work – Italians and Poles to Germany and France; Irish to mainland Britain; from populated areas to relatively empty lands in order to develop them – Germans into Russia and Poland. At this time there was much less migration overseas compared to what would happen in the second half of the century – if money was going to be made the investment opportunities were in Europe. Migration overseas only occurred if valuable raw materials were discovered such as gold in California at the end of the 1840's. Colonialism was still informal, involving co-operation with local élites, rather than direct take-over of territory.[27] Where the industrial revolution helped was with steam power which enabled Europeans to sail up previously unnavigable rivers in Africa, Latin America and Asia.[28]

At the economic level industrial expansion challenged internal barriers to trade, and nowhere more so than in Germany.

Political fragmentation explained the economic backwardness of Germany in 1815 compared with Britain and France. It was not merely the number of states, with their costly customs administrations and widely differing tariff rates that hampered internal trade and encouraged smuggling, but that these states would have enclaves within them belonging to other states or even independent. This situation neither prevented flooding by cheap British goods nor provided the means to fight back against the high tariffs in

countries surrounding Germany. In addition, roads were very poor
and canal and river transport inadequate.[29]

The lead was taken by Prussia, which needed to increase its
revenue from imports and replace the mass of national, provincial,
local and private dues by a single tariff low enough to discourage
smuggling. In 1818–19 two tariffs were introduced, one for the
eastern provinces and one for the western; all internal dues and
prohibitions on exports and imports were abolished, and foreign
enclaves treated for the purpose as Prussian territory. Although the
enclaves resented such treatment, by 1928 they had accepted it and,
together with Hesse Darmstadt joined the Prussian Customs
Union.[30]

In 1828 Bavaria and Württemberg (but not Baden which had a
dispute with Bavaria concerning the Palatinate) formed the South
German Customs Union, while a Middle German Commercial
Union was set up, including Saxony, Hanover, Hesse-Cassel, Nassau, Brunswick, Oldenburg, Frankfurt-am-Main and Bremen.

The following year the Prussian and Southern Unions signed a
commercial treaty providing for goods to be sent to each other duty
free or at reduced rates, uniformity in customs administration, and
reciprocal rights to set up and carry on a business in each other's
territory. Full customs union between the two organisations came
into force on 1 January 1834. In the meantime the Middle Union
had collapsed and a number of its – and other – states joined the
customs union – Saxony and Thuringia (1833), Nassau and Baden
(1835), Frankfurt (1836) and Brunswick (1841). Luxemburg, which
had been partitioned in 1839 with the larger part becoming a
Belgian province, joined in 1842.

The economic transformation of Germany begun by the Customs Union was completed by improvements in transport. Between
1815–29, 2800 miles of new roads were built.[31] The first German
railway, between Nuremburg and Fürth was built in 1835 and by
1846 Germany had 2000 miles of railways, compared to 725 in
Austria.[32] Germans were now coming increasingly into contact with
each other, and industrial regions like Upper Silesia, hitherto
underdeveloped owing to poor communications with potential markets, benefited from the lower transport costs.

The Customs Union had not, however, been set up as a result of
rising German national consciousness. Its members, still particular-
ist, had joined it for their own interests, especially expecting to
benefit from being part of a large and powerful economic unit in

negotiations with foreign states. But the Customs Union did provide a foundation and impetus for unity. At this period there were still a number of problems. One was that not all German states were in the Union and those that were not, like Holstein, Bremen, Lubeck, Oldenburg and Hanover, effectively cut the Customs Union off from the North Sea and the mouths of Germany's chief rivers. The other was that the Customs Union was led by Prussia, but Austria, president of the Germanic Confederation, was not in the Union but desirous of being so. What would be Prussia's reaction?

The political effect of the Industrial Revolution was the growth of political forces based on class – liberalism, communism and socialism.

Through its inventions, the expansion of the banking and credit systems, industry and communications the Industrial Revolution had led to an enlargement of the middle class of persons to operate it – manufacturers, bankers, traders. And what they wanted was not only free competition, with laws passed to free trade from any restraints, including strikes by their workers, but an end to interference by autocratic or privileged government and an extension of democracy. And in this regard it was again Britain that gave the lead. In 1832 the Great Reform Bill eliminated most 'rotten boroughs' (i.e. constituencies with very few electors) and extended the adult male franchise not only to owners of property with an income of £10 per annum but to tenants paying an annual rent. The electorate nearly doubled to almost eight hundred thousand, a much higher proportion of voters in the population than almost anywhere else in Europe.[33]

But this liberalism had its weaknesses. Industrial free competition and the growth of towns had led to hideous living and working conditions because of miserable wages based on the law of supply and demand when there was always more of the former than the latter. Yet any increase in wages or in overhead expenditure to improve conditions of work might lead to decreased profits or a decline in competivity. Social peace could often be obtained only by laws forbidding strikes and trade unions, and using the police to break up demonstrations by workers against their conditions.

In opposition to the liberals and middle class values was the new proletariat class of industrial workers. Their working hours were long – anything up to seventeen a day. Children were employed from the age of six in mines under conditions which destroyed their future health. Women were employed at the most exhausting labour. Drunkenness was widespread. In a factory the worker was bound to the instrument of labour but was excluded from the ownership enjoyed by a craftsman working with his own tools in his own workshop under the pre-industrial system of production.[34]

The reaction to these conditions was led on the one hand by so-called Utopian socialists who appealed to employers in the name of national social solidarity to alleviate them, arguing that ideals such as the health of the nation, family life and human dignity had as high if not a higher value than profits. On the other hand, individual philanthropic manufacturers such as Robert Owen (1771–1858) in Britain and America and Charles Fourier (1772–1837) in France proposed or set up self-help co-operatives, both agricultural and industrial, in which workers would control production and profits.

But the efforts of the Utopians to create reforms might undermine competivity at home and lead to foreign imports flooding the market with the threat of domestic unemployment. To overcome the point that international competition was an obstacle to humanitarian national legislation an Alsatian, Daniel Legrand (1783–1859), proposed that countries should adopt international legislation to rectify abuses. He warned that the constant attention to wealth and profits would lead to masses of people hostile to state institutions and liable to subversion by demagogues.[35]

Again it was Britain that took the lead in national reform. Trade unions were legalised in 1824, and in 1833 the first Factory Act limited child labour and provided for government inspections.

But the pace of reform, slow in Britain, hardly existed on the Continent. It was unsurprising therefore that the proletariat should be attracted by the writings of Karl Marx, born in Trier in the Rhineland to a Jewish family which converted to Protestantism.

The strength of Marxism lay in its ability to explain in world historical terms both how the degradation of the working class had come about, and how things would *inevitably* change for the better. In particular Marx argued that the conditions of economic production determined society. Laws and institutions only reflected the economic system, which in turn reflected the interests of the economically dominant class. The only way to change things, therefore, was to change the economic system. The working class therefore needed to overthrow the existing capitalist system and create a society where the means of production – capital, land, machinery, factories – belonged to all and not just an upper or middle class élite. Marx also argued that the class of mill, mine and factory owners and financiers would not lightly give up their privileged positions based on economic power, or improve working class conditions since this would cut into their profits and make them bankrupt. Their overthrow by the working class would therefore inevitably have to be violent. In the conclusion to the famous *Communist Manifesto*, which came out in February 1848, Marx called on working men of all countries to unite – they had nothing to lose but their chains – they had a world to win.[36] That same year, but for different reasons, revolution broke out in almost every country in Europe.

The second half of the 1840s saw an agrarian crisis brought about by a potato blight, which destroyed the entire crop for many years from 1845 onwards, and loss of the grain harvest in 1846. Prices rose, creating hardship for the working classes, while the decline in spending power affected middle class businesses, threatening debt and bankruptcies. Mass production had reduced the social mobility factor of skilled labour, thus threatening the artisan class with proletarianisation. Political power was still in the hands of landed property owners, so that the increasingly better educated middle class felt excluded (the French electorate was still only two hundred and forty thousand). Intellectuals complained about the censorship in autocratic régimes.

In February 1848 rejection of reforms in Paris led to the overthrow of the monarchy and the establishment of a Second Republic. The uprising spread to Germany, with demands for unification and, amongst radicals, for a republic. A Constituent National Assembly was called in Frankfurt to discuss constitutional reform, among the issues being whether the new German state should be unitary or federal, monarchist or republican, and whether German Austria or indeed all German-speaking Europe should be included. In the Austrian Empire demands for a free press, trial by jury and peasant emancipation led to riots in Vienna and the collapse of the régime. When the news of events in Vienna became known the Italian provinces rose, seeking liberation from autocratic and foreign rule, and a Piedmontese army marched to their aid; Czechs and Hungarians set up national governments and moved to emancipate the peasantry and end aristocratic privileges. In the rest of Italy there were revolts in Naples, Sicily and the Papal States, and a Roman Republic was established. However, the aims of these revolutions were all different. The middle class wanted constitutional reform and to ensure economic and social progress. The working class wanted to improve working conditions which the middle class held incompatible with competition. And the nationalists soon found they had mutually incompatable claims.

The result was that the forces of reaction rallied. In France, Napoleon's nephew Louis Napoleon became President, but in a few years had manipulated power to have himself elected Emperor of the French. In Frankfurt the delegates elected the King of Prussia, Frederick William IV, hereditary German Emperor but he refused a crown 'from the gutter', and with the middle class fearing republican revolutionary radicalism, the move to German unification temporarily came to a halt. In the meantime, troops loyal to the Emperor of Austria routed the Piedmontese at Custozza and Novara and regained control of Northern Italy; the Czechs were bombarded into submission; and the Hungarian rising was also bloodily suppressed although not without help from a Russian army called in under the Holy Alliance.[37] Only two countries remained more or less untouched by these events. One was distant autocratic Russia, where the significance of events could be easily controlled and a plot by some intellectuals (including Dostoevsky) for an armed uprising was soon uncovered.[38]

The other country was Britain, the dominant power in Europe in the mid-century. Its navy was more powerful than any two or three other powers; it had the largest colonial empire; its powerful financial position provided easy capital and investment abroad and returns that covered any deficiencies in the balance of trade so that the country did not have any payments problems; it provided well over half the world's total production of coal.[39] Half the population lived in cities, something that would occur in Germany only in 1900 and France in 1920.[40]

But the experience of the Industrial and French Revolutions ensured that the British socio-economic ethos would differ markedly from that on the Continent.

Because the Industrial Revolution had started in Britain and for the reasons it did, the nation's economic development was led by small independent family firms, and that included the railways. This fostered a tradition of management independence and resistance to the idea that the firm was, let alone should be, part of an institutionalised web including government, banks and organised labour.[41] For conservative Britain the role of the state was not to sponsor the (or any) revolution, let alone stimulate investment and mobilise capital, but to provide a suitable environment – order at home and security against foreign attack.[42] As years went by this would be refined into a 'conservative' view that the government should hold the ring, an impartial mediator between competing groups and interests and not be tempted to descend into the ring and become a player. Society develops as society wishes, using precedent and tradition until the moment comes when these no longer measure up to requirements, whereupon society spontaneously develops a new set of precedents and traditions.

On the Continent, however, the legacy of the French Revolution was that the role of the state was not merely to maintain order and security within which the community might express preferences, but was an instrument by which the population could achieve desired ends, ends or ideals usually proclaimed in written constitutions. Since France and Germany had a smaller middle class and much less capital than Britain it was the state which supported industrialisation and especially the development of the railway system. In Germany this ethos would be taken much further in the second half of the century as the state backed investment banks and promoted big cartels in heavy industry.[43] These differences would play their part in the hostility in Britain to the process of European integration in the last decades of the twentieth century.

12 The Uncertain Giant 1850–1914AD

Apart from the uprisings of 1848–9, for forty years after Waterloo Europe had been at peace. But in the sixteen years from 1854 to 1870 five short wars would change the face of the continent and prepare it for the great wars of the twentieth century. Nationalism was the cause, and no states would be more profoundly affected than the two weakest states in the Great Power system, Austria and the Ottoman Empire.

Russian foreign policy under Tsar Nicholas I, 1825–55, aimed to destroy the Turkish Empire, re-establish the Orthodox Christian religion at Constantinople, dominate the Balkans and control the Bosphorus with its access to the Black Sea. The means by which Russia hoped to achieve these aims was by getting the Turks to agree that Russia should be the protecting power for Christians in the Turkish Empire. In 1774 the Russians had obtained that right in regard to the two Danubian Principalities of Moldavia and Wallachia, while in 1852 France had forced the Turks to allow Latin Christians to share in the administration of the Holy Places in Palestine, leading to a conflict in Jerusalem between Catholic and Orthodox monks.

In 1853 Russia invaded the Danubian Principalities but in the so-called Crimean War Turkey was supported by France and Britain, neither of whom wanted a Turkish collapse and Russian aggrandisement. What shocked the Russians however, was the attitude of Austria. Russia had come to the aid of the Austrians in 1849 and snuffed out the Hungarian revolt, but the Austrians did not side with Russia. They were more concerned about what might happen in Italy and Germany and hoped for western European support there in return for urging Russian evacuation of the Principalities.

This policy was unsuccessful. When the showdown came in Italy and Germany the French were not bought off and Russia's alienation meant Austria's isolation. The Crimean war effectively meant the end of the Concert of Europe.[1]

In Italy one thing was clear. Austria's victories in 1848–9 had punctured boasts that Italians could achieve independence and unification alone. But there were other problems as well. Would the new Italy be monarchist or republican? Liberal or clerical? Regional or central? In the 1848–9 revolution in Italy republicans such as Guiseppe Garibaldi and Guiseppe Mazzini had played a prominent part in the risings against the Austrians in Lombardy and Venice, the absolutist Habsburg or Bourbon rulers in Naples-Sicily and the northern duchies of Parma, Modena and Tuscany, and against the Pope in the Papal States of Umbria, the Marches and Romagna. In 1849 the Pope had even been obliged by the revolutionaries to flee Rome.

The process of Italian unification was begun by the Prime Minister of Piedmont-Sardinia, Count Camillo Cavour. His policy was to create a liberal Italian state under the leadership of the Kingdom of Piedmont. But first he had to get a strong ally, and that ally was Napoleon III, Emperor of the French.

Napoleon III was a complex character, burdened by the reputation of his illustrious uncle. As a youth, exiled from France, he had joined the *Carbonari*, an Italian secret society inspired by the French Revolution and Napoleonic achievements and dedicated to elimination of foreign and autocratic rule in Italy. His experiences made Napoleon III something of an inconstant adventurer or opportunist, and this was reflected in his foreign policies which sought the aggrandisement of France through what became known contemptuously as '*une politique de pourboires*', trying to pick up compensation in return for French action (or inaction) in a given situation. Napoleon's other problem was that he had to placate two powerful and mutually antagonistic forces in France itself, liberalism and catholicism.

In 1858 Cavour and Napoleon struck a bargain. In return for French help in a war against Austria a victorious Piedmont would cede Nice and Savoy to France but gain all northern Italy above the Apennines (Lombardy, Venice, Parma, Modena and the Romagna). Italy would become a federation of three kingdoms – the enlarged Piedmont-Sardinia, Naples-Sicily (perhaps under a new ruler) and a central Italian Kingdom made out of the rest under a sovereign to be chosen. The whole would be under the presidency of the Pope, whose territorial possessions would be restricted to Rome and the surrounding region.

For Napoleon the deal looked good. Acquisition of Nice and Savoy – the natural frontiers of France – and the gratitude of Italy would at least please national pride and the liberal-Bonapartist element in France.

In 1859 the war with Austria duly took place, and within a few weeks the Franco-Piedmontese armies had driven the Austrians out of Lombardy, while risings in the northern duchies led to the expulsion of their rulers.

But the war came to a surprising end. Prussia had mobilised and proposals for mediation by it and the other powers hung in the air. Neither France nor Austria could be certain as to Prussian intentions. At Villafranca Napoleon met the Emperor of Austria, Francis Joseph, and agreed that only Lombardy need be given up while the rulers of the northern duchies would be restored.

This was not nearly good enough for Italian nationalists. In 1860 plebiscites were held in the northern duchies and the Papal states in which those areas voted almost entirely for union with Piedmont. Garibaldi and his 'One Thousand' red-shirts landed in Sicily and within a few months the King of Naples had fled. Plebiscites in Naples and Sicily also overwhelmingly supported annexation by Piedmont, although Cavour himself had doubts about taking over areas of such desperate poverty which would require much northern capital – a problem that would dominate Italian politics even to this day.[2]

That still left Venice, Trento and Trieste with Austria, and there was also the question of Rome which was wanted by almost all Italians as their capital and upon which Garibaldi the republican now wanted to march. The problem was that in 1849 Louis Napoleon, when President and to gain support of French Catholics, had sent a force to Rome to restore the Pope and preserve the Papal States. French troops were still there and Cavour did not wish to antagonise France – and indeed all Catholic Europe – so the issue of Rome had temporarily to be shelved. With the French out of contention, paid off by Nice and Savoy, Italian unification would have to depend on another source of support against Austria, and possibly even France. And that source would be Prussia.

The issue between Prussia and Austria was domination of Germany. Austria was President of the Germanic Confederation but was not a member of the Customs Union. In the 1850s the Customs Union had been a great success, with state revenues and trade greatly increased and had been strengthened by the addition of the Tax Union states of Oldenburg, Hanover and Brunswick, and the Austrians wanted to extend the Customs Union to include not only themselves but their Empire.

In 1862 Otto von Bismarck was appointed Prime Minister of Prussia by King William I. His policies included elimination of

Austria from German affairs and the consequent need to enlarge and modernise the army. When the liberal majority in the Prussian parliament refused to vote the taxes for the army in the budget Bismarck made his famous remark that 'the great questions of the day will not be decided by speeches and the resolutions of majorities that was the blunder of 1848 and 1849 – but by blood and iron', and the money was collected anyhow. It has been said that this showed how shallow were the roots of constitutionalism in Prussia, for a docile population paid taxes to the officials of the state bureaucracy despite their illegal basis. Lack of parliamentary consent meant nothing against royal authority.[3]

Bismarck's pretext for war to eliminate Austria from Germany rose out of the Schleswig-Holstein question. Those two duchies had been ruled jointly since the Middle Ages in personal union with the King of Denmark as their Duke. Schleswig had a large German minority, whereas Holstein was almost entirely German and was a member of the Germanic Confederation.

In 1863 the King of Denmark died and his successor tried to annexe Schleswig outright and separate it from Holstein. But a rival contested his right to the duchies on grounds of the Salic Law and he was supported by German nationalist sentiment in the duchies and the Germanic Confederation. Arguing that the threatened annexation violated an 1852 international agreement on the future of the duchies, Bismarck made an alliance with Austria and in the name of the Confederation attacked Denmark in 1864. The war was soon over and in 1865 the duchies were ceded to the Confederation which accepted the administration of Holstein by Austria and Schleswig by Prussia under the Gastein Convention.

Relations between Prussia and Austria thereupon deteriorated, as Bismarck had hoped and worked for. Prussia proposed that an all-German parliament should be elected that would carry out a reform of the Confederation excluding Austria. The latter accused Prussia of violating both the Treaty establishing the Confederation and the Gastein Convention and asked the Confederation to mobilise against Prussia. Nine states did so, including Baden, Bavaria, Wurttembürg, Saxony and Hanover.[4]

In the meantime, Bismarck had signed a military alliance with Italy guaranteeing Venice in case of victory. As the showdown with Prussia neared, Austria was isolated. The Russians were still resentful over the Crimea; Louis Napoleon still had feelings of guilt about not completing the task of Italian unification in 1859, and Bismarck made some vague suggestions about compensation for France if it remained neutral, possibly Luxembourg.

When the war with Prussia came in June 1866, the Austrians may have had the largest armies but those of its allies were scattered, while there was also the Italian front. The Prussians, on the other hand, not only had inner lines of communication but the railways provided swift transportation of the army to strategic areas. In Italy the Austrians were victorious but the Prussians routed the Hanoverians at Langensalza and at Sadowa in Bohemia won the decisive battle of the war against the Austrians.

The battle of Sadowa had a number of important consequences:

First, Italy, despite defeat, gained Venice as promised. Now only Trento, Trieste and Rome stood in the way of complete unification.

Second, the map of northern Germany was again redrawn. The Germanic Confederation was dissolved. Prussia annexed outright a number of states which had supported Austria – Hanover, Hesse-Cassell, Nassau, Holstein and Frankfurt. Instead a North-German Confederation of twenty-two states was created north of the river Main under Prussian economic and political hegemony, including the Mecklenburgs and Lübeck, coming into effect in 1867. A new Customs Union treaty was signed, which provided for a Customs Council able to take decisions by a majority of the delegates appointed by governments in relation to their respective populations. But it was Prussia which presided over the Council, signed treaties on behalf of the Union and had the right to veto any changes to the regulations.[5] And new military alliances had to be concluded between the North German Confederation and the southern German states to replace those existing under the German Confederation.[6] Austrian political influence in Germany was ended, as were hopes of an Austro-German Customs Union.

Third, with its elimination from German and, more or less, Italian affairs, the focus of Austrian foreign policy became eastern Europe where it would clash with Russia over who should inherit the mantle of the decaying Turkish Empire. And in the decade previous to Sadowa the decay had proceeded further. In 1860 Serbia was allowed to become an autonomous principality and two years later the two Danubian principalities of Moldavia and

Wallachia united to form the state of Romania with the same status. Turkish control in both was now minimal.

But the defeat of 1866 brought about internal reforms as well. Shaken by the defeat and in order to stabilise the realm the Austrians agreed to make the Hungarians full partners with Home Rule. The Austrian Empire henceforth would be the Austro-Hungarian Empire.

The Austrian half (Cisleithania), with a population of twenty-eight million, consisted of German Austria, the Slavs of Bohemia, Moravia, Slovenia, Dalmatia and (Polish) Galicia, and the Italians of Trento and Trieste. The Germans, however, only formed one third of the Austrian half of the Empire. The Hungarian part (Transleithania), with a population of eighteen million consisted of Hungarians (just under fifty per cent), Slovaks, Romanians in Transylvania, Croatians and some Serbs.

The only areas of common responsibility between the two halves of the Empire were foreign affairs and defence, and a common finance ministry which was responsible for finding the money for the other two common activities. Each half had its own parliament and government, armies and financial administration.

The Great Powers welcomed the division of the Empire, seeing it as a source of stability in east-central Europe. And initially the division was also welcomed by the Czechs in Bohemia and Moravia and the Poles in Galicia in the hope that their turn for Home Rule would come. Much would depend on how far these aspirations would be achieved, and how the Hungarians would treat their minorities.[7]

Fourth, the aggrandisement of Prussia seriously alarmed the French. After Sadowa the French again raised the question of compensation – Luxembourg, even some Bavarian or Hessian territory on the left bank of the Rhine. Frustrated, the result would be the Franco-Prussian War of 1870 which would have consequences even more profound than those of the war of 1866.

Since 1869 the Spanish throne had been vacant following revolt against Queen Isabella and her consequent flight into exile. One candidate for her replacement was Prince Leopold of Hohenzollern-Sigmaringen, who was related to the ruling dynasty of Prussia. To the French, having the Prussians on the Rhine and the Pyrenees was as unacceptable as encirclement by the Habsburgs in the sixteenth and seventeenth centuries, and the French government announced that if Leopold did not withdraw his candidature France would consider the matter as a cause for war. When Leopold obliged the French went further and demanded from the King of Prussia, as head of the Hohenzollern dynasty, guarantees that the candidature would not be renewed. At Bad Ems, William I received the French ambassador politely but refused to give the required guarantee, merely stating that he now considered the matter closed and would not see the ambassador again on the subject. William then sent a telegram to Bismarck outlining what had taken place. This telegram Bismarck released to the press but in a version doctored to make it seem that the King had refused to see the ambassador and had therefore *a priori* rejected the formal demands of the French government.[8]

The French were delighted to seize on the perceived insult and in July 1870 declared war, but they were to be severely disappointed. For one thing they were alone. Russia still remembered the Crimea, Austria remembered Italy, Italy remembered Rome and Britain was concerned about French intrigues for 'compensation' in Belgium. For another, the French armies were unco-ordinated and had no answer to superior Prussian mobilisation techniques and the fire power of the steel cannons of Krupp. On 2 September 1870 at Sedan a French army led by the Emperor in person was surrounded, pounded by the Prussian artillery, and capitulated. And with the Emperor's capture his régime, the so-called Second Empire, collapsed.

In Paris the Third Republic was proclaimed and a provisional government formed. But the government had few troops and these were easily repulsed. Paris was besieged until finally surrendering in January 1871 in a state of starvation.

For the French the consequences of the war were disastrous Apart from having to pay a war indemnity of five billion francs, France had to cede to Prussia Alsace-Lorraine. In fact Bismarck was not enthusiastic about incorporating into Germany so many people likely to be hostile but yielded to the views of the Prussian military that if France was again to become a danger, possession of Alsace-Lorraine on strategic grounds, on the left bank of the Rhine, was essential. And then after the siege of Paris had ended the capital was taken over by persons resolved to restore the revolutionary tradition – socialists, anarchists and Marxists – believing in direct proletarian action and reacting against defeat and the bourgeois sentiments of the new French government situated in Bordeaux. The revolt, which included rule by terror and the massacre of hostages, was mercilessly suppressed by the government, with many executions and deportations [9]

For Italy, the defeat of France meant the withdrawal of the French troops from Rome. The Italian national army pushed from the walls the few papal troops defending the city and entered in triumph. Rome was proclaimed the capital of the Kingdom which, to its irredentists, now only lacked Trento and Trieste. All that was left to the Papacy as an independent territory was an enclave on the outskirts of Rome, the Vatican.

Nevertheless, nearly united as it might be, the new state would have fearful problems. These included the enormous disparity in economic standards between north and south, a disparity that would widen when the industrial revolution came to Italy. Central control of the state would seem one way of tackling these differences, but fourteen centuries of independent kingdoms, duchies and republics would create a spirit of regional loyalty that centralism would not break down. And then there was the Pope, Pius IX, the spiritual leader of a country almost totally Roman Catholic, but fiercely resentful of the unification process that had deprived him of his territorial possessions and left him with an enclave of only a few acres. The previous year he had reiterated the doctrine of papal infallibility. Now his hostility to the government led him to forbid Catholics to vote or stand for office – a rift in society that would last for nearly sixty years. [10]

The great winner was Prussia, which brought about the unification of Germany. Bismarck's policy had been to ensure that the southern German states participated in the war against France. They were, after all, military allies and they could be frightened by the threat of territorial losses if the French should win – the folly of the policy of compensation being only too well revealed. But how to get the southern states to join a united Germany under the King of Prussia as Emperor? William I, like his predecessor, did not want a 'crown from the gutter'. And thus it was that Bismarck arranged for King Ludwig II of Bavaria to offer William the title of German Emperor on behalf of his fellow German rulers in the Palace of Versailles, outside the capital of the defeated enemy, on 18 January 1871. [11]

The new Germany, the Second Reich, was similar to the North German confederation. But unlike in Austria-Hungary, the Empire not only controlled defence and foreign affairs but customs, commerce, transport and the postal services. The twenty-five federal states (four kingdoms, six grand duchies, five duchies, seven principalities and three free cities) controlled their own administration, judiciary, education and culture. Alsace-Lorraine would receive its own special administration in 1911. The Reich was funded, however, by contributions from the States.

The chief organ of government was the Upper House, the Federal Council or *Bundesrat* of fifty-eight members representing the States who had legislative powers and could issue decrees, although fourteen contrary votes was enough for a veto. There was also a Lower House, the *Reichstag* of some four hundred deputies which could approve legislation and the imperial budget.

But this federation was dominated by Prussia, which comprised nearly two-thirds of the area and population of the Reich. It was the Emperor, and King of Prussia, who appointed and dismissed ministers, not the governmental organs. He was supreme commander of the armed forces. The Imperial Chancellor was usually Prime Minister of Prussia, and it was he who was responsible for foreign affairs. And because there were seventeen Prussian members of the Bundesrat they could veto any measure of that body they disliked, particularly relating to the armed forces and Reich expenditures.[12]

The great loser was Europe. For the seizure of Alsace-Lorraine, in a famous phrase, 'mortgaged the future'. The French would never be reconciled to its loss, but since the transfer deepened the difference in terms of population and economic strength between themselves and Germany and it was clear that in a one-to-one war they would lose again, they would have to seek allies.

Of this Bismarck, now Imperial Chancellor, was aware, and to guard against the French finding such allies and remaining isolated he created a network of alliances between Germany and the other Great Powers except England. Bismarck also knew that the greatest opportunity for France would come if there was to be another European war and the greatest danger of such a war lay in Austro-Russian rivalry in the Balkans. The principles upon which his system was based were therefore three. First, that in a war between Germany and France the other Powers would be neutral. Second, with regard to Austria and Russia, Germany would defend either against attack but not help the one that was an aggressor. Since Germany was so strong that whatever side it supported would win, that would damp down their rivalry. Third, the French would be encouraged to pursue colonial rather than European ambitions, knowing that this would embroil them in rivalry with Britain and Italy, particularly in Africa.

Thus in 1872 Bismarck promoted the League of the Three Emperors (Germany, Austria–Hungary and Russia), which was renewed in 1881. In 1879 the Dual Alliance was signed between Germany and Austria–Hungary, and this was extended in 1882 to include Italy to create the Triple Alliance. Finally in 1887 Germany signed the so-called Reinsurance Treaty with Russia, under which Bismarck promised diplomatic support for Russia against Turkey.

All would be well as long as Bismarck remained at the helm of German foreign affairs. As for Alsace-Lorraine, the French in isolation could only wait and hope. But while the French waited and hoped the economic development of the continent was altering drastically the relationships between the Powers.

The first industrial revolution had been based on textiles, steam and metals, and was led by Britain. The second was based on chemicals and electricity and was led by Germany. Britain might have had Faraday with the law of electrical induction and electrolysis (1831–3) and Rutherford for radioactivity (1903) and atomic structure (1911), and France might have had Madame Curie and radium (1898), but for Germany there was Runge with the derivation of acids and dyes from coal (1833), Jacobi and the electric motor (1834), Liebig and fertilisers (1841), Kirchhoff and Bunsen with spectral analysis (1859), Siemens and the dynamo (1867) and the electric locomotive (1879), Otto and the 4-cycle gas engine (1876), Daimler and the petrol engine (1884) and with Benz the motor car (1885), Hertz with electro-magnetic wares (1888), Diesel and his engine (1893), Planck with quantum theory and Zeppelin with his dirigible (1900), and Einstein and his theory of relativity (1905).[13]

In 1910 Germany was closing in fast on Britain in terms of coal output, and each of those two countries was producing six times as much coal as France and nearly ten times as much as Russia. In terms of iron Germany had overtaken England and was producing as much as the latter and France. Germany's output of steel was more than that of Britain, France and Russia combined.[14] Germany thus had the instruments of power or the resources to create such instruments should the time come for the European *status quo* to be changed.[15]

If Germany was the leader in Europe's economic development much would depend on how the other Powers followed. All would respond to this economic development and the inventions which would rub off on each other.

The country significantly to emerge was Russia.

Russia had been shocked by the Crimean War, which showed up the country's backwardness in terms of the lack of material and administrative resources. In 1855 Alexander II became Tsar and his government embarked on a series of reforms. The serfs were liberated in 1861. There was an enormous expansion in railroads, banks, joint-stock companies and industrial enterprises with French, Belgian and British technology being imported, and with many (if not most) industrial enterprises being foreign owned. But – and this was the crucial point – the success of every venture, commercial, industrial or financial, depended on state aid. And that meant bureaucratic controls and subsidies for the favoured few rather than an open *laissez-faire* system which could have attracted and then kept flowing the massive foreign investment required but on the other hand had its risk of mismanagement, speculation and business failures.[16] Nevertheless, on the eve of the First World War Russia was the third industrial power in Europe, having grown since the Crimean War at an average rate of five per cent per year. Its output of steel had overtaken that of France and Austria-Hungary, and it was catching up on France in regard to iron, and whereas Russia had practically no statistical output of coal at the time of the Crimean War, its production was two-thirds that of France by 1914. But no matter how impressive these achievements were, Russia was still an industrial dwarf compared to Germany and Britain.[17]

France may have established modern iron, steel and engineering plants, may also even have been the world's leading automobile producer and had an ample supply of mobile capital, but it was still only fourth in terms of the European Powers – its industrial potential about forty per cent of Germany's, its steel production one-sixth, its coal production one-seventh. But most of its plants were small, industrial practices out of date, and protection rather than competition was the order of the day.[18]

The industrial revolution also came to Austria–Hungary. Its industrial growth rate was as good as Russia's, but in comparison with Germany it was still a dwarf. It had already well overtaken France as a coal producer by 1900, but on the eve of the first world war its coal production was only one-sixth of Germany's, its pig-iron one-seventh and its steel one-fifth.[19]

As for Italy, the newcomer to the ranks of the Great Powers there was also a big effort to industrialise, at least in the north. Heavy industry – iron and steel, automobiles, shipbuilding, textiles – was pursued, and thus from practically no base Italian industry grew as fast as anywhere else. But Italy had practically no coal and had to import it in order for its hydro-electricity to function. On the eve of war its iron and steel production was one-seventeenth that of Germany.[20]

The only European country in the same economic league as Germany was, of course, Britain. On the eve of the First World War it possessed the largest empire the world had ever seen, possibly one quarter of the world's population. Britain was still the world's biggest investor, banker, insurer and commodity dealer. True, its output of coal, steel, iron and textiles had increased but already by 1890 Britain had fallen behind Germany in regard to steel and iron. In the sectors of the second industrial revolution Britain soon lost any early lead it might have had. Overall its industrial growth rate was far less than that of its rivals. Its percentage of total world manufacturing output and share of world trade fell by over one-third between 1880 and 1913.[21]

The relative standings of the European Great Powers may have been changing in the second half of the century but that could not hide the fact that one result of the industrial revolutions was the increasing integration of the continent. This could be seen not only in the movements of peoples in search of work but also the sheer expansion of business, and the growth of international agreements in such fields as postal and telegraph services, patents and copyright, and hours of work.

Vital for that business expansion was the idea of limited liability. Before Britain led the way with the 1862 Companies Act a big restraint on business was the fear of shareholders that they would be liable for the debts of a firm should it go bankrupt. With this fear lifted there was a big increase in the number of shareholders and investment in a large variety of firms and projects.

International business expansion was also helped by the fact that from 1815 to 1914 the European economy was based on the so-called Gold Standard. The currencies of the countries of Europe were valued in terms of gold, and Central Banks were obliged to buy and sell gold at that fixed price. The advantages for international trade were that individual traders did not have to worry about changes on the exchange rate and that it was as easy for firms to settle a debt abroad as it was at home.

One effect of the rivalry and industrial expansion of the Great Powers in Europe was to usher in a third stage of colonialism, the stage which would indeed see eighty-five per cent of the entire world come under the domination of the Europeans, and thirty-five per cent of its land surface be colonial dependencies.[22]

The beginning of this third stage dates from the opening of the Suez Canal in November 1869. The main result of this feat of engineering was to cut the time of travel between Europe and the Far East by two-thirds in comparison with the route round the Cape of Good Hope.

What made this stage different from the previous two was that it was no longer a case of Europeans co-operating with local élites in order to acquire raw materials and markets but moving to outright control. Britain had already led the way with the takeover from the East India Company of the Indian sub-continent after the Indian Mutiny of 1857 (although the Princes of the various states still possessed some autonomy), but one reason for all the Powers to establish formal control over an area was strategic: to prevent encroachment by their European rivals who might take advantage of local tribal conflicts. Thus, for example, if India was indeed the 'Jewel in the Crown' of the British Empire, British colonial expansion had much to do with protecting its interests there, particularly occupying Egypt and acquiring direct control over the Suez Canal, annexing Burma and attempting to thwart Russian ambitions by seeking to control Afghanistan.[23]

Around about 1880 began the so-called 'scramble for Africa', the only continent which remained to be conquered. On the eve of the First World War it had been divided up between Britain and France (with by far the largest shares), Belgium (whose King Leopold II was given personal control of the Congo in 1885), Germany (today's Tanzania, Namibia and Togo), Italy (Libya), Portugal (Angola and Mozambique) and Spain. In this division of the continent boundaries were drawn to denote Great Power interests without regard to ethnic and tribal considerations. Only two states on the continent were independent: Liberia, founded by philanthropic American societies in 1820 for freed slaves, formally becoming a republic in 1847; and Abyssinia, today's Ethiopia. These two states joined only five in Asia not under direct European control or divided into

European spheres of influence – Afghanistan, Japan, Persia, Siam (today's Thailand) and Tibet.

But what prompted this enormous expansion? Economic motives are given as the usual answer: control of natural resources to fuel industrial development back home and feed burgeoning populations (except for France, most countries' populations had increase by half as much again in the period 1850–1910; that of Germany had nearly doubled; that of Russia had more than doubled).[24] There was also the not unimportant consideration that the colonies could provide troops. But the Marxist view that the decline in investment opportunities in Europe spurred colonial expansion can be discounted: most European investment was applied either to developing independent countries already controlled by governments of European stock such as the United States, Canada, South Africa, Australia and Argentina or for strategic reasons in other European countries. The level of investment elsewhere in the colonies was low.[25]

Another reason was 'Social Darwinism'. In 1859, on the basis of his research, the explorer and naturalist Charles Darwin published his *On the Origin of Species* in which he propounded the thesis of evolutionary natural selection through the survival of the fittest.[26]

No country was more struck by the issue of survival than France, traumatised by the shock of defeat in the war with Prussia and the loss of Alsace-Lorraine. Around them the French saw large, successful but probably hostile powers – Britain, with the largest empire the world had ever seen; Germany, an ever present menace, with a much larger population, more powerful and dynamic industry and a far larger army. For the French the world was indeed an arena of never-ending conflict between peoples and races, and survival meant having some control of the apparently limited economic resources of the world.

But it was not merely the danger of being eliminated in the fight for survival that alarmed the French. They felt that the world would be a poorer place if French civilisation were to disappear. To them France in the world had a 'civilising mission' based on the values of the French revolution, and there was no chance of France keeping its world standing and carrying out successfully that civilising mission if confined to Europe, a secondary power like Greece or Romania.[27]

Thus Indochina was taken over in the years 1885–95, and Madagascar between 1885–96. When Tunisia was taken over in 1881 and Morocco became first a sphere of French influence and then a Protectorate in the early twentieth century, control of the so-called Magreb region of North Africa had been secured. As a result of the 'scramble for Africa' France created in 1902 a West African Federation of eight colonies (Senegal, Ivory Coast, Dahomey, Guinée, Upper Volta, Mali, Mauretania, Niger) and in 1910 an East African Federation of four colonies (Congo-Brazzaville, Gabon, Tchad and Oubangui-Chari). There was also French Somaliland on the African East Coast.

But what should the attitude of France be towards the peoples they had taken over?

To begin with the answer was assimilation, that the population of a colony should become as French as the French themselves. There were three reasons for advocating this doctrine: the strong moral belief in human equality, tracing its roots through Stoicism and Christianity to the Rights of Man postulated in the French Revolution; that assimilation would be a solid foundation for a centralist and uniform colonial administration as in France; and that it was best way to spread French culture.[28]

Nor was the issue of survival limited to the French. The Dutch too were fearful of annexation by Germany, perhaps arising out of renewed Franco-German war, and South Africa, with its Boer Republics, was seen as a place where they might find a new home.[29]

However, the idea of assimilation soon lost favour. One major problem was that either for climatic or social reasons few French people emigrated to these colonies, apart from Algeria. Second, there was the contrast between French colonialism on the one hand and British and Dutch on the other. The latter were seen as concentrating on imperial prosperity, reconciling native with national interests, maintaining native institutions rather than enforcing dogmatically and rigidly one system over a wide variety of peoples. And evidence of the vast social and cultural differences amongst races soon led the French to switch from the idea of the basic equality of all peoples to the belief that important inequalities existed, and people could not be changed 'by decree'. The doctrine of assimilation was therefore replaced by that of association under which, because of the lack of colonists, the colonised would do the work of developing the land under the guidance of the colonisers and aided by their capital and techniques, and thus progress in a teacher-pupil relationship.[30]

The problems faced by French colonialism brought out one important point about the so-called age of imperialism, namely that as with investment, apart from the military class and civil servants, these newly acquired colonies were never areas for European migration. Between 1850 and 1914 some fifty million persons emigrated from Europe mainly from the British Isles (18 million, a large proportion of whom came from famine and post-famine Ireland), Italy (9.4 million), Austria–Hungary (4.8 million), Germany (4.5 million) and Spain (4.3 million).[31] Their destinations were overwhelmingly the United States and the process of westward expansion after the American Civil War of 1861–5, the gold fields and mines of South Africa, Canada, Australia and South America. By contrast there were only 65 000 Europeans and Eurasians among Indonesia's 35 million in 1903; the British ran India with one thousand senior civil servants and 65 000 British troops – Europeans numbered less than a quarter of a million in a country of 300 million. Of the 1.5 million French persons in their empire nearly one million lived in Algeria (which was considered as an integral part of France), there were about 200 000 in Tunis and Morocco, but only 32 000 in IndoChina, 25 000 in French West Africa and 5000 in French East Africa.[32]

But where for climatic reasons Europeans were reluctant to go they organised migration of non-Europeans to those areas, and this was due to quinine becoming easily and cheaply available in the last quarter of the century. Until then negroes, because of their resistance to malaria, had been the favoured form of labour in the tropics. Now Indians and Chinese would be imported as indentured labourers to make workable areas previously hostile: South Africa, Malaysia, the Pacific Islands, Ceylon, the Caribbean. In many places whole new crops could be grown because of the availability of the workers – sugar in Natal, tea in Ceylon, bananas in the Caribbean. Indeed it was quinine that really made European settlement possible in such areas as the Belgian Congo, French West Africa and the Dutch East Indies.[33]

But the seemingly inevitable take over of the coloured peoples of the world by the Europeans demanded an explanation as to why this should be so. The result was the adaptation of Darwin's idea of struggle and the survival of the fittest to postulate that the world developed not through struggle between nations or classes but between races. It was from this that racial theory developed. The French Count, Arthur de Gobineau, argued that all the world's civilisations flowed from the white race. These civilisations collapsed when they degenerated through mixing the blood of their founders with other races. But since the other races were inferior in terms of their physical and intellectual qualities the only way to ensure survival was racial purity.[34] This theory was taken up by Germans but particularly Houston Stewart Chamberlain, a Germanised Englishman, who sought to explain the triumphant achievements of their country by arguing that Germans were racially pure, that they were the real formers of European history (beginning by overthrowing the mixed race Roman Empire) and that Germans were therefore really the master race. To these racists history really consisted of Jewish conspiracies to overthrow the Germans; Christ might be a Jew by religion and education but by race he was almost certainly Greek.[35] One side effect of racial theory was a reinvigoration of Europe's latent anti-semitism that would have such catastrophic consequences in the next century.

Along with colonial expansion the last half of the century saw renewed efforts by the working class for improvement in their living and working conditions. The utopian socialists of the first half of the century had given way to a four-way fight for the soul of the labour movement.

First, the attempt by the workers to form trade unions in order to bargain collectively for improved conditions was gradually successful. The ban on them lifted in Britain in 1824 was repeated in France and Germany in the 1860's. Soon these trade unions were forming international federations, particularly miners, railwaymen and metalworkers.

Second, there were the Marxists who were arguing that since capitalism would use its political power to defend its economic system, the workers would have to conquer political power and they could only do that by violence. There was also a need for international working-class unity, particularly in order to prevent governments spilling the blood of the workers in wars. In 1864 Marx, together with Friedrich Engels, a German industrialist with factories in England, set up the First International. But it was premature to set up an international organisation of workers before these had developed solid organisations, whether trade unions or political parties, in their own countries.[36]

By the time the Second International was formed in 1889 the lack of working class parties had been largely overcome, with socialist parties being formed (usually from splinter groups) in the 1870s in Denmark, Bohemia, Germany, Portugal and Spain, and in the 1880s in France, Belgium, Austria, Switzerland and Sweden.

Then in the 1890s they would appear in Italy, Poland, Bulgaria, Holland, Hungary and Russia. In Britain the Independent Labour Party was founded in 1893 but the Labour Party as it is today did not come into being until 1900.

But by that time these parties faced a dilemma, namely, whether to work within the parliamentary system, even participate in government, in order to obtain improvements for the working class or simply to overthrow it. This was particularly true in Germany where, in 1883, Bismarck had introduced an unprecedented system of social insurance designed to protect workers against unemployment, illness, accident, disability and loss of income in old age, which was later copied in France and Britain.

Those who were prepared to work within the system, the third group, were denounced by their more extreme Marxist colleagues as revisionists. Much depended on the degree of confidence in the parliamentary system as well as the size of the economic cake to be shared out. Unsurprisingly therefore revisionism was strongest in France (where a socialist joined the Cabinet in 1898) and in the German *Länder*.[37]

In one country, however, there was to be no compromise – Russia. The Tsarist regime, particularly after the assassination of the serf-liberator Alexander II in 1881, would tolerate no challenge to absolutism. The result was an unparalleled expansion in underground revolutionary groupings in an atmosphere of increasing violence. Nihilists believed all authority should be destroyed. The Narodniks – later the Social Revolutionaries – believed that a communist-type revolution should be based on the peasantry, rural values and nationalisation of the land. The Social Democrats, founded by Georgi Plekhanov, were Marxists, believing that it was industrial workers who would create the revolution and that therefore Russia would first have to be industrialised in order to produce an appropriate proletariat working class.[38]

The savage police reaction to the wave of terrorist bombings, assassinations and strikes meant that the leaders of these revolutionary groups were either in prison, exiled to Siberia or taking refuge abroad.

An early member of the Social Democrat Party was Vladimir Ilyich Ulyanov, later to become famous as Lenin. His brother Alexander had been executed in 1887 for his part in a plot to assassinate the Tsar Alexander III. As a law student Lenin was involved in writing and distributing subversive literature, for which he was arrested and sent to Siberia for three years. On his release he went abroad and was one of the founders, with Plekhanov, of the newspaper *Iskra* (the Spark). In 1903 a Congress of the Party meeting first in Brussels and then in London, divided on the issue as to whether the party should organise as a democracy open to all or a small dictatorship with control by a central committee. Lenin, who favoured the latter, won a narrow victory and the Party split, Lenin and his supporters becoming the Bolsheviks (majority) and his opponents the Mensheviks (minority).[39]

From abroad Lenin wrote and arranged for the circulation of his writings in Russia, strengthening his position by gathering around him many of those who would come to prominence in 1917. Nevertheless, they were in reality only a small group of exiles, wandering throughout Europe, usually quarrelling on ideological points amongst themselves, frustrated and bitter at their inability to accomplish anything, waiting for a favourable opportunity.

The fourth group to strive for the allegiance of the working class was the Christian Socialists.

The response of the Roman Catholic Church to the French Revolution and the process of Italian unification had been very hostile. Quite apart from resenting the loss of territory and possessions the heirs of the revolution in both France and Italy had been anti-clerical liberals desirous of secularising society, and (at least in France) wishing to eliminate church schools. In both countries the attitude of the Papacy was to advise Catholics not to participate in state institutions such as political parties. On the other hand, the vision of infinite material progress opened up by the industrial revolution merely seemed to confirm the Enlightenment view that science and free enquiry was the key to progress rather than God. The Church found it difficult to make much impression upon a class infiltrated by the forces of Marxism or republicanism, and which identified the Church with capitalism. Nor did it help that the Church believed poverty and unemployment were best dealt with through charity and good works rather than comprehensive economic and social policies. The result was that the working class was almost entirely lost to the Church, preferring anti-clerical parties and trade unions.

Change came under Pope Leo XIII (1878–1903). In the Encyclical *Rerum Novarum* (1891) it was accepted that the French and Industrial Revolutions had potentially paved the way for a more humane society but so far only the monied élites had benefited.

Marxism, with its emphasis on the collectivity at the expense of the individual was rejected, as was the naked Darwinian individualism of the liberals which treated the worker as a commodity. The spiritual personality of a human being could only find fulfilment within the natural social structures of society such as the family, community or workplace. The encyclical supported the right of workers to form trade unions and even to strike in order to protect their interests, but since Catholics were not allowed to join organisations run on anti-religious lines this opened the door to the establishment of Catholic trade unions. The Pope also agreed that the state could intervene to regulate wages and conditions of work.[40] Later, Leo's successor Pope Pius X would lift the ban in Italy on Catholics voting and standing for office.[41] The result was that in the early years of the century the first small Christian-democratic type political parties and workers organisations began to appear in France and Italy to join the German Catholic Zentrum Party that had already existed since the 1850s.

As it would turn out the fortunes of all the various contenders for working class loyalty would depend on the political future. Certainly the Communists believed that war held out the best prospects, with a likely collapse of the entire European capitalist system. What sent Europe on the road to World War was the change of policy in Germany.

Bismarck's weakness was that he belonged to no political party but was entirely dependent on the favour of the Emperor for being Imperial Chancellor. He had enjoyed good relations with William I, but in 1888 not only William but also his son Frederick III died, and his grandson William II became emperor.

In 1890 Bismarck fell out with William II over how to deal with the rising power of the Social Democrats. To his surprise the resignation he offered was accepted.

Bismarck had always argued that Germany should be a contented power, concentrating on European affairs. Although Germany under his leadership had acquired a few colonies he never believed in a world destiny for his country. His successors now reversed this policy, embarking on an aggressive foreign policy, aimed at achieving German mastery of the Continent prior to becoming a world power. One reason suggested for this was to distract the German people from domestic concerns, the tension between an increasingly large and politically demanding working class and the traditional autocracy of the Prussian ruling class.

The new course was held to require the friendship of Britain.[42] But embarking on such a policy involved risks which turned out to be fatal. To begin with, the Germans refused to renew the 1887 Reinsurance Treaty with Russia which expired in 1890, on the grounds that if its contents became known it would arouse British hostility, as well as being incompatible with the alliance with Austria.[43] That meant, however, that Germany would no longer be in a position to mediate Austro-Russian rivalry in the Balkans, but be an out-and-out supporter of Austria.

The result was that the French swiftly took advantage of Russia's feeling of isolation in order to sign a military alliance in 1892, backed up by massive loans aimed partly at improving Russia's railways so as to speed mobilisation of troops. The ring round France had now been broken and Germany faced the prospect of war on two fronts.

Unfortunately, in compensation Germany basically had nothing with which to induce Britain to make an alliance. And that led to the very unwise tactics on the one hand of putting pressure on Britain by threatening to support colonial rivals – France over Siam and the Belgian Congo, and the Boer Republics of Transvaal and the Orange Free State – while on the other telling Britain that it would have nothing to fear if it joined the Triple Alliance.[44]

The results were not what the Germans expected. It was soon realised that no one could put pressure on Britain as long as the British navy ruled the waves. In the 1880s the British navy had been rather run down. Now plans were brought forward to restore it to its traditional role of being able to match the strength of the two nearest European naval powers, the French and the Russians. And the British, who had hitherto never given the Germans much thought, seeing the French as their traditional rivals, began to sense a growing German hostility. This impression was strengthened when the Germans, realising the British could not be coerced into anything as long as they ruled the waves, began to build a fleet that clearly aimed to challenge, one day, the Royal Navy.[45]

Faced with the new Germany, the British, French and Russians saw the need to compose their differences. In 1898 Britain and France had nearly gone to war when at Fashoda in the Sudan a small French army was forced to withdraw by a superior British force recently victorious over fanatic Arab nationalists that had threatened Anglo-Egyptian control of the area. But the French realised that if they were to get back Alsace-Lorraine a British alliance was essential. In 1904 Britain and France came to a wide range of colonial agreements (the 'Entente Cordiale') which left the British in control of Egypt and the Sudan while the French were given a free hand in Morocco.[46]

Russia, too, was feeling vulnerable. Stalemate in the Balkans had led Russia to pursue a policy of expansion in Asia, threatening India, participating in the economic division of the Chinese empire, and wanting to seize Korea from China because of its ice-free ports and minerals. Its rival over Korea was Japan, a country which had only been open to the West since the 1850's. Japan had embarked on an astonishing series of reforms which had transformed the country in a few decades from feudalism to a state of high technological ability, including modernisation of the army and navy. In 1905 the two countries clashed, and to the world's astonishment the Japanese army defeated the Russians, sank the Russian fleet at Tschushima and occupied Korea. One result of the defeat was a revolutionary outbreak in Russia, with strikes and mutinies and desertions in the armed forces which further revealed the fragile nature of the state. The Tsar, Nicholas II was forced to call a *Duma*, or parliament, but he retained control of the armed forces, foreign affairs and the police. This move enabled the government to split moderates from the extremists in the opposition, and troops loyal to the Tsar crushed the revolt.[47] In 1907 the Russians came to an agreement with Britain to end further colonial rivalry. Tibet and Afghanistan were to be buffer states, while Persia was divided into spheres of influence.[48]

With all sources of friction eliminated between Britain, on the one hand, and France and Russia on the other, Germany now had nothing with which to exploit differences amongst the so-called Triple Entente. And it was Germany which now felt vulnerable and surrounded, linked to relatively weak states like Austria–Hungary and Italy.

The division of Europe into alliances was now leading states into arms races, and nowhere was the effect of an arms race more critical than in naval strength.

The British had been viewing the development of a German fleet with alarm. Then in 1906 the British built a new type of battleship, the 'Dreadnought', which left all previous achievements in speed and gun-firing ability behind. There were two consequences of this event. First, all older battleships were useless compared to Dreadnoughts, so that the strength of a navy could only be reckoned in their number. Second, since the design would be copied, Britain now faced competition in the building of these ships with only a slender lead, and that meant its old unchallenged naval superiority would no longer exist. The building of these ships was very expensive and only one European state had the industrial and financial power to compete against Britain, and that was Germany.

When the Germans began to expand their navy with Dreadnoughts this was seen by the British as a hostile act. Britain needed naval supremacy to protect its trade and its colonies and to ensure national security since it did not have armies at home on the scale of those on the Continent. Germany had few, unimportant colonies, and its fleet would be concentrated in the North Sea. If Britain were defeated in the North Sea a German army could be transported to Britain. As attempts to limit the building of Dreadnoughts failed, and more German Dreadnoughts were launched, British public opinion increasingly saw Germany as the next enemy while the Germans believed that once the British fleet was defeated Germany would indeed dominate Europe, if not the world.

When the war came it was because of events in the Balkans, arising out of the continual decline of the Ottoman Empire.

In 1875 the Christian subjects of the Empire had risen in revolt and the Russian army advanced to their aid, nearing Constantinople. But Austria and England did not want to see Turkey collapse to the advantage of Russia. At the 1878 Berlin Conference, however, Romania, Serbia and Montenegro became absolutely independent; a Bulgarian state received an autonomy, while Austria was given the right to administer Bosnia. Then it was the turn of the Greeks – in 1881 they acquired Thessaly from Turkey, and after a war in 1897, Crete.

However, these states soon began to have ambitions of their own; Serbia wanted to unite all Serbs, and Greeks, Serbs and Bulgarians all coveted Macedonia. Their rivalries with each other and Turkey would lead to a series of wars in 1912–13, at the end of which an independent Albania emerged.

In 1908 a reform movement in Turkey led by army officers resulted in military uprisings and the deposition of the autocratic Sultan. Bulgaria took the opportunity to declare full independence. Austria, fearing for the effect of these reforms on its control of Bosnia or that Serbia might get the Province, came to an agreement with Russia in which Austria would be allowed simply to annex Bosnia while in return Austria would support Russian ambitions as regards Constantinople. Serbia mobilised but Germany made it clear that it would back Austria, and for their various reasons the other Powers refused to intervene.

For Serbs, therefore, dreams of a Greater Serbia or a union of the South Slavs required the destruction of the Austro-Hungarian Empire. For the Austrians, survival of the Empire required destroying a nation increasingly seen as Russia's clients.

On 28 June 1914 the heir to the throne of the Austro-Hungarian Empire, the Archduke Franz Ferdinand, was assassinated by a Serb, Gavrilo Princip, in the Bosnian capital, Sarajevo. Believing that the plot had been hatched by extreme nationalist groups in Serbia, possibly even at the instigation of the Serbian government, and eager to take advantage of the situation to end the Serbian threat once and for all, Vienna presented Belgrade with an ultimatum containing demands for the suppression of anti-Austrian activities so harsh that had Serbia complied it would have become a vassal of Austria as it had once been of Turkey. When the Serbs rejected the ultimatum as a whole (although ready to accept some of the conditions) Austria declared war and invaded Serbia.

The Austrian invasion of Serbia could not be tolerated by Russia. If successful, Austria would dominate the Balkans. Russia mobilised partially against Austria, but the Germans warned that if Russia did not demobilise they would mobilise against Russia. When the Russians refused Germany declared war against Russia.

All that the French had prayed for since 1871 had now come true. Mobilisation was ordered, and when the Germans asked the French to be neutral in the war with Russia they received only the laconic reply that France would act in accordance with its own interests, whereupon Germany declared war on France.

In all five countries the mood was one of rejoicing. Even working class hostility to war was swept aside, appeals for solidarity ignored. The attempt by the French socialist Jean Jaurès to get French and German workers to strike rather than mobilise led to his assassination. In the Reichstag even the Socialists voted for war credits: they did not want their country overrun and working class gains destroyed by autocratic and backward Russia. The war was not expected to last long and the air would be cleared. Everyone expected to win and fulfil long-held ambitions – France to regain Alsace-Lorraine, Russia and Austria to dominate the Balkans, Serbia to unite all Serbs (at least) and Germany, eager to defeat France and Russia before they became too strong, hoped to dominate them all. But three Great Powers were still standing aside: Britain, Turkey and Italy.

And now Germany made a serious blunder.

German military plans had been based on the ideas of the Chief of the General Staff from 1890–1905, Count von Schlieffen: expectation of war against both France and Russia simultaneously, but since Russia would take a very long time to mobilise, Germany should aim to destroy the French armies in the west before the Russians could come to their aid in the east. However, since the French defences facing Germany were very strong the German armies should outflank them by attacking through Belgium, even though Belgian neutrality had been collectively recognised by the Great Powers in 1839.[49] Germany indeed did ask for permission to cross Belgian territory, but when this was refused the invasion went ahead nevertheless, if only because twenty years of logistical planning could not suddenly be changed.[50]

That left Britain with no alternative but to issue an ultimatum to Germany to withdraw its forces. When the withdrawal failed to occur Britain declared war on Germany.

For the Turks matters were easy. Their main enemy was Russia. In the previous years their armies had been trained by Germans, and on the eve of war the Germans had sold them two warships. The bombardment of Odessa by those warships ensured that Turkey enlisted in the Austro-German camp.

The Italians did not honour their commitments to the Triple Alliance. Unification of Italy meant that their real enemy was Austria, and they knew they would not get the Tyrol south of the Brenner, Trento and Trieste if Austria was victorious and would be unlikely to get them if Austria lost but they were not on the winning side. To begin with Italy remained neutral arguing that under the terms of the Triple Alliance they were not obliged to support a partner that had been an aggressor, and Austria's ultimatum to Serbia had made it the aggressor. In March 1915 the Austrians offered Trento to Italy in return for its neutrality but that was not nearly enough.[51] Negotiations had been opened with the Triple Entente and Italy was offered not only what it wanted for unification but much more – a large part of the Dalmatian coast, the Dodecanese Islands, Adalia (a Turkish province in Asia Minor) and colonial expansion in Africa – if it changed sides. This was agreed in the Treaty of London in April 1915 and a month later Italy declared war on Austria–Hungary, although it did not declare war on Turkey until August of that year and on Germany until a year later.[52]

Finally, promised Macedonia, Bulgaria entered the war on the side of Germany and Austria in 1915; Romania, seeking reunification with the Romanians in Transylvania, declared war on Austria–Hungary in 1916, while the Greeks, hoping to enlarge themselves at the expense of the Turks, declared war on the side of the Entente in 1917.

218

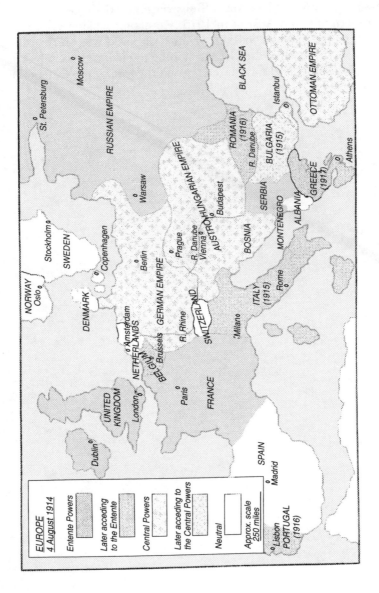

8 Europe – 4 August 1914

EUROPE
4 August 1914

Entente Powers

Later acceding
to the Entente

Central Powers

Later acceding to
the Central Powers

Neutral

Approx. scale
250 miles

13 The Zenith of Nationalism 1914–1945AD

The mood of rejoicing when the war began did not last when it became clear that the troops would not be home for Christmas.

The Russian armies advanced into Germany from the east quicker than expected and as a result part of the German army that had crossed Belgium and invaded France had to be put on trains and despatched to the east. The crushing victory over the Russians at Tannenberg by Generals Hindenburg and Ludendorff hardly compensated for the failure to destroy the French armies and take Paris as in 1870. Instead, on the Marne the German army was halted and the attempts by the German and Franco-British armies to outflank each other led to a race to the sea. Trench warfare set in, and for both sides barbed wire, machine-gun defences and massive artillery barrages ensured huge slaughter of troops attempting to pierce the enemy line. There was relative stalemate too on the eastern front as the large but clumsy Russian armies manoeuvred over great distances against the equally cumbersome forces of the Austro-Hungarian empire.

The result was a number of attempts to break out of the deadlock. In 1915 the Germans used gas against the French at Ypres and initiated submarine warfare, declaring that any shipping in the waters around the British Isles would be sunk without warning. The Allies landed at Gallipoli, hoping Turkish defeat would lead to the creation of pressure on the Austro-German south-eastern flank. But the Gallipoli campaign ended in defeat and the submarine campaign was called off after protests from the United States, especially at the sinking of the liner *Lusitania*. The stalemate resumed. In 1916 two of the bloodiest battles in world history – at Verdun and the Somme – ended inconclusively, while in the North Sea, off Jutland, the failure of the German surface fleet to defeat the British would ensure a return to unrestricted submarine warfare. And warfare took on new dimensions with the introduction of the tank by the Allies and increasing use of airplanes.

1917, however, would see two events which would vitally affect the course of European history.

The first was revolution in Russia.

The nation had been exhausted and disorganised by the war. Nearly fifteen million men had been called up, many being sent to the front lacking adequate clothes and weapons. There were far too few victories to compensate for the horrific casualties. Desertions began, aided by seditious propaganda.

In February 1917 the lack of food and essential supplies led to riots and strikes. The police disintegrated and troops refused to fire on the demonstrators. A few days later the Tsar abdicated and three centuries of autocratic rule came to an end. A Provisional Government of liberals and democrats was set up, but it immediately faced a challenge from Bolshevik-dominated Soviets (Councils) of Workers and Soldiers Deputies, the Soviets demanding an immediate end to the war and drastic reforms at home. The Provisional Government needed money to provide supplies and restore order but the Allies would only provide the money if the Provisional Government continued the war and thus kept German and Austro-Hungarian troops tied down in the East rather than freeing them to reinforce their armies facing France and Italy. Reluctantly the Provisional Government agreed.

It was at this point that the Germans arranged for Lenin, then living in Zurich in neutral Switzerland, to return to Russia, counting on him to take charge of the revolution.

From then on it was Lenin and his *Bolsheviks* who dictated the course of events. When the new offensive ordered by the Provisional Government was crushed the demand for 'All Power to the Soviets', an end to the war, the nationalisation of banks and land, and the establishment of a Soviet republic proved irresistible. In October 1917 the Provisional Government collapsed, to be replaced by a Council of People's Commissars. Three decisions quickly taken were to end the war, nationalise the property of large landowners without compensation and to grant the peoples of Russia self-determination.

With Russia out of the war German troops could be switched to the western front where it was now vital to win a quick victory, and that was because of the second event of 1917, the entry of the United States into the war.

Since the end of the Civil War in 1865 America had grown to be the leading economic power in the world. The population had trebled to over ninety million, thanks to twenty million European immigrants.[1] There had been massive European investment in the railroads, and the oil and steel industries. In 1914 the United States

uch coal as Britain and Germany t̀
, France and Germany together and .
nce, Germany, Russia and Austria–Hu
per cent of the world's manufacturing proc
wo-and-a-half times that of Germany, three
and-a-half times that of Britain.[2]

During the war Americans had continued to trade with Europe, shipping food, raw materials, steel and armaments, mostly to the Entente powers and particularly Britain with which they had the strongest commercial connections. The Germans were now determined to cut this lifeline by resuming unrestricted submarine warfare while offers were made to Mexico of Arizona, New Mexico and Texas should the United States declare war on Germany. In February 1917 American ships began to be sunk and the Americans learned of the approach to Mexico. On 6 April the United States declared war on Germany.

The all-out German assault in the west was launched in March 1918 but had ground to a halt by mid-summer. And with the arrival of fresh, well-armed American troops it was clear that the war could not be won, and this conclusion was soon confirmed by news elsewhere. Allied forces landing in Salonika forced Bulgaria out of the war and prepared to attack Austria–Hungary in the rear. Turkey capitulated as its armies in Palestine and Syria were defeated by British forces from India and Egypt. Austria–Hungary was disintegrating as the by now ill-equipped starving regiments on the Italian front began to melt away, demoralised, to join the ethnic nations of the empire which were beginning to proclaim their independence. And at home *Soviets* of workers and soldiers had begun to foment mutiny in the armed forces and seize control in Germany's leading cities. Offers of an armistice were made to President Woodrow Wilson of the United States, and on 11 November 1918 the war came to an end.

It had cost the lives of some eight million combatants out of a total of some thirty-six million casualties.[3] The losses were overwhelmingly among the cream of the nation, young men aged twenty to forty. Many of the surviving casualties were gassed or mentally scarred, and the war was followed by an influenza epidemic which struck at the starving, weakened population of the continent, carrying off more victims than the war itself.

It was the timely arrival of the Americans that had won the war for the Allies and Wilson was the man of the hour. The peace was

..o be on the basis of his ideas, announced during th..
..peeches to the American Congress. The first, on 8 Janu..
..contained fourteen points and had been accepted by th..
..tral Powers in October. Apart from general principles such as
..pen negotiations on problems, freedom of the seas, equality of
trading conditions, disarmament 'to the lowest levels consistent with
national safety' and 'impartial' adjustment of colonial claims, Wilson called, amongst other things, for the evacuation and restoration
of Belgium, Serbia, Romania and Montenegro (with Serbia being
given access to the sea); the return of Alsace-Lorraine to France; the
peoples of Austria–Hungary to be given the freest opportunity of
autonomous development; the frontiers of Italy to be readjusted
'along clearly recognisable lines of nationality'; the erection of an
independent Polish state; and the formation of a general association
of nations to guarantee the independence and integrity of states
great and small.[4]

More dramatically, in his second speech, on 11 February, Wilson
called for peace on the basis of the self-determination of peoples –
that people and provinces were not to be bartered about from
sovereignty to sovereignty in a discredited game of balance of
power, but that any settlement should be made in the interest and
for the benefit of the populations concerned.[5]

The problem about Wilson's pronouncements was that the world
of January–February 1918 when the Allies looked like losing was
very different from that at the end of the year when they had won.

The key issue of the future was clearly going to be the relationship of the German people with those around them, particularly the
French. France had suffered proportionately heavier casualties than
Germany. Its industrial north-east had been devastated. Yet hardly
a shot had been fired on German territory, and the framework of
German industry was intact. And not only had the German Empire
collapsed, so too had the Austro-Hungarian, Russian and Turkish.
The emperors of Germany and Austria–Hungary had abdicated
and been replaced by republican régimes; the Tsar of Russia had
been shot by the Bolsheviks. By the time Wilson arrived in Paris for
the Peace Conference it was no longer a question of autonomy for
the peoples of these empires but their *de facto* independence in
Czechoslovakia, Estonia, Finland, Georgia, Latvia, Lithuania and
Poland. And what about German Austria? The day after the collapse of the Empire the parliament in Vienna voted for Austria to
join Germany.

Nor were the European allies interested in self-determination. The French did not want to have restricted their intention to see that Germany was kept down, including being reduced in size. For the Italians self-determination was in conflict with the Treaty of London. Not only would they not get Dalmatia but if their northern frontier was to be drawn on 'clearly recognised lines of nationality' they would also not get the Southern Tyrol with the militarily superior Brenner frontier against the German world. The Italians therefore declared they did not accept the Fourteen Points as the basis for the peace.[6] As for the British, self-determination was also dangerous. Irishmen seeking independence had risen in revolt in Dublin at Easter 1916, and in elections held in December 1918 nationalists seeking separation from Britain had taken three-quarters of the votes and seats in Ireland.[7] Nor was nationalism confined to Ireland – it was rife in Egypt and India as well.

Thus at the Peace Conference in Paris Wilson faced the vengeful French, the grasping Italians and the British far more concerned with Empire than Europe, and the resulting attempt to reconcile the high principles of self-determination with French and Italian intentions to keep the Germans down led to decisions which struck a moral blow at the peace settlement and fundamentally undermined the political and economic stability of the continent, leaving far too many Europeans bitter and hostile, and so ensuring that the optimism which greeted the peace soon turned to pessimism over its permanence.

Under the Peace Treaty of Versailles with Germany the latter had to accept responsibility for the war, and that meant paying for it. Besides having to deliver raw materials and rolling-stock to the Allies, Germany had to pay them 269 billion gold marks over thirty-five years, mainly because they in turn needed to repay to the United States the sums borrowed during the war.[8] In order to check German militarism the army was reduced to 100 000 men, and the navy to a token force of a few warships, with no submarines. All German territory west of the Rhine had to be demilitarised. Alsace-Lorraine was returned to France, and Posen and Upper Silesia were given to the new state of Poland. The Saar was placed under the mandate of the newly-established League of Nations for a period of fifteen years, after which a plebiscite would decide its fate. All German colonies were confiscated and also placed under the mandate of the League, to be administered by Germany's former enemies. And a 'corridor' separating East Prussia from the rest of Germany gave Poland access to the Baltic. Lastly, the Treaty was 'negotiated' in humiliating circumstances. The German delegation at Versailles only met the Allies face to face on two occasions – the presentation of the draft text and its signature. There were only written, no oral exchanges on the draft. When the text was presented the Germans were given two weeks to make representations on it. These representations were almost all ignored. The new German government was given one week to decide whether or not to accept the Treaty with the threat that the war would be resumed if it was not, even though that government had nothing to do with the régime that had conducted the war. All this fixed in the consciousness of the Germans that the peace was dictated and therefore not morally binding.[9]

As for Germany's former allies, under the Treaty of St Germain (German) Austria had to give up South Tyrol, Trento, Trieste and the Istrian peninsula to Italy and Slovenia to the new Yugoslavia. The country was forbidden to unite with Germany, forbidden even to call itself 'German' Austria. Under the Treaty of Trianon the newly independent Hungary lost two-thirds of its territory, having to give up Transylvania to Romania, Slovakia and Ruthenia to the new Czechoslovakia, and Croatia to the new Yugoslavia. Under the Treaty of Sèvres Turkey had to give up eastern Thrace, the Aegean Islands and Smyrna (Izmir) to Greece, Rhodes and the Dodecanese Islands to Italy and Cyprus to Britain. Syria, Lebanon, Palestine and Iraq were placed under the mandate of the League of Nations, the first two under French and the last two under British administration. Under the Treaty of Neuilly Bulgaria had to give up south-west Thrace to Greece.

But for the Allies, and particularly the French, it was not just a question of reducing the size of the vanquished states. To ensure that they were kept in their place the states around them needed to be strengthened, and it was this which created problems for application of the principle of self-determination.

Nineteenth century nationalism had postulated monocultural states. Heinrich Luden, Professor of History at Jena, believed that only a state built upon the ethnic principle could be a true fatherland, that state and nation must coincide.[10] And as the multinational empires began to collapse this was certainly the expectation of their putative successors. But the states created, or restored, or expanded in order to fulfil their watchdog functions found they contained almost as many cultural minorities as the multinational empires they had sought to overthrow.

Poland, for example, had a dual role; to watch over Germany and act as part of the *cordon sanitaire* being thrown up against Bolshevik Russia. It had been hoped to strengthen it economically by the access to the sea through the Danzig corridor. But as a result, only two-thirds of the population of the restored Poland's thirty-two million were Poles. There were five million Ukrainians, over one million Germans and three million Jews.

The frontiers of the new Czechoslovak state were drawn on military grounds. This led to a large number of ex-Austrian Germans (thirty per cent of Bohemia, twenty per cent of Moravia) being incorporated into the Czech lands, in the so-called Sudetenland, and the inclusion of Ruthenia in order that Czechoslovakia should have a common frontier with Romania. This would enable Czechoslovakia to act as a watchdog over not only Germany, but Austria and Hungary. But of Czechoslovakia's population of fourteen million only just over half were Czechs. There were two million Slovaks, over three million Germans, 700 000 Hungarians (in Slovakia), and 600 000 Carpatho-Ukrainian Ruthenians. The Czechs wanted their Slovak Slavonic kin in to balance the Germans, but the Slovaks had never been enthusiastic. It was the Americans, putting pressure on Slovak exiles in the United States who obtained an agreement that Slovakia should have an autonomous status in the new state. For the Slovaks the agreement was that there should be a Czech *and* Slovak state whereas Czechs simply wanted one Czechoslovakia.[11]

Romania, which was eager to act as a watchdog over Hungary and be part of the *cordon sanitaire* against Bolshevik Russia, had acquired one-and-a-half million Hungarians in Transylvania, as well as 700 000 Germans, out of a population of eighteen million.

Yugoslavia too had a function to guard against Austria and Hungary. Its twelve million population had five million Serbs, three-and-a-half million Croats, one million Slovenes and half a million each of Germans and Hungarians. The saying was that Yugoslavia was one country with two scripts (Roman and Cyrillic), three languages (Serbo-Croat, Slovene, Macedonian), four religions (Catholic, Protestant, Orthodox, Moslem), and five nations (Serbs, Croats, Slovenes, Macedonians and Montenegrans). But this new Yugoslavia was very fragile, created under external pressure. Italy's claims in 1918 had pushed Slovenes and Croats to go in with the perceived lesser danger, Serbia, after the fall of the Habsburg empire. The state would soon be in conflict with Italy over Istria and with Bulgaria over Macedonia.

The victorious allies did not apply the principle of self-determination in their empires (an independent Ireland was born in violence), nor did they do so in setting up the new states. Apart from the plebiscite held in industrially-important Upper Silesia in 1921 which ended with partition of the area between Germany and Poland, plebiscites to ascertain the wishes of the inhabitants were held only in a few unimportant areas (North Schleswig, Eupen-Malmedy, Allenstein, southern Carinthia). But there were no plebiscites for Slovaks and Ruthenians, for Germans in South Tyrol, Sudetenland, and the Polish corridor, nor for Hungarians in the borderlands of Slovakia, Romania and Yugoslavia, nor for Austria's *anschluss* with Germany.[12] Agitation for independence or unification with their kin by all these embittered minorities would provide plenty of scope for destabilising the Paris peace settlement.

Nor was the fragmentation of central and eastern Europe into a dozen nationalistic states likely to be a good thing should there be an economic crisis. For example, half of the population of the new Austria lived in Vienna, a city which had once governed an empire of fifty million and was far too large to govern a state one-tenth that number. The famous saying by the Czech historian Frantisek Palacky that had Austria (i.e. the empire) not existed it would be necessary to create it[13] referred to the fact that the empire was as much an economic unit and the various parts would find it hard to exist by themselves. Yet Austria, which had not been allowed to unite with Germany, and later would not even be permitted to have a customs union with that country, was now separated from the industries of Bohemia and the rich agricultural lands of Hungary.

Possibly the continent could control potential crises if there was a balance of power. But the American government had refused to ratify the Treaty of Versailles, refused to join the new League of Nations, and refused to join in a military alliance with France on the traditional grounds of shunning European involvements. The British, too, refused to make an alliance with France, preferring to pursue the concerns of empire. Nor was France's previous ally, Russia, available. Russia's new masters were expecting capitalism to collapse and to that end were fomenting red revolution in Berlin, Bavaria and Budapest, and invading Poland and the Baltic states. Worse for France, the Bolsheviks had repudiated the debts incurred by the Tsarist régime. There was hardly a family in France which had not subscribed to bonds to modernise the Russian army.[14] For the Europeans Russia was now a pariah and several western governments provided aid for so-called 'White' Russians fighting the Bolsheviks as the country degenerated into civil war. That left France and Italy – but particularly France – to face the prospect of eventual German revenge. Germany might be weak at the moment but few believed it would accept its present position for long. All the French could do was make hardly compensatable alliances with and promote military agreements between the countries on the borders of Germany, Austria and Hungary – Belgium, Czechoslovakia, Poland, Romania and Yugoslavia.

It also explained why the French would make one of the most disastrous moves of the inter-war period.

The republic that had come to power in Germany in 1918 was no threat to France, being weak and deeply divided. Under its constitution, drafted in the city of Weimar, voting was by proportional representation, which ensured that no single party would ever hold an absolute majority in the Reichstag. Since 1919 the largest party in government coalitions had been the socialists, but the machinery of government – civil servants, police, judiciary, as well as army officers – was almost entirely conservative, if not monarchist, and deeply suspicious of socialism. On the other hand, that socialism was far too moderate and bourgeois for the communists, who accused it of not wanting to introduce revolutionary reforms.

Although the sum to be paid by Germany in reparations had been reduced by the Allies by one-half,[15] in 1922 the French maintained that Germany had defaulted in regard to the delivery of raw materials and, with Belgium, invaded the Ruhr and tried to promote the secession of the Rhineland. The Germans put up a passive resistance and workers went on strike, bringing production to a halt. Coming a year after the German mark had started to decline, the invasion set off its collapse – from 400 to the dollar in the summer of 1922 to 50 million in the summer of 1923 to 630 billion by the end of the year. While the upper classes and property owners still had their land and factories and those in work could be paid barrow-loads of falling marks at the end of each day, the inflation destroyed the investments, pensions and savings of the middle class, thus affecting all those who had worked hard and loyally as servants of the Second Reich, threatening to reduce them to the level of the working class. With their bitterness and humiliation the dispossessed middle class promised a mass of recruits for any party or individual that undertook to restore its status and overthrow the iniquitous peace settlement.

And that party, and that individual, were waiting in the wings.

Adolf Hitler was born in Braunau, an Austrian town on the Bavarian border in 1889, the son of a junior customs official. He tried unsuccessfully to make a living as a painter in Vienna, where he was attracted to pan-Germanism and anti-semitism, coming to despise the multinational Habsburg empire. In 1913 he moved to Munich and when war broke out joined a Bavarian regiment. By the end of the war he had been wounded, gassed and decorated with the Iron Cross.

Two months after the war he became a member of the small *Nazional-Sozialistische Deutsche Arbeiter Partei* (NSDAP), and within two years was its leader with a programme of unification of all Germans (including Austrians) in a Greater Germany, abrogation of the Treaties of Versailles and St. Germain, and exclusion of Jews from citizenship and public offices.[16] He denounced the government in Berlin as the 'November Criminals of 1918', socialists who had stabbed the German nation and army in the back by insisting on peace and accepting the Versailles Treaty. When in 1923 the German government called off its passive resistance against the Franco-Belgian invasion of the Ruhr Hitler tried to mount a coup in Munich. It failed, but he took full responsibility for his actions and his speeches at his trial provided him for the first time with an audience outside Bavaria.[17] Sentenced to five years imprisonment (although soon released) he wrote his political manifesto *Mein Kampf* (My Struggle).

During these years Hitler's attention had been increasingly focused on another country where similar dissatisfaction with the peace, weak government, inflation and industrial unrest were crippling the nation – Italy.

The elections of November 1919 were the first by proportional representation and the first in which Catholics were able to vote for a party founded on Catholic values, the *Partito Popolare*. But no party had an overall majority. And that made it difficult to deal, on the right, with patriotic, nationalistic groups of unemployed ex-combatants angered that the government had accepted the Paris Peace settlement rather than insisting on what had been promised in the Treaty of London, particularly Dalmatia, and on the left with an urban and agrarian proletariat hit by inflation, inspired by the

Russian revolution and which had been occupying factories and land and fomenting industrial and social unrest.

It was also in 1919 that the ex-socialist and ex-soldier Benito Mussolini founded the *Fasci di Combattimento*, political action squads, with the aim of restoring national unity and national greatness. The Fascist squads began to take violent action against socialists and communists, even *Popolari*, breaking up their meetings, strikes, and factory and land occupations. The fascists were supported particularly by the industrialists of northern Italy who saw in Mussolini a better chance of restoring order than in the existing weak-willed government. By November 1921 the action squads had turned themselves into a political party, the *Partito Nazionale Fascista*, with thirty-five seats in Parliament.[18]

In August 1922 a general strike was called by the Left and Mussolini declared that if the government did not prevent the strike the Fascists would. When the Fascist columns began to head for Rome the King, Victor Emmanuel III, invited him to form a government, and shortly after his investiture he was granted full powers to institute reforms by a parliament relieved at the prospect of an end to what appeared imminent civil war.[19]

Fascists denounced the inter-party parliamentary squabbles that were perceived as weakening the nation's ability to deal with the economic and social crisis. They denounced the class war between employers and workers which hampered economic recovery. They denounced the communist party and communist-dominated trade unions as having a prior loyalty to Moscow and thus weakening national solidarity. Their response was the one-party, corporate state.

In 1923 the electoral law was changed to provide that the party with the highest votes should receive two-thirds of the seats in parliament, and in the following year amid violence and intimidation, the Fascist Party polled sixty-five per cent of the vote. Thereafter opposition parties were dissolved and their leaders arrested.[20]

The so-called 'corporate state' was created, aimed at ending class divisions by institutionalising collaboration between employers and workers. Public corporations were founded, funded by the state, in regard to whole sectors of production so that the public sector in Italy became larger than in any other capitalist country. Only fascist trade unions were allowed – indeed one could only get a job if one belonged to such a union. But the trade unions had to give up the right to strike. On the other hand, employers recognised the fascist unions as the sole representatives of the workers in collective bargaining. In 1926 twelve national confederations were founded, six each for unions and employers and workers. But since fascist party members occupied all-important positions all the important sectors of Italian economic life were under party – and therefore state – control.[21]

The state was to be the expression of national unity, and the slogan of fascism was 'Everything for the State, nothing against the State, nothing outside the State',[22] and for those inhabiting the Italian peninsula and islands that meant the unity of the Italian nation. Censorship of the press stifled political opposition. It even meant Italianisation through cultural genocide not only of the ethnic groups who had suddenly found themselves Italian citizens because of the Paris Peace Settlement – German South Tyrolese and Istrian Slavs – but also the French-speaking inhabitants of the Aosta valley, part of the Kingdom of Savoy since the Middle Ages. Education in their language was forbidden, as were names which 'offended Italian sentiment' and those not fluent in Italian were dismissed from public posts.[23] Enrolment in Party youth organisations, Party uniforms, banners, slogans, parades, were all used to create a sense of solidarity in the struggle for national, political, economic and social regeneration. To Fascists the new Italy was the spiritual heir of the Roman Empire.[24]

Hitler would indeed be impressed.

And in two other countries nationalism would affect destiny.

In Turkey national sentiment was outraged at the Treaty of Sèvres – indeed the Sultan only signed it after the Allies occupied Constantinople. Armed resistance was prepared by General Mustafa Kemal (Atatürk) at Ankara and when the Allies authorised the Greeks to intervene Kemal routed the Greek armies and seized Smyrna and eastern Thrace expelling the Greek populations there. These gains were ratified by the 1923 Treaty of Lausanne between the Allies and Turkey. Kemal went on to abolish the Sultanate and become the first President of the Turkish Republic, turning the country into a western-leaning secular state. The Latin alphabet replaced Arabic, western civil and criminal codes were introduced and women emancipated.[25]

And in Ireland, following the strong nationalist gains in the 1918 elections, separation from a Britain perceived to have discriminated against Catholics and done little for the population during the famine could not be restrained. Revolt broke out which Britain could not contain. But in six counties in the northern province of Ulster, the wealthier industrial part of the island, the pro-British Protestant majority refused to accept the prospect of being part of a poor, agrarian, priest-ridden state. In 1921 a Treaty between Britain and the Irish nationalists led to the establishment of an independent Irish (Free) State in the South leaving Northern Ireland with Britain. However, Irish pressure to unify the island on the one hand, and Ulster Protestant anxieties about their place in Britain on the other would ensure that the Irish catholic minority in the north would be regarded with hostility, with the result that relations between the two communities in the north, between the two parts of Ireland, and between Britain and Ireland would continue to be in crisis.[26]

For the first ten years after the War, except on its fringes, an uneasy peace continued. The European economy was restored, largely due to loans from the United States. But psychologically the continent was a prey to fear and doubt: fear that peace was temporary, fear of communism. Theoretically Europe might still be the political centre of the world, but most sensed that the days of European domination were ending and that the future lay either with the bright, technological, wealth-generating life style of the United States or the realisation of a Communist millennium. And as few penetrated into Russia one only heard alarmist stories or sycophantic propaganda as to how the communist experiment was proceeding.

One attempt to ensure that the devastation of war did not occur again was the establishment of the League of Nations.

The seat of the League was Geneva, and at its height it would have a membership of over sixty states. These were grouped in a General Assembly, but the controlling organ of the League was the Council. Originally this was to consist of five permanent members – the United States, Britain, France, Italy and Japan (but after the withdrawal of the United States the number fell to four until Germany joined the League in 1926) – and (eventually) nine members chosen by the General Assembly.

The League was based on two principles – judicial settlement of political disputes (if necessary by referral to the newly-created Permanent Court of International Justice at The Hague), and collective security, i.e. that if a member state was attacked (or threatened) the Council would advise on action to be taken.

In its work the League ran the Mandates system and tried to achieve reductions in armaments. It also supervised the so-called minorities treaties, treaties between the Allies on the one hand and Poland, Czechoslovakia, Romania, Greece and Yugoslavia on the other, designed to ensure equality of rights and provide some cultural protection for ethnic, linguistic and religious minorities in those states.

But for all its hopes the League had a number of disadvantages. Decisions had to be by unanimity. It had no forces of its own to ensure decisions were carried out but had to rely on the Member States. Such decisions were political, and the most serious weakness of the League was that it was too closely associated with the peace settlement and thus the political *status quo*. Nor were important countries members of the League – the United States not at all, Germany only from 1926 to 1933 and the Soviet Union only from 1934.

There were a few minor successes – mediating disputes between Sweden and Finland over the Aland Islands in 1921 and Italy and Greece over an incident in Corfu in 1923 – but the lack of solidarity among the European nations held little promise for the future. It was this lack of solidarity which led the French Prime Minister, Aristide Briand, in 1929 to propose a closer European integration within the League system in order to solve problems of security and economic co-operation. But many Germans saw the idea as an indirect means of maintaining existing boundaries (if at Locarno in 1925 they had agreed to accept their western borders as final they had not accepted their eastern borders); and the British feared that it would weaken the League and that they would be manoeuvred into European commitments at the expense of Imperial ones.[27]

What broke the fragile peace was the October 1929 stock market crash in the United States. American loans, which had restored European and particularly German prosperity ceased or were called in, causing liquidity to dry up, prices and production to fall, and many firms to go bankrupt. Unemployment leapt up, provoking social unrest. Countries tried to protect their industries by putting up tariffs against foreign imports, but this only invited retaliation. Germany was particularly hard hit. During 1929–32 exports and imports fell by sixty per cent, and unemployment rose from two to six million.

The result was widespread disillusion with the liberal-democratic parliamentary system which was proving incapable of dealing with the crisis, and increasingly people turned to the extremes of right or left.

On the left Communism held out the promise of an end to class privilege, the provision of equality of opportunity, full employment and a fair standard of living. To sympathetic observers this new society was being created in the Soviet Union. The Soviet attempt in 1920 to 'invade' the West to bring down capitalism had failed, Polish forces beating back the Red Army. On the other hand, western governments had recoiled from full-scale intervention to bring down communism in Russia because of war-weariness and much working-class sympathy for the new Soviet experiment.

This enabled the 'Reds' to defeat the 'Whites' in the civil war, but nevertheless the debate as to whether the Soviet Union should continue to seek world-wide revolution or consolidate first at home continued, and was involved in the struggle for succession to the leadership of Russia after the death of Lenin in 1924.

On the one hand Leon Trotsky, Commissar for War and architect of victory in the civil war, argued that backward Russia needed the victory of the proletariat in the West. If the revolution failed to spread from Russia to western Europe either it would succumb to conservative, capitalist Europe or it would become stagnant, nationalistic even, corrupted by Russia's backward economic and cultural environment. On the other hand Josef Stalin, General Secretary of the Communist Party, rejected this view that Russians could not bring socialism about by their own efforts, but even if they did there was no guarantee that it would survive. Russia therefore needed not only to be organised on socialist lines but developed to such an extent that it could hold off any attack by capitalist forces.[28]

As a result of inter-party power struggles Trotsky was expelled from the Communist Party and banished from Russia, while Stalin assumed the leadership and embarked on an economic and social revolution even more tumultuous than that of 1917.[29]

Economic development was ensured through five-year plans, the first 1928–32, the second from 1933–7, designed to transform Russia into a modern industrialised, self-sufficient state. The emphasis was deliberately on industry, which had a special place in Marxist thought: that the revolution is made by an industrial proletariat, and that industrial power was the basis for economic and military power. During the two plans production of coal, iron, steel, oil and gas tripled, electric power increased six-fold, the output of chemicals and the machine and metal industry tenfold.[30]

Agriculture was collectivised – 240 000 collective farms replacing twenty-five million separate peasant holdings. Soviet Russia became the world's largest producer of agricultural machinery, and this mechanisation enabled agricultural labour to be freed for industry.[31] As a result, the rural population of Russia declined from 82 to 67 per cent while the urban nearly doubled from 18 to 33 per cent. All these developments took place without foreign loans or foreign firms, although a few foreign technicians and experts were called in.[32]

Russia was transformed into a complete 'command economy'. All the means of production were nationalised. The Five Year Plans fixed production targets for each unit of production, whether factory or farm. All resources – natural, financial, labour, equipment, were allocated to fulfil the Plans. Prices were fixed administratively without heed to the laws of supply and demand. The state controlled foreign trade and foreign currency, and exports and imports were considered only in relation to the requirements of the Plans.

But there was a very heavy price to pay for Russia's 'Great Leap Forward'.

The emphasis on industrialisation left little room for the provision of consumer goods. Wealthier peasants, the so-called *Kulaks*, owning larger plots of land resisted collectivisation, often preferring to slaughter their cattle or burn their crops rather than hand them over to the state, or receive low state prices for them. As a result the state determined to exterminate the *Kulaks* as a class, murdering them or deporting them to the ever-growing number of forced labour camps (the so-called Gulag Archipelago) in northern Russia and Siberia where they would be put to developing the infrastructure – canals, ports, roads, railways, and building towns.[33] They would be joined there by all those millions, including non-Russian minorities, denounced as 'class enemies', 'economic saboteurs' or 'foreign spies' in the mass hysteria arising out of the internecine struggle for power and survival in the Communist Party as Stalin sought to purge it of his rivals. The purges decimated not only the Party leadership and many foreign communists who had fled to Russia from events abroad, but also the High Command of the army, imperilling the ability of the Soviet Union to resist attack should it occur.[34]

Finally, all sources of information – press, radio, the arts – were controlled by the Party. Contact with foreigners was suspect. The result was that the population had no knowledge as to what was happening in the country or the rest of the world other than information and interpretation of that information by the Party. This applied also to education with the curriculum at all levels approved by the Party.

Nevertheless, for the casual foreign observer or dedicated visiting foreign communist, state investment into housing, health and education was paying off. Russians were more literate, more healthy, better housed and in full employment.

If the communists in Russia seemed to have found the answers to the economic depression, so apparently did the Nationalist Socialists (Nazis).

After the Wall Street crash Hitler's fortunes revived spectacularly on the pattern of the fascist Italy. The deteriorating economic and social situation provoked communist and socialist demonstrations, and Nazi action squads, the *Sturmabteilung* (SA), four times the size of the army allowed under the Versailles Treaty, broke them up. The Nazis began to win local and state elections and money began to flow into the coffers of the Party from industrialists happy to see the red menace tackled. With the difficulties of creating even a coalition government with a majority in the Reichstag to deal with the crisis three elections were held between March 1930 and November 1932 and the Nazis became the largest party, even though not with an overall majority, with the communists in third position.

On 30 January 1933 Hitler was invited by President Hindenburg to become Chancellor, and it was agreed to hold yet another Reichstag election in March. The Nazis polled seventeen million votes, nearly 44 per cent, and gained 288 seats but this was still not a majority in the 647 seat parliament. Hitler therefore formed a coalition with the German National Party which gave him that majority.

Thereafter Nazi seizure of total power in Germany was swift. An Enabling Act which required and, after intimidation, received a two-thirds majority in the Reichstag gave the government the power to legislate without that body. But in any case the Reichstag was shortly rendered superfluous when, first the Communist and Socialist parties were proscribed and their assets seized, and then the NSDAP was declared the only permissible political party. The trade unions were dissolved and their members merged into a new German Labour Front, under Nazi control. When President Hindenburg died in 1934 Hitler became Head of State and

Commander-in-Chief of the armed forces, to whom members of the latter would personally have to swear allegiance.[35] The police force, the media and the arts were also brought under Party control. And, as with Stalin, potential party rivals of the old guard – particularly in the SA – were eliminated, with the *Schutzstaffel* (SS), Hitler's former bodyguard, becoming the Party's new élite.[36]

With regard to the ideology of the state, Hitler insisted on the classic German interpretation of society, namely that everyone belonged inescapably to a cultural community (nation) through ties of blood and language, and the object of the state was to protect that community. The result was the absolute subordination of the individual to the state and the political and racial doctrines of those who controlled it, particularly promotion of the Germans as the Master Race. Concentration camps were set up to which opponents of the régime – socialists, communists, trade unionists, churchmen – were dispatched. Anti-semitism became state policy: Jews were first removed from the civil service and professions, then deprived of German citizenship and forbidden to marry *aryan* Germans.[37] Those that could left the country and, as with the persecution of the Jews by Catholic Spain and Protestants by Catholic France, other countries would benefit from their skills, particularly in the field of science. But too many others stayed, unable to believe what was happening, especially those who had served their country with distinction in war and peace.

Having consolidated his hold on the German people it was time to turn to foreign affairs. Hitler had made no secret of his intentions to destroy the Versailles Treaty and create a living space (*Lebensraum*) for a Greater Germany, unifying not only all ethnic Germans and the lands which historically they had settled and redeemed with their blood and sweat, but areas considered part of the German cultural sphere. Two things in his favour were the absence of Russia and the attitude of Britain. The British had never believed in the harsh penalties imposed on Germany in 1919, and the French would not move without Britain.

Within two years Hitler had withdrawn Germany from the League of Nations and denounced the military clauses of the Versailles Treaty. Conscription was introduced. An agreement was reached with Britain under which Germany would limit its naval strength in all categories of surface ships to 35 per cent of the British and 100 per cent in the case of submarines.[38] German rearmament leapt forward, particularly in the production of tanks and aircraft.

As the rearmament programme was coupled with a massive programme of public works the two together provided for a dramatic rise in employment and a corresponding rise in the popularity of the régime. When the Saar returned to Germany as a result of the plebiscite required in 1935 and German troops entered the demilitarised Rhineland unchallenged the following year, it seemed as if at last Germans were in control of Germany. Nevertheless the failure of the British and French to do more than protest at violations of Versailles had repercussions. The Germans saw that by standing up to the Allies they got much more than the weak Weimar Republic. Hitler had brushed aside the fears that the allies would intervene, and the more he was proved right the more difficult would it be to restrain him or, for those disgusted by his treatment of political opponents and Jews, to overthrow him. And there was the Soviet Union. Alarmed at the rise of the uncompromisingly anticommunist Nazis it had joined the League of Nations in 1934 and made an alliance with France in 1935, supplemented by an agreement with Czechoslovakia providing for Soviet aid if the French helped that country against German attack.

Hitler's next steps concerned Austria and Italy. Since Hitler came to power Nazis in Austria had been agitating for union with Germany, and in 1934 had even assassinated the Austrian Chancellor, Engelbert Dollfuss. Mussolini, fearing a German take-over of Austria, had moved troops to the Brenner. But in 1935 Italy attacked Ethiopia and the League of Nations ordered sanctions against it. Italy withdrew from the League and began to be wooed by Germany, joining it and Japan in the 1937 Anti Com(munist)intern (ational) Pact.

When in 1938 the situation in Austria deteriorated further Hitler put pressure on the government to include Nazis, align Austrian foreign policy with that of Germany and establish close relations between their armies. The Austrians refused to do these things without a plebiscite whereupon German troops entered Austria and took it over without resistance. The plebiscite was held, and 99 per cent voted for annexation by Germany. This time Italian troops did not march in support of Austria.

And Hitler pursued the link with Italy in order to break the ring around Germany. The dictators sent forces to Spain where in 1936 the right, under General Francisco Franco, had risen against the socialist-dominated Second Spanish Republic, which in turn was being aided by the Soviet Union. The refusal of Britain and France to help the republic ensured victory for Franco, who would rule a Fascist-type state until his death in 1975.

And to ensure Mussolini's support Hitler refused to intervene to help the South Tyrolese. In 1939 they would be given a choice either to abandon their 1300-year homeland and move to the Reich, thus preserving their culture, or to stay in Italy and accept Italianisation. Under Nazi pressure some eighty-five per cent of them voted for the former and only the course of the Second World War prevented this population transfer being fulfilled.[39]

Austria's incorporation into the Reich now left Czechoslovakia exposed. As with Austria, Hitler's arrival in power was the signal for Sudeten Germans to agitate for union with Germany. One month after the annexation of Austria the Germans urged the Slovaks to demand full autonomy and the Hungarians to seek the return of territory ceded at Trianon, while they made arrangements to invade the country. As before, many senior German generals believed that the French would intervene to help the Czechs, and this would bring in the Russians, but as before, the Western powers buckled. At a conference in Munich in September 1938 Britain, France, Germany and Italy agreed to give the Sudetenland to Germany. No representatives of Czechoslovakia were present. Munich confirmed the growing Soviet view that France and Britain would not resist Hitler. It also ended the hopes of a number of senior officers and ambassadors of attempting a coup against Hitler.[40]

After Munich, Czechoslovakia had not long to live. In November 1938 the government was forced by Germany to cede to Budapest much of the territory inhabited by the Hungarian minority, a move which strengthened all those in Hungary who believed that by throwing in their lot with Germany the Treaty of Trianon would be destroyed.

In March 1939 German troops simply marched into what was left of the state. Bohemia and Moravia became German protectorates, and in Slovakia a Catholic priest, Monsignor Josef Tiso proclaimed independence, while Hungary seized Ruthenia.

One week after the dissolution of Czechoslovakia, Germany demanded from Poland the return of Danzig and part of the Polish corridor so that East Prussia should be connected to the Reich. Since it was plain that Hitler intended to play with Poland the same game as he had played with Czechoslovakia, in March 1939 Britain and France agreed to guarantee Poland's existence. The Germans replied by making a formal alliance with Italy.

But Hitler did not intend to make the German mistake of 1914 and fight a war on two fronts. In August he astounded the world by making a non-aggression pact with his arch enemy, Stalin, under which, in the event of war between Germany and Poland, Russia would remain neutral but Latvia, Estonia and eastern Poland would belong to its sphere of influence while the rest of Poland and Lithuania would lie in that of Germany.

On 1 September 1939 Germany attacked Poland and with a Russian invasion on 17 September that unfortunate state collapsed. A subsequent treaty gave the Russians a free hand in Lithuania. In November the Russians gratuitously attacked Finland, for which they were expelled from the League of Nations. In June and July of 1940 they simply took over the three Baltic states and incorporated them into the Soviet Union.

In the meantime in April 1940, in order to get control of the North Sea Hitler turned west, invading and establishing pro-Nazi governments in the neutral countries of Belgium, Denmark, Norway and Holland. British, Belgian and French armies were routed, the former lucky to be evacuated from the continent. Italy joined the war on the side of Germany, attacking France, Egypt and later Greece. Under the weight of defeat the Third French Republic collapsed in June, to be replaced by a collaborative rump state centred on the spa town of Vichy, while all northern and western France and the Atlantic ports were taken over by Germany although theorctically remaining under French administration. Only a few 'Free French' rallied under General Charles de Gaulle to the Allies in London.

The British might have been driven off the continent but under the inspired leadership of Winston Churchill, who had become Prime Minister in 1940, they did not surrender. Defeat of Britain required control of the sea and the air. When the British held off the German airforce in the 'Battle of Britain' in September 1940 the only alternative was a return to the submarine warfare of the first world war to starve Britain out.

But above all Hitler was anti-Communist, and that meant war eventually with the Soviet Union, with the aim of seizing all the economic resources at least of Russia up to the Urals, providing living space for the German people and in the process annihilating most of the Slavonic races there and treating the rest as slaves.

Hitler hoped to attack in mid-May 1941 so as to give himself plenty of time to destroy the Russians before winter set in. What upset his timetable were the misfortunes of his Italian ally. The Italian attack on Greece had been a failure and the Germans decided to send help through Yugoslavia. But in March the pro-German government of that country was overthrown in a coup. Enraged, Hitler ordered Yugoslavia to be crushed. In Croatia a pro-German state was set up but throughout the country there was fierce resistance by Serb royalists (*Cetniks*) and communists, the latter led by Josip Broz (Tito). The bitter harvest of the ensuing years which saw not only war against the Axis invaders but civil war between communists and non-communists would be reaped in the division of Yugoslavia fifty years later. But the effect of the German intervention was crucially to delay the invasion of Russia by five weeks. It was not until 22 June that three German armies, later joined by Hungarians and Romanians in an anti-Communist crusade, attacked the unprepared Russians, driving all before them. Millions of Russian soldiers were captured, and many Russians at first welcomed the Germans as liberators from Stalin's rule. But the German policy of treating them as sub-human soon turned them back into implacable enemies. And the distances were too vast, there always seemed to be more Russians, and it was not possible to land a knock-out blow, especially as Stalin had factories dismantled and moved beyond the Urals. Nevertheless, by 2 December 1941 German troops had reached the outer suburbs of Moscow.

A few days later everything would change.

In the United States the desire not to get involved in world affairs was still very strong and the 1935 Neutrality Act forbade the sale of arms to belligerents. Nevertheless the administration of President Franklin Roosevelt was increasingly concerned at the expansion in power of the dictatorships and military régimes, particularly Japan which, in 1932, had taken advantage of civil war between nationalists and communists in China to seize Manchuria and then try to conquer the rest of the country.

After the Munich Conference the United States began a programme of rearmament, and this was accelerated after the fall of France. Roosevelt was concerned to get round neutrality legislation and in March 1941 got Congress to adopt the Lend–Lease Act, giving him the power to supply war materials to any country whose defence he considered vital to the defence of the United States, without immediate payment. Besides sending equipment to help the Chinese government one hundred destroyers were sold to Britain in exchange for sovereign rights for ninety-nine years over bases in the

West Indies; Iceland was occupied in July; and in order to mitigate the British merchant shipping losses at the hands of German submarines the American navy began escorting transatlantic convoys to mid-Atlantic where the Royal Navy took over. In October the first American warships were being torpedoed. Nevertheless the Germans did not react to these unneutral activities.[41]

In the meantime, in the Far East the United States had terminated its trade treaty with Japan. The Japanese believed this was setting the stage for a complete embargo on the sale of raw materials. Japan's main difficulty was that it had few raw materials of its own and needed them, particularly oil, to prosecute the war in China.

This placed the Japanese government before a choice: either to attack Soviet Siberia to the north for its oil, or the British, French and Dutch empires to the south for the oil of the Dutch East Indies and the rubber of Malaya and Indochina. But in August 1939 Japanese and Soviet troops had clashed on the Siberian border and the Red Army had given the Japanese a thrashing.[42] On the other hand, invasion of south-east Asia would enable the Japanese to pose as liberators of the people from western colonialism. Indeed, after the fall of France in 1940 and the establishment of the Vichy régime the Japanese simply took over Indochina, to which the Americans replied by freezing Japanese assets.[43]

Since it was assumed the United States would not stand idly by, the final Japanese decision to attack to the south had to include eliminating the American presence in the Pacific, and that meant invading the Philippines (which Spain had sold to the United States in 1898) and destroying the American fleet at Pearl Harbor in the Hawaian Islands.

The Japanese decision to attack south rather than Siberia was known to the Russians through the spy Dr Richard Sorge, a communist working in the German embassy in Tokyo. It enabled Stalin to transfer his Siberian divisions to the Moscow front where on 6 December 1941 they burst upon the surprised German army and threatened to destroy it completely.[44]

The following day the Japanese attacked Pearl Harbor. Because of communication difficulties the Japanese envoys in Washington were not able to present the declaration of war before the attack. Believing that a state of war virtually existed between the two countries Hitler did not hesitate to support his ally and declared war on the United States.[45]

But like the Germans in the First World War Hitler badly under-
estimated the United States' industrial capacity. In 1938 the United
States was producing more steel than Germany even though,
because of the recession, two-thirds of American steel plants were
idle. Once the enormous spare capacity of the United States'
economy was put to work the sheer volume of airplanes, ships
and tanks soon outstripped those of Germany and its allies.[46]
Material aid could be sent to the Soviet Union, and within less
than a year American troops were crossing the Atlantic – helping
the British to defeat the German and Italian armies in North Africa,
and then going on to land in Italy itself. In September 1943
Mussolini was deposed by the Fascist Grand Council, which provoked German intervention in Italy as well, with the result that a
rump fascist régime continued the war in the north while in the
south a democratic government was established which declared war
on the side of the Allies.

In June 1944 American, British and Canadian forces landed in
France and swept on to Germany. Superior allied airpower was
ensuring that Germany was bombed around the clock while the
sheer weight of numbers in warships gradually eliminated the submarine threat to allied merchant shipping. In the meantime in the
east the Red Army had continued the offensive, pushing the Germans back to the frontiers of the Reich. And as they did so evidence
was continually found in numerous deathcamps of the attempt to
exterminate European Jewry and opponents of Nazism.

At the end of April 1945 American and Russian soldiers linked
up at Torgau on the Elbe in the heart of Germany, and on 7 May
the war ended in Europe. The Soviet army had captured Berlin.
Hitler had committed suicide and Mussolini been executed by
partisans. Three months later, after the United States had dropped
an atomic bomb on Japan, that country surrendered and the war
was over.

The Second World War was the most expensive in history in terms
of casualties – some fifty-five million dead and thirty-five million
wounded, a large proportion of them civilians.[47] But not only Nazi
Germany, almost all Europe was in ashes from end to end with the
exception of the Iberian peninsula, Switzerland and Sweden. Capitalist democracy and communism had been thrust together to defeat a
system that had threatened to destroy them both.

What would Americans and Russians do with the continent they
had conquered?

14 Division and Integration 1945–1995AD

At the end of the war Europeans could reflect on the lessons of the past fifteen years and come to three conclusions:

First, the internationalisation of economies and advances in the destructive fire-power of weapons meant that their nation states individually no longer had the capacity to carry out their traditional functions of ensuring the economic and military security of their citizens.

Second, their standing in the world had been shaken by the democratic message of arriving American troops, communist ideology and early Japanese victories over the hitherto invincible Europeans, and this would increase the pressure for independence in North Africa, Indochina, the Indian sub-continent, Burma, Malaya and Ceylon.

Third, as the photograph of American and Russian soldiers shaking hands at Torgau in the middle of the ruins of Nazi Germany implied, for the foreseeable future their destinies would be decided by the superpowers.

And indeed almost at once Europeans found themselves caught up in the collapse of the fragile alliance that had defeated National Socialism.

The Soviet Union was very conscious of its weaknesses – the high loss of life, the shattered industry, and aware that the greatest capitalist state, the United States, denounced so vituperatively for decades, possessed the atom bomb. Why should not the Americans try to finish off what the Germans had planned to do and destroy communism in its heartland? The Soviet leadership therefore decided to put as big a barrier as possible between Russia and the West. As Winston Churchill put it, an Iron Curtain was rung down on central and eastern Europe. In the countries through which the Red Army had marched political parties other than Communist ones were either abolished or neutered, their leaders and other 'class enemies' liquidated. The state took over land and industry without compensation – indeed, most industrial plant still surviving was stripped and sent off to Russia as war reparations. The press was heavily censored and anything western was discouraged, if not forbidden. School and university teaching and research had to reflect Marxist–Leninist values. And the hysterical pre-war denunciations of capitalism and bourgeois socialism were resumed, with calls on trade unions to sabotage economic reconstruction in the west by strikes and industrial unrest. A glum night of secrecy, hostility and disappointment quickly dispelled the joy of liberation from National Socialism. The only east European country not to succumb was Yugoslavia, which, although communist, escaped the Russian grip because it had liberated itself under Tito without the help of the Red Army.

These events caused consternation in the West. Had countries like Poland and Czechoslovakia been liberated from the totalitarian Nazis only to be swallowed up by the totalitarian Communists? And in two of western Europe's largest countries, France and Italy, Communists dominated the trade unions and enjoyed great prestige because of their record in the Resistance. Why should not Communism, with its strident anti-western propaganda, not exploit the economic chaos of the first years of the peace, the unemployment, the inflation, the black market, to take over western Europe as well? To the Americans, the loss of western Europe with its market potential, skilled workers and (with the exception of the Iberian peninsula) democratic way of life would amount to a dangerous shift in the balance of power against them.

These developments raised in turn the question of the future of Germany.

At the Yalta Conference between the allied leaders Roosevelt, Stalin and Churchill in February 1945 it had been agreed that Germany should remain as one but each of the Allies should have a zone of occupation and the country would be administered by a Control Commission in Berlin in which decisions would be taken by unanimity. Others, particularly France, had wanted Germany dismembered and indeed, as in 1919, the Saar was separated from Germany, being joined with France in a customs union. It soon became clear that the Russians would not agree to anything that would weaken their hold on their zone of occupation in the east – Prussia, Saxony, Thuringia and Pomerania, and including Berlin, which also had its Soviet and western zones of occupation.

The American reactions to the threats of Communism were two. The economic reply was the Marshall Plan, named after the American Secretary of State General George Marshall, under which between 1949 and 1952 nearly fourteen billion dollars in food, raw materials and currency were made available to war-torn western European countries on condition that they co-operated in their economic reconstruction, that they should draw up the plans for developing production, relaxing restrictions on trade and payments, increasing employment and maintaining currency stability.[1] One international organisation, the Organisation for European Economic Co-operation (OEEC) was set up to implement the plan and another, the European Payments Union (EPU) to overcome the problems of currency shortage. By 1952 the OEEC's membership included 17 west European countries – Austria, (a separate country again), Belgium, Britain, Denmark, France, (West) Germany, Greece, Iceland, Ireland, Italy, Luxembourg, Netherlands, Norway, Portugal, Sweden, Switzerland and Turkey.

The Soviet Union was asked to participate in the Marshall Plan but refused, and ensured that the countries it controlled also refused, fearing penetration of American influence. And when the Soviet Union got trade unions to go on strikes against the Plan and communist ministers in western coalition governments to oppose it, it was clear further co-operation between the capitalist and communist allies that had won the war was impossible. The communists were ejected from their ministries and non-communists broke away from communist-dominated trade unions to set up their own.[2] After a momentary semblance of unity the continent was now confirmed to be deeply divided.

In its economic aims the Marshall Plan was a great success. It saved western Europe from imminent ruin. It laid the foundations for twenty years of sustained economic growth. It provided the incentive and institutional machinery for permanent inter-state co-operation.[3] And by including West Germany in these developments rather than applying punitive isolation it was a brilliant contrast to the fiasco of the post-first world war years.

The military reply to the communist threat required ending the traditional American policy of refusing entangling alliances with European states. In March 1948 Britain, France and the Benelux countries had come together in the Brussels Treaty to take common action in the event of an armed attack in Europe, but clearly their forces would stand little chance against the Red Army. They had no atomic weapons – it would not be until 1951 that Britain developed its nuclear capacity. What was wanted was the commitment of American military – and nuclear – might. Was this possible? Things were made easier by the actions of the Russians.

Only a few days after the signature of the Brussels Treaty the Soviet Union closed all road and rail communications with Berlin which lay ninety miles within the Soviet Zone of Germany. The object was to eliminate an island which was providing an escape route for all who wished to flee to the West and from which western press and broadcasting could challenge communism. The West replied by airlifting thousands of tons of fuel and food daily for more than a year. In May of 1949 the blockade was ignominiously called off but not before the Soviet action had effectively stilled isolationist voices in the American Congress and the North Atlantic Treaty Organisation (NATO) had been set up, under which the signatory states (the United States, Canada, Britain, France, Belgium, Holland, Luxembourg, Denmark, Iceland, Italy, Norway, Portugal – and later Greece and Turkey) agreed that an armed attack on any of them in Europe or North America would be an attack on all of them. The Organisation seemed all the more necessary when later that year the Soviet Union carried out a nuclear test, and clearly was about to embark on a nuclear military programme designed to rival that of the United States.

In the meantime the Americans had been making no secret of their view that the western European democracies should develop their inter-state co-operation much further and create a United States of Europe. Thanks largely to Britain and France decision-making in the OEEC was still traditional, by unanimity, so that states did not need to accept having imposed on them action with which they disagreed, and this tended to slow progress.[4]

The attitude of the Americans was very welcome to Europe's federalists, particularly those in France. Formed from those who in the war on the one hand, had a background in the non-communist resistance, and on the other hand from business circles which had either participated in the German economic mobilisation of the continent or the Allies' global economic mobilisation,[5] they had already put forward five reasons for the creation of a united federal Europe, namely, that only federal union would prevent wars between the continent's states, allow the Germans to participate in the life of the continent without endangering others, solve the problems of ethnic and linguistic minorities, safeguard democratic institutions in countries with insufficient political maturity, and advance the economic reconstruction of the continent.[6]

These federalists hoped to set up a supranational organisation to which national states would transfer their powers, so that Europe would, so to speak, be created 'from above'.[7] On the other hand there were others, pragmatic politicians and business men, also convinced of the need for an integrated Europe who felt that the federalists were unrealistic. States were involved in the process of reconstruction and their peoples wanted a return to pre-war normality. It would be far better to have states begin by functional integration of their economies, sector by sector. With Europe having been gradually built up 'from below' it would be easier for political unity to arrive on the wings of economic unity.[8]

The strongest supporters of the process of western European integration were the various Christian Democratic parties, advocates of international, national and class reconciliation. Socialist parties were far less keen on integration seeing it as a process organised by capitalists and Catholics. German socialists were particularly negative, seeing Russian hostility to integration as ensuring the permanency of the division of Germany.[9]

It was the federalists who made the running by setting up the Council of Europe in 1949. But it was not destined to be the institution for the creation of a federal western Europe, and the main reason was the implacable opposition of Britain, and particularly its Labour government that had come to power in 1945. There were three reasons for British hostility:

First, because of the Commonwealth the British considered themselves a world power in terms of interests and commitments, and rejected the implication of becoming a regional power. Europe was also perceived as unstable.

Second, the British rejected the idea that by a majority vote they might have to accept policies with which they disagreed.[10] Labour was suspicious that a Europe made by clerics and capitalists might require Britain to dismantle the Welfare State and nationalisation programmes which Labour had introduced and of which it was very proud.

Third, unlike the other European countries Britain had no written constitution. The country was governed and society developed through the rule of the Crown in Parliament. It was Parliament that was sovereign, not a code, and no Parliament had the power to bind its successor. Clearly these constitutional arrangements would be difficult – if not impossible – to fit in with the written constitution a politically integrated western Europe would probably require.[11]

The founders of the Council of Europe had envisaged an Assembly composed of MP's from national parliaments and a Committee of Ministers as a kind of Cabinet. The British argued that in order to avoid a clash of competence between decisions of the Committee of Ministers and the policy of a government responsible to its national parliament, decisions by the Committee of Ministers would have to be by unanimity, and therefore the Assembly could only be consultative and could only adopt recommendations to the Ministers.[12]

This effectively reduced the Council of Europe to a 'talking shop'. Furthermore, at British behest defence and the economy were removed from its remit on the grounds that defence organisations already existed and neutral countries such as Ireland, Sweden and Switzerland would find it difficult to belong, while economic issues were already being handled by the OEEC.[13] Later attempts to have the Council of Europe take over defence and the economy and get the power to pass European-level legislation binding on all Member States without the need for ratification by national parliaments were rejected by the Committee of Ministers.[14]

Nevertheless, the Council of Europe was able to promote western European integration through the adoption of conventions in two areas.

The first was human rights. Fascism, nazism and communism had shown that the main threat to an individual's liberties was not a foreign government but his own, and the need was to get governments to allow themselves to be sued in an international court by individuals or groups for redress of grievances. The 1950 European Convention on Human Rights and Fundamental Freedoms listed seventeen rights (later protocols would add more) and provided for the appropriate international machinery. Second, the Council promoted the harmonisation of standards relating to health and working conditions, culminating in the 1961 Turin Social Charter.

The federalists had failed in their attempt to emasculate nation states; henceforward it would be the functionalists that would lead the way.

Jean Monnet has been described as the architect of the European Community. He had been the French Deputy Secretary-General of the League of Nations and during the War had worked in Washington co-ordinating the Allies economic resources. In 1945 he became head of the French Planning Council. Early in 1950 he proposed to his friend Robert Schuman, Foreign Minister of France, that European countries, particularly France and Germany, should pool their coal and steel resources. France was still concerned about Germany. Since these were 'war industries', pooling them would ensure that war between France and Germany was impossible. It would bind Germany to the West and end possible flirtations with neutrality in return for unification. These industries were also essential for reconstruction – but for much more than that: if Europe did not want to be an economic backwater between and dominated by the United States and the Soviet Union it needed to develop to match them.

The result was the establishment in 1951 of the European Coal and Steel Community (ECSC), consisting of six countries – Belgium, France, West Germany, Italy, Luxembourg and the Netherlands. As the world's first supranational body it was radically different from traditional international organisations.

To begin with, decisions were taken not by governments but by a group of nine independent individuals, the so-called High Authority, appointed by but not responsible to governments. Decisions by the High Authority were by majority and binding on governments. Instead of member states paying a quota of the budget the ECSC had its own source of funds, levies of up to one per cent on the turnovers of all coal and steel firms, public or private, in the Community. The organisation had its own Court of Justice, and any disputes in the coal and steel sectors involving the Member States, the Organisation or the firms had to be referred to it, and its decisions were binding. The High Authority was responsible not to governments but to an Assembly composed originally of Members of national parliaments but with provision for it to be directly elected although it had no legislative functions. Governments were represented on a Council of Ministers, the duty of which was to harmonise the action of the High Authority with governments and thus see that vital national interests were not impaired.

Monnet was chosen as the first President of the ECSC, the work of which involved elimination of trade barriers, subsidies and discriminatory pricing in the two sectors (including transportation of the goods in question), re-training and housing of workers, as well as their freedom of movement to take up work anywhere in the Community, and research into safety and health in mines and mills.[15]

Britain was asked to join the ECSC but refused on the grounds that the decision-making process was undemocratic and it would not be able to decide its own coal and steel policies.[16]

If supranationality seemed acceptable in economic affairs, the attempt to extend it to defence was revealed as premature, with suspicions of Germany still lingering.

Following the attack in 1950 of communist North Korea on a South Korea that was under American protection, the United States had proposed that western Europe's defences should be strengthened by the rearmament of West Germany. This was highly unpopular in western Europe and to soften the blow the French government proposed a European Defence Community (EDC) into which German troops could be integrated. But most French public opinion was against any form of German rearmament. Supranationality implied loss of sovereignty and the French military feared that their army, engaged in a colonial war in Indo-China, would lose its independence. Those in favour could only argue that it was essential to have the Germans participating in European defence, and it was better to have them in an integrated community than with their own independent army, and if the EDC did not go ahead the Americans might rearm the Germans anyway. But to no avail. The weakness of the scheme was that an army is an instrument of a political authority and it was not possible to agree on one.[17] In any case the British refused to participate and when Stalin died in March 1953 a period of détente set in and the Korean war was wound down. Anti-EDC sentiment in the French parliament ensured that the proposal was rejected in 1954.

The defence crisis was solved by a package deal proposed by the British. Germany (and Italy) would join the Brussels Treaty Organisation, which would be renamed Western European Union (WEU), and then NATO. National contingents at the disposal of the WEU would remain under national governments. Full sovereignty was granted to the West German government which was recognised as the only government entitled to speak for the German people in international affairs. On the other hand, the Germans agreed not to fabricate chemical, biological or nuclear weapons or to resort to force to achieve unification. Finally, the future of the Saar would be settled by a plebiscite. In 1955 West Germany and Italy duly entered NATO and in reply the Soviet Union set up the Warsaw

Pact, consisting of itself and the countries under its control, and recognised East Germany as a sovereign independent state.

But the setback to western European integration was only temporary. In June 1955 the Foreign Ministers of the Six, meeting at Messina, decided to go all out for a united Europe by embarking first on full-scale economic integration,[18] and a Committee under the chairmanship of the Belgian Foreign Minister, Paul-Henri Spaak, was set up to examine the issues.

Once again Britain was invited to participate in the process of European integration, and for a time an official from the Board of Trade was sent to the Spaak Committee, but before long he was withdrawn. The British believed in free trade and saw the future Common Market as a protectionist organisation that could well conflict with the OEEC. And they preferred the intergovernmental OEEC to the supranationality postulated for this Common Market. And Britain still had illusions of grandeur, whereas the defeated or occupied or smaller European states accepted the Monnet analysis that only by coming together could they perhaps regain their influence and stand with the superpowers. The British also saw western Europe as being dominated by them together with the French, and simply did not believe that the French would accept the supranationality of the Common Market, particularly as they had rejected the EDC.[19]

What ended British illusions and decisively affected the future course of western European integration were the crises over Suez and Hungary in the autumn of 1956.

In 1952 the Egyptian monarchy had been overthrown and a year later power was seized by a fervid Arab nationalist, Colonel Abdel Gamal Nasser. He wanted to end western colonialism and spheres of influence in the Middle East and to get rid of the state of Israel established in 1948 out of the old Palestine mandate. Nasser began denouncing pro-western Arab leaders and supporting a revolt by Arab nationalists in Algeria, then an integral part of France.

When, on the grounds that he was buying arms from the Soviet block to attack Israel, a state under American protection, the United States used its influence with the World Bank to have withdrawn the offer of a loan to build a dam at Aswan, Nasser seized the international Suez Canal company in order to use the revenue from tolls on shipping to finance the dam.

For the British the Suez Canal was the lifeline of their Empire, and Nasser's action threatened their standing as a world power.

And encouragement of Arab nationalism might lead to other pro-Western leaders being overthrown and oil supplies being jeopardised. For their part the French had just been forced out of Indo-China; they were not going to be forced out of Algeria.

Believing that the United States would tolerate such action Britain and France in collusion with Israel invaded Egypt. But they had miscalculated. The American attitude was hostile. It was a presidential election year. Anti-colonial sentiment was still deeply rooted. And there was the fear that the Russians would exploit the situation and American efforts to build up an anti-Soviet alliance of Arab states would be undermined.[20]

When a run on the pound, a reserve currency, began, the Americans only agreed to back a loan by the International Monetary Fund (IMF) if the operation was called off.[21] Within days the Suez campaign was over.

For the British the Suez crisis brought home the fact that their country was no longer a great power: it could no longer act independently in its own interests. It also ended illusions about the Empire/Commonwealth – most of its members had denounced the British action. The British failure strengthened the drive for independence in those African and Caribbean countries still lacking it and within ten years would achieve it. What the British concluded from the crisis was that no independent action would be possible without the *'nihil obstat'* of the United States, and therefore every effort should be made to have a close relationship.

What the French concluded, however, was that the Americans would never let the vital interests of their allies stand in the way of their own interests and hence a virulent anti-Americanism began to permeate French politics. Prior to Suez the French had also believed in an Anglo-French condominium over western Europe. But the British clearly could not be trusted to be anything but American agents. And the British were wrong about something else. The French wanted to escape continual economic crisis and were prepared to meet the challenge of big internal changes that membership of the Common Market implied.[22] But a new partner would have to be sought in the creation of a Europe that could stand up to the superpowers and in which France would have the dominant role, thus regaining its position of power in the world. That partner was Germany.

And the moment was right. In October 1955 the last source of friction between the two powers, the Saar, had been solved amicably when the Saarlanders voted overwhelmingly (as in 1935) to return to Germany.

But there was another effect of the Suez crisis for the French. Already at the end of 1954 those around Monnet were proposing that Europe should have its own sources of nuclear power both to provide energy for industry (consumption of electricity was doubling every ten years) and defence.[23] The threat to oil supplies which lay behind the Suez crisis seemed to make the switch to nuclear power essential while on the other hand during the crisis itself the Russians had actually threatened to bombard London and Paris with rockets. The Russians also took the opportunity of the Suez crisis to crush a reformist communist government in Hungary which had hoped to declare neutrality and establish a multi-party political system. The French bitterly resented their military impotence, and felt the only answer was to acquire atomic autonomy.[24] A nuclear weapons programme was soon begun.

Thereafter, with the Suez and Hungarian crises over, the pace of negotiations on European integration quickened. On 25 March 1957 the Six signed in Rome two treaties, one establishing the European Economic Community (EEC) and the other the European Atomic Energy Community (EURATOM).

The aim of the EEC Treaty according to the Preamble was 'to lay the foundations of an ever closer union' among the peoples of Europe (without actually defining what was the ultimate aim or shape of this union). Its task was to establish a common market, progressively approximate the economic policies of the Member States, promote a harmonious development of economic activities, a continuous and balanced expansion, an increase in stability, an accelerated raising of the standard of living, and closer relations between the Member States.

This would be achieved by a timetabled and automatic elimination of customs duties and quantitative restrictions between the Member States and the erection of a common external tariff *vis-à-vis* the rest of the world within a transition period of twelve years beginning on 1 January 1958; free movement of goods, persons, services and capital; a common agricultural and transport policy; fair competition; and approximation of the laws of Member States to ensure the proper functions of the market. In addition a social fund would be created to improve employment opportunities for workers through training; an Investment Bank would be set up to help develop the poorer regions of the Community; and overseas territories and colonies of the Member States would receive financial and technical assistance and preferential access to the Community through an Association Agreement.

Institutionally both the EEC and EURATOM would, like the ECSC's High Authority, be run by a Commission appointed by Member governments but not responsible to them. They would use, for the same purposes as the ECSC, the latter's Assembly and Court of Justice, as well as a new Economic and Social Committee. There was also provision for the EEC to be funded by its own resources once the transition period was over. The motor of the integration process would be the Commission which, besides administering sectoral Directorates-General such as Agriculture, Transport, External Relations, Economic and Financial Affairs, Social Affairs, Competition and the Internal Market, would be solely responsible for initiating legislation in the form of regulations and directives for approval by the Council of Ministers on the basis of qualified majority voting (QMV). The Assembly would have little meaningful power. As with the ECSC it could dismiss the Commission but its only input into the legislative process was the right to give a formal Opinion on draft legislation, which, however, the Council of Ministers could ignore.[25] Later, in 1965, it would be agreed to have one Council and one Commission to run all three Communities, ECSC, EEC and EURATOM.[26]

The Common Market had thus been established and it was hoped that other countries, even Britain, would eventually join. But comfortable assumptions about the integration process and its future were shattered when in the very year that the Treaty of Rome came into effect the fourth French Republic fell because of its inability to solve the Algerian crisis and General Charles de Gaulle came to power.

De Gaulle harboured a deep-seated enmity for the 'Anglo-Saxons' (Americans and the Brtish) for his humiliation at their hands during the war, when he was leader of the Free French, and afterwards.[27] His vision was one of a loose confederation based on a Franco-German condominium but in reality led by France. The supranationalist spirit of the Treaty of Rome was rejected on the grounds that only states had political legitimacy – the peoples of Europe did not as yet have the will to exist as one independent state. Until they did Europe should progress by intergovernmental decision, i.e., unanimity.[28]

On one issue he disagreed fundamentally with President John F. Kennedy of the United States. The President saw western Europe as part of a vast North Atlantic free trade area defended by American nuclear power to which the process of western European integration was a preliminary step, whereas De Gaulle saw a Europe integrated economically and militarily as the precondition for disengagement from American domination, and assumption of the role of arbiter between the two superpowers.[29]

De Gaulle saw Europe as being endangered by the Cold War. Either the superpowers would come to an agreement over the heads of the Europeans or, if there was war, Europe would be reduced to ashes.[30] Since he believed that the Russians would not leave eastern Europe as long as the Americans were in western Europe he aimed at diminishing their influence there,[31] and he led the way by withdrawing French forces from the military wing of NATO, forcing the American government to pay its trade deficit in France with gold, and trying to get Europeans to think of their own defence rather than sheltering behind the United States. He even envisaged France's nuclear weaponry programme being combined with the more advanced one of Britain as the basis for a European nuclear defence.[32] But British thinking on Europe and its relations with America would clearly have to change, and there were some signs of this happening. When the negotiations on the Treaty of Rome were reaching their conclusion the British saw that tariffs would be raised against them and to begin with wondered if there could be a link between the free trade OEEC and the protectionist Six. A Working Party of the OEEC concluded that a free trade area incorporating the Common Market was feasible but in one of his earliest decisions De Gaulle rejected any pursuit of the matter.[33] As a result Britain, together with Austria, Denmark, Norway, Portugal, Sweden and Switzerland formed the European Free Trade Association (EFTA) under which barriers to trade in industrial goods would be dismantled but not in agriculture and fisheries.

But it was not long before the British government, increasingly aware of national economic decline and shrinking Commonwealth markets realised that EFTA did not amount to much (half the total market was British) whereas the EEC held out prospects of real economic gain.[34] Accordingly in 1961 the British Conservative Government applied to join the EEC. De Gaulle was sceptical about this Damascus-like conversion. He believed Americans were behind the move. British public opinion, most of the Labour opposition and many Conservatives were against membership – for one thing, food under the Common Agricultural Policy's system of

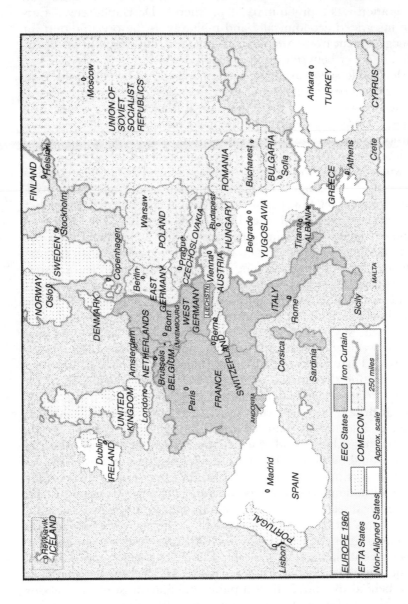

9 Europe – 1960

community preference would be more expensive than Common-wealth imports; indeed, all Commonwealth trade links would be weakened, and thus the Commonwealth itself. De Gaulle believed Labour would win the next election, and the French feared that while the British team at the negotiating table might declare finally that it accepted (with a few minor changes and a long transition period) the Treaty of Rome, once in the British would try to get things changed [35] As for Britain's supposed commitment to Europe, in December 1962 De Gaulle saw Britain at Nassau agree to surrender its nuclear independence to the United States, integrating its nuclear armaments into NATO and accepting American delivery systems. [36]

On 14 January 1963 De Gaulle vetoed the British application (accession of new members to the EEC required unanimity) stating that while the Six had many points in common Britain was 'insular, maritime in all her doings, habits and traditions... profoundly different from those on the Continent'. If Britain joined, the other EFTA countries would eventually do so and then there would be one gigantic North Atlantic Community under American domina-tion with Britain having played the Trojan Horse to bring this about. [37] And in 1967 De Gaulle vetoed a second application by Britain, this time led by Labour, on the grounds that in view of the decline in the British economy retention of the pound as a reserve currency would create very difficult problems for the EEC particu-larly should it embark on economic and monetary union. [38]

Second, De Gaulle brought to a sudden and jarring halt the idea that the Commission of international civil servants was the motor of European integration, and placed the ball firmly in the court of the Member States and their governments.

When the Commission proposed that the Community budget, decided by the Council of Ministers, and, after 1965, on the basis of QMV, should be funded from three sources, namely, all customs duties, a percentage of the VAT base and levies on agricultural imports, some Member States proposed that in view of the total sum involved there should be some democratic control, perhaps by giving the European Parliament the power to amend the budget unless the Council rejected the amendment by a 5/6 majority. De Gaulle was alarmed that France could be outvoted on agricultural spending, a vital French national interest, and when the other Member States insisted on democratic control France boycotted all institutions and forums for six months. De Gaulle railed against the Commission...('a technocratic body of elders, stateless and responsible to no one') and the Parliament...('an assembly of members from various national parliaments [who have] no mandate except in the national sphere').[39]

It was not until January 1966 that the crisis was patched up with the vague compromise that in cases of important interest to one or more member states, discussions in the Council of Ministers would continue until unanimous agreement was reached. It was also agreed that a number of decisions should henceforward require unanimity: financing the Common Agricultural Policy (CAP), market organisation of various agricultural products, and fixing of common prices.[40]

As a result of the so-called Luxembourg compromise the natural and expected evolution of European integration through decision-making by QMV was stopped in its tracks, not to resume for another twenty years. Nevertheless, after De Gaulle resigned as President of France in 1969, the European Community continued to expand and develop an ever-increasing solidarity.

In terms of membership, only a few months after De Gaulle's departure France agreed to let negotiations begin again on the accession of Britain to the EEC, together with Denmark, Ireland and Norway, partly because its partners, angered at Britain's continued exclusion, threatened to paralyse the Community by refusing to embark on economic and monetary union (EMU) and to agree on 'own resources' for the budget, and thus the CAP, and partly for pragmatic reasons – the Community needed Britain for its technology and the financial power and expertise of the City of London, both vital if it was to hold its own against the superpowers. And the negotiations were successful. Britain, Denmark and Ireland became Members of the Community on 1 January 1973, Britain accepting the CAP and agreeing vaguely to run down the pound as a reserve currency.[41] The Norwegian people, however, rejected membership in a referendum mainly because of fears relating to proposed revision of the Common Fisheries Policy (CFP) which had been agreed in 1970. Greece joined the Community in 1979 and Spain and Portugal, after the end of their respective dictatorships in the 1970s, in 1986.

In terms of policies the 1970 Common Fisheries Policy was revised in 1982 to take into account the international move to extend state sovereignty to 200 miles from national coasts. And a Regional Policy for the poorer regions of the Community was developed, starting in 1975 with a fund and a quota system for states and extended later to a system by which the Community increased the amount of money available and applied it directly to the most needy regions, classified by five (later six) categories. The only set back was in regard to plans for EMU, blown off course in the 1970s by the departure of the United States from the Gold Standard and the high inflation, unemployment and currency instability triggered by a thirteen-fold increase in oil prices led by the Middle Eastern countries of OPEC. But currency stability was generally restored with the 1979 Economic and Monetary System (EMS).

In terms of the institutions and management of the Community a vital step was taken in the adoption in 1986 of the Single European Act (SEA), the brain child of the ambitious and dynamic French President of the Commission, Jacques Delors. His programme aimed to bring about complete freedom of movement in goods, persons, services and capital by 1992, and by a big increase in decision-making by QMV rather than unanimity. Some three hundred directives concerned the elimination of non-tariff barriers, including the harmonisation of health and safety standards, the mutual recognition of professional qualifications, the exercise of the banking, medical and pharmaceutical professions, harmonisation of sea and air transport regulations, environmental standards, elimination of discrimination in awarding public procurement contracts, elimination of customs controls between member states, and making available harmonised financial services (mortgages, insurance, stocks and shares).

The SEA also provided formal machinery for Community cooperation in the sphere of foreign policy. And it also provided a more prominent role for the European Parliament, directly elected since 1979, giving it the right to reject draft legislation by the Council of Ministers which the latter could only override by unanimity.[42]

The significance of the Single European Act, however, was that with voting by qualified majority it restored the initiative for the process of European integration to the Commission from the Council of Ministers (and thus the Member States) as the founding fathers of the Treaty of Rome would have wished.

And what gave the Community even more strength *vis-à-vis* the Member States was the heightened profile of the European Court of Justice. Already in landmark decisions in the 1960s the Court had ruled that European law stemming from the Treaties and their implementation in regulations and directives had primacy over national legislation and that state laws should conform to European laws.[43] Furthermore, European law had immediate applicability and could not be made subject to other national rules of implementation.[44] These rulings amounted to a permanent and severe limitation of the sovereign rights of states.

All these events raised questions about the *raison d'être* of the European Free Trade Area and the European Community. Negotiations between the two opened, resulting in the signature of the Oporto Treaty in 1992 on the creation of a European Economic Area which was seen as a preliminary step to the countries in EFTA joining the Community. Free movement of goods, services, capital and labour throughout the area was agreed; the EFTA countries had to accept the entire *corpus* of Community directives and regulations on industrial and environmental standards, consumer protection, company law, social policy, competition and mutual recognition of qualifications. However the CAP would not apply to the EFTA countries, nor would they contribute to the Community's 'own resources'.[45]

In the meantime, as western Europe progressed steadily on the road to integration, the solidarity and permanency of the Soviet Empire had come to be taken for granted. The collapse of that empire and communism itself in 1989 was utterly unexpected.

Since the death of Stalin in 1953 there had been a lessening of the severity of the Communist régime in Russia and its satellite states. What was essential was that these states remained loyal to the principle of Communist control. Hungary's mistake in 1956 was to propose multi-party elections and to become neutral, and in 1968 in Czechoslovakia reforms introduced also seemed to threaten Communist control. In both cases the Soviet Union invaded the country and crushed the reform. On the latter occasion the General Secretary of the Soviet Union, Leonid Brezhnev, pronounced the doctrine of legitimate intervention to maintain not merely Communist but the Soviet model of control in the Soviet sphere of influence.[46] Nevertheless, in order to dampen down grievances in regard to political liberty and drab living standards known to be slipping behind the booming consumer society in the West, the Soviet Union felt obliged to provide massive financial investment in eastern Europe.[47]

But what would turn out to be crucial was the growing gap in technological power, affecting both military and civilian life, between East and West. Nikita Khrushchev, leader of the Soviet

Union 1955–64 had boasted that the Soviet Union would become the world's leading producer of coal and steel, implying that when it did so the capitalist world would be shown up as inefficient and doomed. The Soviet Union did indeed become the world's leading coal and steel power, only to find that the West had moved on into silicon chips, fourth generation computers and high technology industries.

Then in the late 1970s the Soviet Union went into a steep financial decline. In order to alleviate its financial burden the Soviet Union had allowed eastern Europe to borrow massively from the West.[48] But the 1970's oil crisis had affected eastern Europe as adversely as western Europe. The countries were soon heavily in debt and the Russians had to mount costly rescue packages. In addition the Soviet Union was drawn into a war in 1979 in Afghanistan to prop up a pro-Communist government against attacks by the Mujahedeen, Islamic fundamentalists.[49]

In 1985 Mikhail Gorbachev became President of the Soviet Union. He inherited an ailing economy. Central planning required a huge bureaucracy that discouraged initiative and ossified management. Guaranteed employment and a lack of incentives had bred apathy, complacency, absenteeism and drunkenness. It was the same in agriculture: peasants preferred working their own plots rather than collective farms. And transport was inefficient. There was little investment in consumer goods; it was the military which benefited from high technology resources. Patriotism and ideological commitment withered away.[50]

Reforms were clearly necessary, but the limited free enterprise embarked on did not go nearly far enough for radical reforms while changes to the system were resented and rejected by die-hard Communist party functionaries and bureaucrats. Gorbachev soon saw that economic reform was useless without political reform. One aspect of Gorbachev's reform programme (*perestroika* or restructuring) was *glasnost* (openness) under which criticism of the party, state policies in regard to health and the environment (particularly the nuclear disaster at Chernobyl), corruption, and inefficiency was allowed. In 1987 the principle of two-candidate elections was introduced. Dissidents, and many other inhabitants of labour camps were released, and eventually in 1990 political parties other than the Communist party were allowed.

But it was in the military field that the Soviet Union felt most critically behind. The United States developed first the Cruise

missile, with its ability to fly at very low levels following the contours
of the ground, thus making it difficult to detect, and then embarked
on the Strategic Defense Initiative (SDI), the so-called 'Star Wars',
in which it was plain that the United States had not only the
technological capacity but the financial means and the political
will to put manned platforms up in space that would be able to
destroy Soviet missiles before they reached American soil.

With insufficient financial resources to counter SDI Gorbachev
opted out of confrontation with the West[51], and thus in December
1990 at their meeting in Malta Presidents George Bush of the
United States and Mikhail Gorbachev of the Soviet Union declared
that the Cold War was over.

But already the countries of eastern Europe were slipping out of
Soviet control. In the summer of 1989 the stagnation, corruption
and oppression of the East German régime had led to a massive
flight of refugees to the West via the by now relatively liberal
Communist state of Hungary. When Gorbachev made it clear
that the Soviet Union would no longer follow the Brezhnev
doctrine, that spelt the end. In November, amid massive demonstrations, the entire border was opened. The Berlin Wall, erected in
1961 between the eastern and western sectors of the city to choke
off the flow of refugees from eastern Europe to the West, was torn
down by enthusiastic crowds. New political parties emerged, multi-
party elections were held and a non-Communist government was
formed. The intention had been for the two Germanies to negotiate
eventual unification, but the massive flight by those in the East
seeking jobs and better wages in the harder currency of the West
precipitated first economic union and then on 3 October 1990,
political union.

Within two years central and eastern Europe was transformed.
One by one states threw off Communism and began pursuing their
own destinies. Two states went further and dissolved on ethnic lines
– Czechs and Slovaks divorcing amicably, and Yugoslavia dividing
into five new states, Serbia, Croatia, Slovenia, Bosnia and Macedonia.

And astonishingly enough, that too, was the fate of the Soviet
Union. With *perestroika* and *glasnost* ethnic communities, so long held
down by the iron grip of Communism, re-emerged, reintroducing
nationalism into Russian politics. Often it was liberal or reform
minded communists who took the lead, renouncing the leadership
of the Communist Party of the Soviet Union. In 1990 Lithuania,

Latvia, Estonia, Georgia, Azerbaijan and Belarus (White Russia) broke away and declared independence followed in 1991 by Armenia and the Ukraine. And in that same year the leaders of Russia, the Ukraine and Belarus declared that the Soviet Union had ceased to exist and would be replaced by a Commonwealth of Independent States. Now that there was no longer a Soviet Union there was no role for the man responsible for these enormous changes. As if to signify the triumph of the West, on 25 December 1991 Mikhail Gorbachev resigned as President of the Soviet Union and the next day the Soviet flag was hauled down from the masthead of the Kremlin in Moscow, to be replaced by the red, white and blue of Russia. The new leader of Russia was Boris Yeltsin, also a former Communist, who wanted to press on with reforms to bring about a market economy.

The speed of the collapse of Communism and the Soviet block meant that the European Community now had to address urgently a number of issues. Within the Community there were two problems.

First, there was the globalisation of economy and society. Like West Germany before it the Community was an economic giant but a political pygmy. In terms of population it was significantly larger than its market rivals, the United States and Japan. It was the world's biggest trading block partner with fifteen per cent of world exports and sixteen per cent of world imports. It led the world in agricultural trade. Through the Lomé Conventions since 1975 the Union had Association Agreements with over eighty of the less-developed countries of the world. Nevertheless it lagged badly behind both in regard to research, especially on technology. Crime too, in the shape of drugs, fraud and terrorism, had been globalised. Political disunity hampered decision-making on these world-wide issues so that the Community was hardly in a position to face up to its global responsibilities as might be expected. To meet the challenge closer integration would be necessary.

Second, there were the economic and political implications of a unified Germany. The new Germany would be by far the most populous and economically powerful nation in the Community. The *Deutschmark* was by far the most powerful currency in the Community, *de facto* a world reserve currency. There were many, including many Germans, who feared it might use its power in its own interests, and argued that therefore the Community should become even more integrated – even absolutely unified – in order to lock the Germans in.

However, would the closer integration implied as the answer to these problems be acceptable to all the Member States, particularly Britain?

Outside the Community there were also two problems. One was the integration of EFTA. The other was the political instability in Eastern Europe, and the prospect that a number of countries of the former Soviet block would apply for Community membership. Was it feasible for them suddenly to throw off the Communist economy and take up market forces? And what would it cost the Community?

The response was the Maastricht Treaty on European Union of 7 February 1992, containing proposals designed to strengthen the Community and limit even further the ability of Member States to act independently.

It was envisaged that by 1999, if their economies had converged sufficiently in terms of low inflation rates and reduced government debt and borrowing, control of those economies would be transferred to the, by now European Union, through economic and monetary union. A single currency, the *Euro*, would replace national currencies. An independent European Central Bank would replace national Central Banks in regard to decisions on interest rates, lending policy and public expenditure levels. A common foreign and security policy would be developed possibly through qualified majority voting in the Council of Ministers, with the hope that in time a common defence policy would follow, based on the Western European Union. The European Court of Justice would be able to fine Member States which failed to respect the Treaties or a judgement of the Court. The European Parliament would be able to reject definitively proposals by the Council of Ministers. Joint decisions, possibly by qualified majority voting, would replace individual Member State policy in regard to such internal matters as asylum, immigration, drugs, fraud, and judicial, police and customs co-operation. Every national of a Member State would automatically be a citizen of the Union, free to move to and reside anywhere in the Union and vote and stand for office in all except national elections. The only sop to sensitivity about the increasing involvement of the Union in the affairs of its Member States was the agreement to operate on the principle of 'subsidiarity', according to which the Union would only act in areas outside its exclusive jurisdiction if objectives could not be achieved by Member States alone.[52]

With regard to the Union's external problems, the integration of the EFTA countries seemed on the surface to present few difficulties. Two-thirds of their trade had been with the Union, and most of their economic and social policies had been aligned with it. And with the end of the Soviet Union neutrality was much less of an issue. However, with the failure of Switzerland to ratify the Oporto Treaty (mainly because of the fear that it would be swamped by foreign workers)[53] hopes for EFTA joining the union *en bloc* were dashed, and this spurred individual applications for membership by Finland, Austria, Sweden and Norway. The first three became members of the Union in 1995. Norway, as in 1972, rejected membership in a referendum because of fears that its waters would be fished out under the Common Fisheries Policy and cheap food imports would ruin farmers.[54]

Integration of the countries of the former Soviet block into the Union would not, however, be so easy.

After the collapse of Communism central and eastern Europeans had euphorically expected that entry into the Union would be quick in order to consolidate democracy and raise living and technical standards. But the euphoria soon turned to bitterness and recrimination as high inflation and unemployment set in and many people saw their living standards slip below the poverty line. Instead of being cordially invited in they felt they were being kept at arms length. What they needed was a Marshall Plan but instead western investment was grudging and the Union was applying barriers to trade in key eastern European sectors such as agriculture, iron and steel, chemicals, textiles and cement at the same time that the Russian market for their processed and finished goods had collapsed.

For the Union, on the other hand, the integration of Eastern Europe could not be allowed to jeopardise western European integration. Before the east European countries could join they would have to fulfil the obligations of membership, including acceptance of the *acquis communautaire*, the corpus of Union directives and standards. It would be useless admitting countries with 'sensitive' products the output of which the Union itself was seeking to reduce. In the view of the Union there was the feeling that thanks to decades of the command economy there was little understanding of the dynamics of capital and investment. Change could therefore only come about gradually, not overnight. In any case membership of such countries would require reform of the CAP and a switch in resources on regional development would adversely affect financial transfers to the poorer areas of the Community.

In the meantime Association Agreements were made with eleven central and eastern European countries covering such matters as approximation of laws with the Union, technical and financial co-operation and trade liberalisation. But the complaint in the East was that Union exports to the East, usually high quality technical goods, were growing much faster than eastern exports to the Union so that instead of the surplus required for economic development the East's trade with the Union was an ever-growing deficit.[55]

Nor would the question of closer European integration seem likely to be easier, the main reason being the continuing lack of direct democracy in the governance of the Union. Although the idea of European Union was popular in some countries, particularly those benefitting from Union funds, the perception in others was of a process driven by political élites with little regard for the person in the street. The Maastricht Treaty required ratification by all the Member States, either by their parliaments or by popular referendum. Yet Denmark rejected the Treaty in a first referendum and was humiliatingly sent back to vote again, accepting it only after having secured opt-outs from its EMU sections.[56] In France the referendum in favour was wafer-thin, 51–49 per cent.[57] The British parliament only narrowly ratified the Treaty because opt-outs from the social as well as the economic and monetary sections had been secured. And policies designed to secure compliance with EMU convergence criteria have provoked disturbances in a number of other countries as unemployment has grown.

The root of the problem is that on the one hand the only European institution allowed to initiate legislation is the unelected Commission which, if the Parliament can dismiss, it has no powers to appoint, while on the other hand the decision-making Council of Ministers is not, as a body, accountable. Individual members may be removed by a change of government but not the Council as a whole, while the European Parliament only has the negative function of being able to block legislation by the Council. This situation pleases neither those ardent Europeans who seek absolute Parliamentary democracy in a single European state nor those in the Member states who feel helpless before the torrent of legislation pouring out and imposed on them by qualified majority voting in Brussels.

And in no country has this helplessness been more resented than in Britain. Rightly or wrongly the British believed in the early 1970s that they were entering a Common Market rather than a European state in the making. It was the economic benefits that their leaders stressed, although the final aim was always in the fine print.[58] They believed the Gaullist veto would protect them and when that was given up with the 1986 Single European Act they suddenly found that the Union's fanatical attempts to get a level playing field for the economic Common Market was destroying their political culture and invading perniciously the 'nooks and crannies' of their everyday existence, including business practices and procedures.

Since 1500 almost all the peoples of Europe have experienced different régimes – monarchist or republican, democratic or totalitarian, regional or central. Almost all today's states have been invaded, imposed their rule on others or had others impose their rule on them. Some states only came into being in the nineteenth century, others in the twentieth, and some only in the last decade of the twentieth. Some states have come, gone and come again. Few have retained their original shape. Would the collective wisdom of rule by Brussels be either so bad or so different? On the other hand, apart from the Swiss and the Swedes, only the English have been able to develop their political traditions – the concept of rule by the Crown in Parliament with change as and when required and responding to circumstances – spontaneously and uninterrupted by foreigners, in their case since Magna Carta in 1215. Yet of what use is the Crown or Parliament if legislation requires not the monarch's signature or parliamentary majority but conformity with Union regulations and directives?

Together with the secularisation of western society which, amongst other things, has undermined the Church of England, the emasculation of their three most prestigious institutions – Church, Crown and Parliament – has demoralised at least the English, making them sour, uncertain of their role, and causing them to be labelled as the 'awkward partner' in the Union, continually seeking 'opt-outs' from parts of the integration process.

Nevertheless on the eve of the third millennium the Founding Fathers of European integration would have much reason to be satisfied. The Union has become a region of political stability. Democracy has been strengthened with Greece, Spain and Portugal brought in from the cold of dictatorship. Economically it has developed into one of the three most prosperous areas of the world together with North America and Japan, although lagging behind both in terms of 'high tech' research. The great Communist enemy has collapsed. The German people have been well integrated into Europe, overcoming the utter destruction of 1945 to be, once again, the leading economic power on the continent. In the Union the position of ethnic and cultural minorities has greatly improved. The process of European integration has meant that with the exception of Northern Ireland, formally claimed by the Irish Republic in its constitution, all borders and territories are respected and thus such minorities no longer need be seen as potential threats to the integrity of states. As a result, since the 1970s many ethnic communities have received far reaching autonomies – Basques and Catalans in Spain, the South Tyrolese in Italy, Flemings and Walloons in Belgium, while devolution for the Scots and Welsh has become high on the British political agenda. These, and the high standard of cultural rights postulated in the Charters and Conventions of the Council of Europe provide a lesson for Eastern Europe where the collapse of Communism has led to the reappearance of ethnic hostility. Russians in the Baltic states where they were once masters, Hungarians in Slovakia and Romania are regarded with suspicion, while in Yugoslavia the attempt to create a Greater Serbia has led to civil war and horrific ethnic cleansing, particularly in Bosnia.

Looking beyond the integration of Eastern Europe, the founding Fathers would probably be speculating on the future relations between Russia and the Union. Russia has become a member of the Council of Europe, thus encouraging belief in the fulfilment one day of Mikhail Gorbachev's vision of one European home stretching from the Atlantic to the Pacific. Russia is one of the richest areas of the world in terms of raw materials, particularly energy and minerals lying in the harsh terrain of Siberia. Development of that area will provide the Union with great opportunities for investment and technological assistance in competition with the United States and Japan.

But the Founding Fathers might also like to reflect on the great weakness of the Union and the integration process: that for too many of those on the street, as opposed to political élites, it is no longer a cause and therefore lacks a soul. It was born either for negative reasons – to prevent conflict – or material ones – to increase prosperity. The Greeks and early Romans championed the ideas of the rule of law and political liberty in the face of despotism. Europe in the Middle Ages was synonymous with Christianity. From 1500 to 1914 it was the fount of progress, social as well as scientific. One was ready to die for liberty at Marathon or at the Bastille, for Christianity at Poitiers, Jerusalem or Lepanto, or at the stake for one's version of it at Basel and Spitalfields, and in spreading the Gospel across the seas. But who is there ready to sacrifice their lives for the materialism of the social market and the bureaucracy that organises it?

On how Europe responds in providing a focus for loyalty and enthusiasm to replace the still strong pull of nation and ethnicity will depend the success of the Union in the coming millenium.

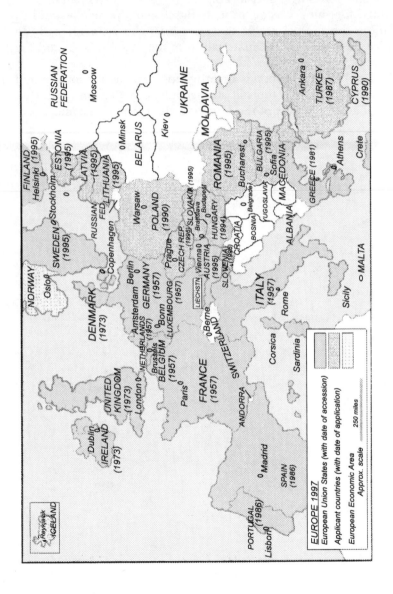

10 Europe – 1997

EUROPE 1997
European Union States (with date of accession)
Applicant countries (with date of application)
European Economic Area
    Approx. scale   250 miles

Notes

1 ANCIENT GREECE 2000–280BC

1. *Penguin Atlas of World History*, vol. 1 (Harmondsworth: Penguin, 1974) p. 33.
2. Boardman, J., Griffin, J., Murray, O., *The Oxford History of the Classical World* (Oxford. Oxford University Press, 1986) pp. 27–34.
   Spielvogel, J. J. (ed.), *Western Civilisation* (New York: West Publishing Co., 1994) p. 68.
3. Aristotle, *The Politics*, ed. T. A. Sinclair (London: Penguin Classics Series, 1981) Bks 3–6.
4. Hogarth, D. G., *The Ancient East* (Oxford: Home University Library, 1950) pp. 231–2.
5. Aristotle, *op.cit.*, Bks II (v) & V (i).
6. De Burgh, W. G., *The Legacy of the Ancient World* (Penguin, 1955) p. 104.
7. Dickinson, G. L., *The Greek View of Life* (London: Methuen, 1912) pp. 66–80, 163–174.
8. *Oxford History*, p. 36, p. 222.
9. *Western Civilisation*, pp. 85–92.
10. *Ibid.*, pp. 101–2.
11. Hogarth, D. G., *op.cit.*, p. 235.
12. Fuller, J. F. C., *The Decisive Battles of the Western World*, ed. J. Terraine, vol. 1 (London: Paladin, 1970) p. 112.
13. Hogarth, *op.cit.*, p. 239.
14. *Oxford History*, pp. 266–7.
15. Hogarth, *op.cit.*, p. 238.
16. *Ibid.*, pp. 240–8.
17. *Oxford History*, pp. 323–6.

2 ROME: REPUBLIC AND EMPIRE 753BC–565AD

1. *Western Civilisation*, pp. 131–3.
2. De Burgh, W.G., *op.cit.*, pp. 246–7.
3. *Ibid.*, p. 244.
4. *Western Civilisation*, *op.cit.*, p. 142.
5. Grant, M., *The World of Rome* (New York: Mentor, 1964) p. 23. *The Oxford History of the Classical World*, *op.cit.*, p. 395.
6. De Burgh, W.G., *op.cit.*, p. 266.
7. De Burgh, W.G., *ibid.*, pp. 253–61.
8. Grant, M., *op.cit.*, pp. 23–4; De Burgh, W.G., *op.cit.*, p. 253; *Western Civilisation*, pp. 154–5.
9. *Western Civilisation*, p. 156; Grant, M., *op.cit.*, p. 25.
10. *Western Civilisation*, p. 160.
11. *Ibid.*, pp. 166–8.

12. Fuller, *op.cit.*, p. 157.
13. *Western Civilisation*, pp. 165–6.
14. *Ibid.*, pp. 166–8.
15. Fuller, *op.cit.*, p. 181.
16. Grant, M., *The Fall of the Roman Empire* (London: Nelson, 1976) pp. 26–27.
17. *Ibid.*, p. 66.
18. *Ibid.*, pp. 73–84 and 100.
19. *Ibid.*, pp. 74–75.
20. *Ibid.*, pp. 203, 221.
21. *Ibid.*, p. 158.
22. *Ibid.*, p. 56.
23. *Ibid.*, p. 51.
24. Jones, A.M.H., *The Decline of the Ancient World* (London: Longman, 1968) pp. 362–3.
25. Norwich, J.J., *Byzantium – The Early Centuries* (London: Penguin, 1990) p. 311.
26. Starr, C.G., *The Roman Empire, 27BC–476AD* (Oxford: OUP, 1982) p. 81.
27. Mackenzie, Lord T. *Studies in Roman Law* (London: Butterworth, 1862) particularly pp. 7–28 *et passim*.
28. Norwich, *op.cit.*, pp. 196–7.
29. Mackenzie, *op.cit.*, pp. 30–31.
30. Cross, G. & Hand, G.J., *The English Legal System*, 5th ed. (London: Butterworth, 1971) p. 15.

3   CHRISTIANITY 100BC–1200AD

1. De Burgh, *op.cit.*, vol. 1, p. 9.
2. Grant, *The World of Rome*, pp. 181–3.
3. *Ibid.*, pp. 183–4.
4. *Ibid.*, p. 207.
5. *Ibid.*, pp. 208–11.
6. Dowley, T., (ed) *The History of Christianity* (Berkhamstead: Lion Publishing, 1977) pp. 130–1.
7. *Ibid.*, pp. 131–2
8. Norwich, *op.cit.*, pp. 42, 59–63.
9. Dowley, *op.cit.*, p. 134.
10. *Ibid.*, p. 179.
11. *Ibid.*, p. 134.
12. *Ibid.*, p. 135.
13. *Ibid.*, p. 183.
14. *Ibid.*, p. 180.
15. De Burgh, *op.cit.*, vol. 2., p. 378.
16. Burman, E., *Emperor to Emperor* (London: Constable, 1991) pp. 74–8.
17. Dowley, *op.cit.*, p. 140.
18. *Western Civilisation*, p. 204; Downley, *op.cit.*, pp. 142, 193–4.
19. Downley, *Ibid.*, p. 190.
20. *Ibid.*, pp. 191–3.
21. *Ibid.*, pp. 173–8, 243–4.

22. *Ibid.*, pp. 245–7.
23. Mayr-Harting, H., *The Coming of Christianity to Anglo-Saxon England* (London: Batsford, 1972) p. 52.
24. Hughes, K., *The Church in Early Irish Societies* (London: Methuen, 1966) p. 35.
25. Mayr-Harting, *op.cit.*, p. 86.
26. Whitelock, D., McKitterick, R., Dunville, D., *Ireland in Early Medieval Europe* (Cambridge: University Press, 1982), p. 120. Hughes, *op.cit.*, p. 105.
27. Hughes, *op.cit.*, p. 105.
28. *Ibid.*, p. 106.
29. Killen, W. D., *Ecclesiastical History of Ireland* (London: Macmillan, 1875) vol. 1., pp. 130–3, 141. Whitelock, *op.cit.*, p. 120.
30. Killen, *op.cit.*, p. 210.
31. Keith, D., *A History of Scotland* (Edinburgh: Paterson, 1886) vol. 2., pp. 290–307.

4 THE PAPACY AND THE FOUNDATION OF THE HOLY ROMAN EMPIRE 700–1000AD

1. Bryce, Viscount J., *The Holy Roman Empire* (London: Macmillan, 1919) pp. 90–5.
2. Davis, R. H. C., *A History of Medieval Europe* (London: Longman, 1957) pp. 90–3.
3. *Ibid.*, pp. 96–9.
4. Burman, *op.cit.*, p. 29.
5. Norwich, J.J., *op.cit.*, vol. 1, pp. 364–5.
6. Chamberlin, R., *Charlemagne* (London: Grafton, 1986) p. 183.
7. Norwich, *op.cit.*, p. 375.
8. Norwich, *op.cit.*, vol. 1, p. 380; vol. 2, p. 3.
9. *Ibid.*, vol. 2, pp. 3–4.
10. *Ibid.*, p. 12.
11. Jones, G., *A History of the Vikings* (Oxford: Oxford University Press, 1984) pp. 182–202.
12. *Ibid.*, pp. 213–18.
13. *Ibid.*, pp. 228–32.
14. Pounds, N. J. G., *An Economic History of Medieval Europe* (London: Longman, 1974) pp. 72–84.
15. Bloch, M, *Feudal Society* (London: Routledge & Kegan Paul, 1962) p. 154.
16. *Ibid.*, p. 157.
17. *Ibid.*, pp. 153 ff.
18. *Ibid.*, pp. 243–54.
19. *Ibid.*, p. 147.
20. *Ibid.*, pp. 190 ff.
21. *Ibid.*, pp. 211 ff.
22. *Ibid.*, p. 443.

5 EASTERN EUROPE 600–1100AD

1. Browning, R., *The Byzantine Empire* (London: Weidenfeld & Nicolson, 1980) pp. 46–7 and 63–64.

2. Vernadsky, G., *A History of Russia (hereinafter History)* (New Haven: Yale, 5th ed. 1961) pp. 24–8. Browning, *op.cit.*, p. 51
3. Browning, *Ibid.*, p. 53.
4. Baynes, N.H., *The Byzantine Empire* (London: Oxford University Press, 1962) p. 130; Browning, *Ibid*, pp. 49–50 and and 63–5.
5. Hosch, E., *The Balkans* (London: Faber, 1972) p. 59.
6. Dowley, *op.cit.*, p. 310.
7. Jones, *The Vikings, op.cit.*, pp. 246–7.
8. Vernadsky, *op.cit.*, pp. 29–34; Norwich, *op.cit.*, vol. 2, p. 66; Jones, *Vikings*, p. 266.
9. Vernadsky, *op.cit.*, p. 40; Jones, *Vikings*, p. 263.
10. Vernadsky, *op.cit.*, p. 41.
11. *Ibid*, pp. 50–2.
12. *Ibid.*, pp. 44–6; Vernadsky, G., *A History of Russia, vol. 3, The Mongols* (New Haven: Yale, 1948) pp. 372–3;
13. Vernadsky, *History*, pp. 47–50.
14. Browning, *op.cit.*, p. 94.
15. Norwich, *op.cit.*, vol. 2., pp. 316–7.
16. Browning, *op.cit*, pp. 87–92.
17. Norwich, *op.cit*, vol. 2, pp. 340–1.

6 THE HIGH MIDDLE AGES: THE POWER OF THE PAPACY 1000–1300AD

1. Pounds, N. J. G., *An Economic History of Medieval Europe (hereinafter Medieval Europe)* (London: Longmans, 1974) pp. 90–107. Roerig, F., *The Medieval Town* (Batsford, 1967) p. 73.
2. Pounds, N. J. G., *An Historical Geography of Europe (hereinafter Historical Geography)* (Cambridge: Cambridge University Press, 1990) pp. 124–5.
3. Crump, C. G., *The Legacy of the Middle Ages* (Oxford: Clarendon, 1926) pp. 25 and 48.
4. *Ibid.*, p. 42.
5. *Ibid.*, pp. 328–55.
6. Bryce, *op.cit.*, pp. 233–4.
7. *Ibid.*, p. 261.
8. *Ibid.*, pp. 209 and 225.
9. Norwich, J. J., *The Normans in the South* (London: Longman, 1967) p. 197.
10. *Western Civilisation*, p. 279.
11. Davis, *op.cit.*, p. 245.
12. *Penguin Atlas of World History* (Harmondsworth, 1974) vol. 1, p. 153.
13. Trevor-Roper, H., *The Rise of Christian Europe* (London: Thames & Hudson, 2nd ed. 1966) p. 126.
14. Barraclough, R. R. (ed.), *Eastern and Western Europe in the Middle Ages* (London: Thames & Hudson, 1970) p. 60.
15. *Ibid.*, p. 65.
16. Barraclough, *op.cit.*, pp. 70–1.
17. Tilly. C. and Blockmans, W. P., *Cities and the Rise of States in Europe, AD 1000–1800* (Oxford: Westview, 1994) pp. 32–6. Roerig, *op.cit.*, p. 56.

18. Pounds, *Medieval Europe*, p. 362.
19. Kam, V., *Accounting Theory* (New York: Wiley, 1990) pp. 14–18.
20. Lovell, C. R., *English Constitutional and Legal History* (Oxford: Oxford University Press, 1962) p. 80.
21. Stubbs, W., *The Constitutional History of England, 5th ed.* (Oxford: Oxford University Press: 1903) vol. 1, section 155, pp. 569 ff.
22. Lovell, *op.cit.*, pp. 60–1.
23. *Ibid.*, pp. 62–5, 109–10, 138.
24. *Ibid.*, p. 117.
25. *Ibid.*, pp. 183–6.
26. *Ibid.*, p. 194.
27. *Ibid.*, p. 190.
28. Vernadsky, G., *The Mongols and Russia* (New Haven: Yale, 1963) pp. 334–47.

7 THE END OF THE MIDDLE AGES AND THE RISE OF STATES 1300–1500AD

1. Ziegler, P., *The Black Death* (London: Collins, 1969) pp. 233–47.
2. *Ibid.*, pp. 267–77.
3. *Ibid.*, pp. 240 and 273.
4. Holmes, G., *Europe: Hierarchy and Revolt 1320–1450* (London: Fontana/Collins 1975) pp. 169–79.
5. *Ibid.*, pp. 183–191.
6. Lee, S. J., *Aspects of European History 1494–1789* (London: Methuen, 1984) p. 11.
7. Holmes, *op.cit.*, pp. 189–91.
8. *Ibid.*, p. 158; Dowley, *op.cit.*, p. 341.
9. Bryce, *op.cit.*, p. 222.
10. Holmes, *op.cit.*, pp. 195–201; Dowley, *op.cit.*, pp. 338–9.
11. Holmes, *op.cit.*, p. 56.
12. Tilly, *op.cit.*, pp. 101 and 109.
13. Roerig, *op.cit.*, pp. 182–6.
14. Lee, *op.cit.*, p. 93; Crump, *op.cit.*, p. 483.
15. Lee, *op.cit.*, pp. 95–6.
16. See Kohn, H., 'The Modernity of Nationalism' in Tipton, C. L. (ed.), *Nationalism in the Middle Ages*, (New York: Holt, Rinehart & Winston, 1972) pp. 7–13.
17. Strayer, J. R., 'Laicisation and Nationalism in the Thirteenth Century', in Tipton, *op.cit.*, pp. 32–4.
18. Hertz, F., 'The Role of the Medieval Church', in Tipton, *op.cit.*, pp. 65–9.
19. Lovell, *op.cit.*, pp. 70–71; Stubbs, *op.cit.*, vol. 3, pp. 300–1, 342.
20. Hertz, *op.cit.*, and Keeney, B. C., 'England' in Tipton, *op.cit.*, pp. 55 and 87–97.
21. At the Lateran Council of 1139, Microsoft (R), Encarta (R) 96 Encyclopaedia, Microsoft Corporation, 1993–5.
22. Hertz, *Ibid.*, pp. 55–6.
23. Tipton, *op.cit.*, p. 4.
24. Galbraith, V. H., *Language and Nationality*, in Tipton, *op.cit.*, p. 45.
25. *Ibid.*, p. 52.

26. Schmickler, E. D., 'Thuringia's Cultural Landmark' in *German Comments*, (Osnabruck, Fromm, n. 40), 1995, p. 92.
27. Browning, *op.cit.*, pp. 160–74.
28. *Ibid.*, p. 176.
29. *Ibid.*, p. 179.
30. Hay, D., *The Renaissance Debate* (New York: Holt, Rinehart & Winston, 1965) pp. 31, 43–47, 65–9, 99–105; Holmes, *op.cit.*, pp. 301–11; Lee, *op.cit.*, p. 8.
31. Holmes, *op.cit.*, pp. 231–5.
32. Grey, I., *Ivan III and the Unification of Russia* (Harmondsworth: Pelican, 1973) p. 20.
33. Grey, *Ibid.*, p. 21; Vernadsky, *Mongols*, pp. 377–8.
34. Sumner, B., *Survey of Russian History* (London: Methuen, 1961) pp. 75–6.
35. Vernadsky, *Mongols*, p. 374.
36. *Ibid.*, pp. 346–9.
37. *Ibid.*, pp. 368–9.
38. *Ibid.*, p. 358.
39. *Ibid.*, pp. 355–65.
40. Barraclough, *op.cit.*, pp. 167–74.

8 THE EXPANSION OF EUROPE AND THE FIRST COLONIAL EMPIRES 1500–1650AD

1. Jones, G., *op.cit.*, pp. 298–304.
2. Hobhouse, H., *Seeds of Change – Five Plants that Transformed Mankind* (London: Papermac, 1992) pp. 106–8.
3. Kennedy, P., *The Rise and Fall of the Great Powers* (London: Unwin, 1988) pp. xvi, 19–20.
4. Davis, R., *The Rise of the Atlantic Economies* (London: Weidenfeld & Nicolson, 1973) pp. 125–32.
5. Hobhouse, *op.cit.*, pp. 28–30 and 44–60.
6. Davis, *op.cit.*, pp. 125–9.
7. Hobhouse, *op.cit.*, pp. 68–9; Davis, *op.cit.*, pp. 262–3.
8. Davis, *ibid.*, pp. 235–49.
9. *Ibid.*, pp. 242–6.
10. Jayne, K. G., *Vasco da Gama and his Successors* (London: Methuen, 1970) pp. 31–2.
11. Howard, M., *War in European History* (Oxford: Oxford University Press, 1984 ed.) pp. 32–3.
12. Kennedy, *op.cit.*, pp. 52–3; Tilly, *op.cit.*, p. 168.
13. Tilly, *ibid.*, pp. 24–5.
14. Tilly, *ibid.*, p. 175; Kennedy, *op.cit.*, p. 54.
15. Elliott, J. H., *Imperial Spain 1469–1716* (Harmondsworth: Penguin, 1970) pp. 110–11.)
16. *Ibid.*, pp. 305–8.
17. *Ibid.*, p. 311.
18. *Ibid.*, pp. 312–5.
19. Tilly, *op.cit.*, p. 211.
20. Davis, *op.cit.*, pp. 180–5.

21. Lilly, *op.cit.*, p. 197.
22. Davis, *op.cit.*, p. 113.
23. Howard, *op.cit.*, p. 55.

9 REFORMATION, COUNTER REFORMATION AND
   RELIGIOUS WAR 1500–1650AD

1 McGrath, A. E., *A Life of John Calvin* (Oxford: Blackwell, 1993) p. 9.
2. *Ibid.*, p. 11.
3. Lee, *op.cit.*, p. 24; McGrath, *op.cit.*, p. 273; Dowley, *op.cit.*, p. 360.
4. Elton, G. R., *Reformation Europe, 1517–1559* (Glasgow: Fontana/Collins, 1971) p. 152.
5. Schmickler, E. D., 'Thuringia's Cultural Landmark', in German Comments, no. 40, Oct. 1995 (Osnabrück: Fromm,) p. 92.
6. Lee, *op.cit.*, pp. 21–2.
7. Weber, M., *The Protestant Ethic and the Spirit of Capitalism* (London: Routledge reprint, 1992) pp. 80–5.
8. McGrath, *op.cit.*, p. 1.
9. *Ibid.*, pp. 102–4, 168; Weber, *op.cit.*, pp. 101–4.
10. Weber, *op.cit.*, pp. 106–11.
11. Weber, *op.cit.*, pp. 85, 157–62; McGrath, *op.cit.*, pp. 232, 245.
12. Weber, *op.cit.*, p. 141.
13. McGrath, *op.cit.*, pp. 230–1.
14. *Ibid.*, pp. 180–6.
15. Lee, *op.cit.*, pp. 41–2.
16. *Ibid.*, pp. 42–5.
17. McGrath, *op.cit.*, p. 202.
18. Elliott, J. H., *Europe Divided 1559–1598* (Glasgow: Fontana/Collins, 1974) p. 307.
19. The term originates from the German word '*Eidgnoss*' or 'confederate', referring to the Swiss reformers; McGrath, *op.cit.*, p. 88.
20. Dickens, A. G., *The English Reformation* (Glasgow: Fontana/Collins, 1972) p. 138.
21. *Ibid.*, p. 154.
22. *Ibid.*, p. 158.
23. *Ibid.*, pp. 162–74.
24. *Ibid.*, pp. 229–39.
25. *Ibid.*, pp. 183, 193.
26. Ellis, S. G., *Tudor Ireland* (London: Longman, 1985) p. 27; Dickens, *op.cit.*, pp. 304–5.
27. Dickens, *ibid.*, p. 364.
28. *Ibid.*, pp. 408–13.
29. Mattingley, G., *The Armada* (Boston: Houghton Mifflin, 1959) pp. 397–400.
30. Alcock, A. E., *Understanding Ulster* (Lurgan: Ulster Society, 1994) pp. 10–11, 22–3.
31. Heater, D., *The Idea of European Unity* (Leicester: University Press, 1992) pp. 21–33.

32.   Parker, G., *Europe in Crisis 1598–1648* (Glasgow: Fontana/Collins, 1979) p. 216.
33.   Howard, M., *op.cit.*, pp. 57–60; Parker, *ibid.*, pp. 209–11.
34.   Wedgwood, C. V., *The Thirty Years War* (London: Cape, 1968) pp. 510–21; Lee, *op.cit.*, pp. 113–23.
35.   Lee, *ibid.*, p. 119.
36.   Trevelyan, G. M., *England under Queen Anne*, vol. 1 (Blenheim), London, Fontana/Collins, 1965, p. 116.

10   CONTINENTAL ABSOLUTISM AND ENGLISH POLITICAL LIBERTY 1650–1789AD

1.   Hobbes, T., ed. C. B. Macpherson, *Leviathan* (Harmondsworth: Pelican, 1968) esp. chs. 13, 14, 29, 30; Warrender, H., *The Political Philosophy of Hobbes* (Oxford: Clarendon, 1970) pp. 103–45: von Leyden, W., *Hobbes and Locke* (London: Macmillan, 1987) pp. 177–8.
2.   Cobban, A., *A History of Modern France, vol. 1, 1715–1799* (Harmondsworth: Penguin, 1973) p. 29.
3.   Lee, S. J., *op.cit.*, p. 260.
4.   Cobban, *op.cit.*, p. 10.
5.   *Ibid.*, pp. 11–13; Rudé, G., *Revolutionary Europe, 1783–1815* (Glasgow: Fontana/Collins, 1964) pp. 15–16.
6.   Rudé, *Ibid.*, p. 115.
7.   Hufton, R., *Europe: Privilege and Protest 1730–1789* (Glasgow: Fontana/Collins, 1980) p. 59.
8.   Cobban, *op.cit.*, pp. 29–30.
9.   *Penguin Atlas of World History, vol. 1* (Harmondsworth: Penguin, 1974) p. 259.
10.   Cobban, *op.cit.*, p. 58.
11.   *Penguin Atlas, op.cit.*, p. 259.
12.   Rudé, *op.cit.*, p. 41.
13.   Cobban, *op.cit.*, pp. 74–5.
14.   Craig, G. A., *The Politics of the Prussian Army* (Oxford: Clarendon, 1955) pp. 1–7; Feuchtwanger, E. J., *Prussia – Myth and Reality* (London: Wolff, 1974) pp. 29–31.
15.   Craig, *op.cit.*, pp. 7–8.
16.   *Ibid.*, p. 15.
17.   Feuchtwanger, *op.cit.*, pp. 48–9.
18.   Craig, *op.cit.*, (quoting Ergang, R., *The Potsdam Führer – Frederick William I, Father of Prussian Militarism* (New York, 1941) p. 122).
19.   Craig, *ibid.*, p. 19.
20.   Yanov, A., *The Origins of Autocracy* (Berkeley: University of California, 1981) pp. 2–3, 115.
21.   *Ibid.*, p. 18.
22.   Kochan, *op.cit.*, pp. 54–5.
23.   Yanov, *op.cit.*, pp. 53–4, 247.
24.   Sumner, *op.cit.*, pp. 131–4.
25.   Guroff, G, and Carstenson, F. V., *Entrepreneurship in Imperial Russia and the Soviet Union* (Princeton University Press, 1983) pp. 32–62; Sumner, *op.cit.*, p. 100.

26. Kochan, *op.cit.*, pp. 108–9.
27. *Ibid.*, pp. 106, 111–2; Treasure, G., *The Making of Modern Europe* (London: Methuen, 1985) p. 576.
28. *Ibid.*, p. 110.
29. Treasure, *op.cit.*, p. 553.
30. Lee, *op.cit.*, pp. 77–83.
31. Treasure, *op.cit.*, pp. 527–48; Hufton, *op.cit.*, pp. 134–6.
32. Cipolla, C. M., *The Fontana Economic History of Europe, vol. 3 (The Industrial Revolution)* (Glasgow: Fontana/Collins, 1973) p. 512; Lee, *op.cit.*, p. 262.
33. Lee, *op.cit.*, p. 254.
34. Stone, *op.cit.*, pp. 67–77.
35. *Ibid.*, pp. 82, 99–102.
36. *Ibid.*, p. 85.
37. *Ibid.*, pp. 91–3.
38. *Ibid.*, pp. 118–38.
39. Locke, J., ed. Laslett, P., *Two Treatises of Government* (London: New English Library, 1965) pp. 115, 395, 402–3; von Leyden, *op.cit.*, p. 188.
40. Dickinson, H. T., *Bolingbroke* (London: Constable, 1970) pp. 197–202.
41. Stone, *op.cit.*, p. 147.
42. Colley, L., *Britons* (London: Pimlico, 1994) pp. 77–9.
43. Heater, *op.cit.*, pp. 66–90.
44. *Ibid.*, pp. 93–4.

11 THE INDUSTRIAL AND FRENCH REVOLUTIONS 1750–1850AD

1. Stearns, P. N., *The Industrial Revolution in World History* (Oxford: Westview, 1993) p. 5.
2. *Ibid.*
3. Mannion, A. M., *Agriculture and Environmental Change* (Chichester: Wiley, 1995) pp. 86–8.
4. Cook, C. and Stevenson, J., *The Longman Handbook of Modern European History 1763–1991* (London: Longman, 1992) p. 235.
5. Hobhouse, *op.cit.*, pp. 148–57.
6. Fuller, J. F. C., *op.cit.*, vol. 2, pp. 16–17.
7. Weber, M., *op.cit.*, p. 175; Stearns, *op.cit.*, p. 39.
8. Cobban, *op.cit.*, p. 136.
9. *Ibid.*, p. 144.
10. Kohn, H, *Prelude to Nation States* (New York: Van Nostrand, 1967) p. 26.
11. Wordsworth, W., *The Prelude, Bk. IX, 1. 108*, ed. E. de Selincourt (Oxford: Clarendon, 1959).
12. Freeman, M., *Edmund Burke and the Critique of Political Radicalism* (Oxford: Blackwell, 1980) pp. 14, 29.
13. O'Sullivan, N., *Conservatism* (London: Dent, 1976) pp. 11–12.
14. Cobban, *op.cit.*, p. 184.
15. Cobban, A., *National Self Determination* (London: Oxford University Press, 1944) p. 5.

16. Bernard Le Nail, in Doherty, M., 'Brittany: An Example of the Continuing Strength of French Centralism' (M. Phil. thesis: University of Ulster, 1990) p. 59.
17. Kohn, *op.cit.*, pp. 88–90.
18. *Ibid.*, pp. 53–6.
19. *Ibid.*, p. 71.
20. *Ibid.*, pp. 119–21.
21. *Ibid.*, pp. 170–83.
22. *Ibid.*, p. 226.
23. *Ibid.*, p. 257.
24. *Ibid.*, pp. 275–7.
25. Heater, *op.cit.*, pp. 102–10.
26. Droz, J., *Europe between Revolutions* 1815–1848 (Glasgow: Fontana/Collins, 1977) pp. 16–17.
27. Kuitenbrouwer, M., *The Netherlands and the Rise of Modern Imperialism* (Oxford: Berg, 1991) pp. 11–12.
28. Stearns, *op.cit.*, p. 82.
29. Henderson, W. O., *The Zollverein* (London: Cass, 1968) pp. 10, 21–33.
30. *Ibid.*, pp. 41–9.
31. *Ibid.*, p. 55.
32. *Ibid.*, pp. 143–7.
33. Droz, *op.cit.*, p. 135; Colley, *op.cit.*, p. 348 gives a figure of 656 000.
34. Alcock, A. E., *History of the International Labour Organisation* (London: Macmillan, 1970) pp. 4–5.
35. *Ibid.*, p. 6.
36. Marx, K and Engels, F., *The Communist Manifesto (ed. Taylor, A. J. P.)* (Harmondsworth: Penguin, 1967) p. 121.
37. Lee, S. J., *Aspects of European History 1789–1980* (London: Methuen, 1982) pp. 56–62.
38. Kochan, *op.cit.*, p. 156.
39. Kennedy, *op.cit.*, pp. 154–6.
40. Stearns, *op.cit.*, p. 131.
41. Dyson, K. and Wilks, S (eds), *Industrial Crisis: A Comparative Study of the State and Industry* (Oxford: Robertson, 1983) p. 64; Duchene, F. and Shepherd, G. (eds), *Managing Industrial Change in Western Europe* (London: Pinter, 1987) p. 149.
42. Mathias, P., *The First Industrial Nation* (London: Methuen, 1969) p. 32.
43. Stearns, *op.cit.*, pp. 46–7.

12   THE UNCERTAIN GIANT 1850–1914AD

1. Taylor, A.J.P., *The Struggle for the Mastery of Europe, 1848–1918* (Oxford: Oxford University Press, 1971) p. 61; Lee, *1789*, p. 70.
2. Procacci, G., *History of the Italian People* (Harmondsworth: Penguin, 1970) pp. 318–21.
3. Thomson, D., *Europe since Napoleon* (Harmondsworth: Penguin, 1974) p. 309.
4. *Ibid.*, p. 313.
5. Henderson, *op.cit.*, pp. 316–8.

6. Feuchtwanger, *op.cit.*, p. 195.
7. Hoensch, J., *A History of Modern Hungary, 1867–1986* (London: Longman, 1989) pp. 16–18.
8. Thomson, *op.cit.*, pp. 316–7.
9. *Ibid.*, pp. 321, 395.
10. Procacci, *op.cit.*, pp. 331–2.
11. Feuchtwanger, *op.cit.*, p. 196.
12. *Penguin Atlas of World History, op.cit.*, vol. 2, p. 77.
13. *Ibid.*, p. 65.
14. Cook, C. and Stevenson, J., *The Longman Handbook of Modern European History 1763–1991* (London: Longman, 1992) pp. 246 50.
15 Kennedy, *op.cit.*, p. 211.
16. Guroff and Carstenson, *op.cit.*, pp. 77–82.
17. Kennedy, *op.cit.*, pp. 233–4.
18. Kennedy, *op.cit.*, pp. 222–3.
19. Taylor, *op.cit.*, pp. xxix–xxx.
20. Kennedy, *op.cit.*, p. 204.
21. *Ibid.*, pp. 224–8.
22. Pounds, *An Historical Geography of Europe* (Cambridge University Press, 1993) p. 349.
23. Kuitenbrouwer, *op.cit.*, p. 353.
24. Cook and Stevenson, *op.cit.*, pp. 236–8.
25. With regard particularly to Britain see Bayly, G. (ed.), *Atlas of the British Empire* (London: Guild, 1989) p. 250.
26. Thomson, *op.cit.*, pp. 278–80.
27. Roberts, S.H., *The History of French Colonial Policy 1870–1925* (London: Cass, 1963) pp. 18, 100–1.
28. *Ibid.*, pp. 27, 100–3.
29. Kuitenbrouwer, *op.cit.*, pp. 209–10.
30. Roberts, *op.cit.*, pp. 105–113.
31. Pounds, *op.cit.*, p. 361.
32. Yacono, X., *Histoire de la Colonisation Française* (Paris: Presses Universitaires de France, 1979) p. 62; Kuitenbrouwer, *op.cit.*, p. 280; Bayly, *op.cit.*, pp. 97, 131.
33. Hobhouse, *op.cit.*, pp. 30–2.
34. De Gobineau, A., *Essay sur l'Inegalité des Races Humaines (1854)* (Paris: Firmin-Didot, 1940) vol. 1, pp. 24, 214–23.
35. Chamberlain, H.S., *The Foundations of the Nineteenth Century (1899)* (New York: Fertig, 1977) vol. 1, pp. 202–5.
36. Alcock, A.E., *op.cit.*, p. 7.
37. *Ibid.*, p. 8.
38. Moorehead, A., *The Russian Revolution* (Glasgow: Collins–Hamish Hamilton, 1958) p. 49.
39. *Ibid.*, pp. 58–63.
40. McSweeney, B., *Roman Catholicism* (Oxford: Blackwell, 1980) p. 78; Corbett, J.A., *The Papacy* (London: Macmillan, 1956) p. 82.
41. Procacci, *op.cit.*, p. 378.
42. Taylor, *op.cit.*, p. 328.
43. *Ibid.*, pp. 328–9; Liddell Hart, B., *History of the First World War* (London: Pan, 1970) p. 6.

44. *Ibid.*, pp. 344, 349, 365.
45. Liddell Hart, *op.cit.*, pp. 6–7.
46. *Ibid.*, p. 9.
47. Moorehead, *op.cit.*, p. 75.
48. Taylor, *op.cit.*, pp. 443–5.
49. Liddell-Hart, *op.cit.*, p. 41; Taylor, *op.cit.*, p. 340.
50. Taylor, *ibid.*, p. 529.
51. Alcock, A.E., *The History of the South Tyrol Question* (London: Michael Joseph, 1970) p. 18.
52. Taylor, *op.cit.*, pp. 546–7, n. 5.

13 THE ZENITH OF NATIONALISM 1914–1945AD

1. *Penguin Atlas of World History, vol. 2*, p. 117.
2. Taylor, *op.cit.*, pp. xxix–xxx.
3. Cook and Stevenson, *op.cit.*, p. 135.
4. Scott, J.B., *President Wilson's Foreign Policy* (New York: Oxford University Press, 1918) pp. 354–63.
5. *Ibid.*, p. 368 ff.
6. Albrecht-Carrié, R., *Italy at the Peace Conference* (New York: Columbia, 1938) pp. 61–5; Seymour, C., 'Woodrow Wilson and Self-Determination in the Tyrol' in *Virginia Quarterly Review*, vol. 38, n. 4 (1962), p. 574; Baker, R.S., *Woodrow Wilson and World Settlement*, (London: Heinemann, 1923) vol. 2, p. 133.
7. Lyons, F.S., *Ireland Since the Famine* (Glasgow: Collins, 1973) pp. 367–70, 398–9.
8. Watt, R.M., *The Kings Depart* (Harmondsworth: Penguin, 1973) pp. 491, 557.
9. *Ibid.*, pp. 454, 503–4.
10. Kohn, *op.cit.*, p. 226.
11. Pearson, R., *National Minorities in Eastern Europe 1848–1945* (London: Macmillan, 1983) pp. 151–5.
12. Watt, *op.cit.*, pp. 348, 383–4.
13. Pearson, *op.cit.*, p. 51.
14. Ullman. R.H., *Intervention and the War* (Princeton University Press, 1961) pp. 69–70.
15. Watt, *op.cit.*, p. 557.
16. Bullock, A., *Hitler – A Study in Tyranny* (Harmondsworth: Penguin, 1962) p. 75.
17. *Ibid.*, p. 115.
18. Hibbert, C., *Benito Mussolini* (Harmondsworth: Penguin, 1962) pp. 42–7.
19. *Ibid.*, pp. 49–50.
20. *Ibid.*, pp. 64–5.
21. Procacci, *op.cit.*, p. 430; Thomson, *op.cit.*, p. 659.
22. Sabine, G.H. and Thorson, T.L., *A History of Political Theory*, 4th ed. (Orlando: Harcourt Brace, 1973) p. 818.
23. See, for example, Alcock, *South Tyrol, op.cit.*, pp. 33–40.
24. Sabine, *op.cit.*, p. 815.
25. *Penguin Atlas, vol. 2*, p. 167.
26. Alcock, *Understanding Ulster*, pp. 35–76 *passim*.

27. Heater, D., *op.cit.*, pp. 133–48.
28. Deutscher, I., *Stalin* (Harmondsworth: Penguin, 1966) pp. 284–7.
29. Kochan, *op.cit.*, p. 279.
30. Sumner, *op.cit.*, pp. 342–3.
31. *Ibid.*, pp. 108–9, 343.
32. *Ibid.*, p. 349.
33. Kochan, *op.cit.*, pp. 287–8.
34. For the details see Conquest, R., *The Great Terror* (Harmondsworth: Penguin, 1971) especially ch. 7.
35. Bullock, *op.cit.*, pp. 269–77, 309.
36. *Ibid.*, pp. 284–307.
37. Bullock, *op.cit.*, pp. 279, 339.
38. Churchill, W.S., *The Second World War, Vol. 1* (London: Cassell, 1948) pp. 108–9.
39. Alcock, *South Tyrol*, pp. 45–59.
40. Bullock, *op.cit.*, p. 452.
41. Morison, S.E., *The Two-Ocean War* (New York: Ballantine, 1963) pp. 26–31.
42. Moynahan, B., *The Claws of the Bear* (London: Arrow, 1990) p. 84.
43. Kennedy, *op.cit.*, p. 343.
44. Moynahan, *op.cit.*, pp. 117–8; Toland, J., *The Rising Sun* (New York: Bantam, 1970) p. 139.
45. Bullock, *op.cit.*, p. 662.
46. Kennedy, *op.cit.*, p. 331.
47. *Penguin Atlas, vol. 2*, p. 218.

14 DIVISION AND INTEGRATION 1945–1995AD

1. Mahotière, S. de la, *Towards One Europe* (Harmondsworth: Pelican, 1970) p. 19.
2. Mayne, R., *The Recovery of Europe* (London: Weidenfeld & Nicolson, 1970) pp. 148–9; Alcock, *ILO., op.cit.*, p. 211.
3. Mayne, *ibid.*, p. 107.
4. *Ibid.*, p. 127.
5. Hoffman, S. (ed.), *A La Recherche de la France* (Paris: Editions de Seuil, 1963) p. 71.
6. Lipgens, W. (ed.), *Documents on the History of European Integration* (Berlin: De Gruyter, 1985) vol. 1., pp. 680–1.
7. Brugmans, H., *L'Idée Européenne 1920–70* (Bruges: De Tempel, 1970) p. 132.
8. Mowat, R. C., *Creating the European Community* (London: Blandford, 1973) p. 26.
9. Mayne, *op.cit.*, p. 198.
10. Brugman, *op.cit.*, p. 149.
11. Spaak, P. H., *Combats Inachevés* (Paris: Fayard, 1969) vol. 2., p. 26.
12. Mayne, *op.cit.*, p. 168.
13. Mowat, *op.cit.*, p. 28.
14. Spaak, *op.cit.*, p. 48.
15. Text of the ECSC Treaty in *European Community Treaties* (London: Sweet & Maxwell, 1980) pp. 3–47.
16. Mowat, *op.cit.*, pp. 102–12.
17. Camps, M., *Britain and the European Community 1955–1963* (London: Oxford University Press, 1964) pp. 14–17.

18. The Messina Resolution in Camps, *ibid.*, pp. 520–2.
19. Charlton, M., 'How and Why Britain Lost the Leadership of Europe' in *Encounter* (London) vol. 57, n. 2, pp. 9–22.
20. Thomas, H., *The Suez Affair* (Harmondsworth: Penguin, 1970) pp. 55–61.
21. *Ibid.*, pp. 163–4.
22. Charlton, *op.cit.* in '*Encounter*', vol. 57, n. 3, pp. 22–33.
23. Bromberger, M. and S., *Jean Monnet and the United States of Europe* (New York: Coward–McCann, 1969) pp. 146–9.
24. *Ibid.*, p. 172.
25. Text of the EEC Treaty in Sweet and Maxwell, *op.cit.*
26. Text of the so-called Merger Treaty of 8 April 1965 in Sweet & Maxwell, op.cit., pp. 233–42
27. See for example Werth, A., *De Gaulle* (Harmondsworth: Penguin, 1965) Chapters 4 and 5.
28. Kolodsiej, E. A., *French International Policy under De Gaulle and Pompidou* (London: Cornell, 1974) pp. 241–4.
29. Werth, *op.cit.*, pp. 325–6.
30. Kolodsiej, *ibid.*, p. 42.
31. *Ibid.*, pp. 320–21.
32. Newhouse, J., *De Gaulle and the Anglo-Saxons* (London: Deutsch, 1970) p. 207.
33. Kolodsiej, *op.cit.*, pp. 281–3; Marjolin, R., *Le Travail d'une Vie* (Paris: Laffont, 1986) pp. 314–17.
34. Graduate Institute of International Studies, *The European Free Trade Association and the Crisis of European Integration* (London: Michael Joseph, 1968) p. 165; Beloff, N., *The General Says No* (Harmondsworth: Penguin, 1963) p. 136; Marjolin, *op.cit.*, p. 336.
35. Marjolin, *op.cit.*, p. 330.
36. Newhouse, *op.cit.*, p. 227; Camps, *op.cit.*, p. 502.
37. De Gaulle, C., *Discours et Messages* (Paris: Plon, 1970) vol. 4, pp. 61–79.
38. Wilson, H., *The Labour Government 1964–1970* (London: Weidenfeld & Nicolson and Michael Joseph, 1971) p. 393.
39. De Gaulle, *op.cit.*, (pp. 373–81; Marjolin, *op.cit.*, pp. 343–9.
40. Text of the so-called Luxembourg Compromise in Sweet & Maxwell, *op.cit.*, pp. 249–50.
41. Kolodsiej, *op.cit.*, pp. 405–15.
42. Text of the SEA in *Official Journal of the European Communities*, no. L169 of 29 June 1987, Luxembourg, office of the official Publications of the European Community.
43. *Costa* v. *Enel*, Case 6/64 in European Court of Justice, Court Reports 1964, Luxembourg, office of the official Publications of the European Community, pp. 585–616; Louis, J. V., *The Community Legal Order*, Commission of the European Communities, Luxembourg, 1990. pp. 135–9.
44. *Van Gend & Loos*, Case 26/62, European Court of Justice, Court Reports 1963, Luxembourg, office of the official publications of the European Community, pp. 1–30; Louis, *ibid.*, p. 109.
45. Commission of the European Communities, *Agreement on the European Economic Area*, Luxembourg, office of the official Publications of the European Community, 1992.

46. Pearson, R., *The Rise and Fall of the Soviet Empire* (London: Macmillan, 1997) p. 80.
47. *Ibid.*, pp. 61, 72–3.
48. *Ibid.*, p. 84.
49. *Ibid.*, p. 102.
50. *Ibid.*, pp. 90–1.
51. *Ibid.*, p. 111.
52. Text of the Maastricht Treaty on European Union in *Official Journal of the European Communities*, no. C. 224 of 31 August 1992, Luxembourg, Commission of the European Communities.
53. *The Times* (London), 8 December 1992.
54. Keesing's *Record of World Events*, vol. 40, no. 11, 1994, p. 40297.
55. See, for example, *Is the West Doing Enough for Eastern Europe?* (Brussels: Philip Morris Institute for Public Policy Research) no. 5, November 1994.
56. Keesing, *op.cit.*, vol. 38, no. 6, p. 38942 and vol. 39, no. 5, p. 39483.
57. *Ibid.*, vol. 38, no. 9, p. 39082.
58. Bonn Declaration of 18 July 1961 and statement by the Rt. Hon. Edward Heath, 10 April 1962, in Camps, *op.cit.*, pp. 522–30; *Membership of the European Communities*, Cmnd. 3269 (London: HMSO, May 1967).

Select Bibliography

Albrecht-Carrié, R., *Italy at the Peace Conference*, New York: Columbia, 1938.
Alcock, A. E., *The History of the South Tyrol Question*, London: Michael Joseph, 1970.
—— *History of the International Labour Organisation*, London: Macmillan, 1970.
—— *Understanding Ulster*, Lurgan, Ulster Society, 1994.
Aristotle, *The Politics* (ed. T. A. Sinclair), London, Penguin Classic Series, 1981.
Baker, R. S., *Woodrow Wilson and World Settlement*, London: Heinemann, 1923.
Barnett, C., *The Swordbearers*, Harmondsworth: Penguin, 1966.
Barraclough, R. R. (ed.), *Eastern and Western Europe in the Middle Ages*, London.
   Thames & Hudson, 1970.
Bayley, G., (ed.), *Atlas of the British Empire*, London: Guild, 1989.
Baynes, N. H., *The Byzantine Empire*, London: Oxford University Press, 1962.
Beloff, N., *The General Says No*, Harmondsworth: Penguin, 1963.
Bloch, M., *Feudal Society*, London: Routledge & Kegan Paul, 1962.
Boardman, J., Griffin, J. and Murray, O., *The Oxford History of the Classical World*,
   Oxford: University Press, 1986.
Braudel, F., *The Mediterranean and the Mediterranean World in the Age of Philip II*, 2 vols.,
   London: Collins, 1992–3.
Bromberger, M. & S., *Jean Monnet and the United States of Europe*, New York: Cow-
   ard–McCann, 1969.
Browning, R., *The Byzantine Empire*, London: Weidenfeld & Nicolson, 1980.
Brugmans, H., *L'Idée Européenne 1920–70*, Bruges: De Tempel, 1970.
Bryce, Viscount J., *The Holy Roman Empire*, London: Macmillan, 1919.
Bullock, A., *Hitler – A Study in Tyranny*, Harmondsworth: Penguin, 1962.
Burke, E., *Reflections on the Revolution in France* (1790), ed. C. C. O'Brien, London:
   Penguin, Classics, 1986.
Burman, E., *Emperor to Emperor*, London: Constable, 1991.
Camps, M., *Britain and the European Community 1955–1963*, London: Oxford Uni-
   versity Press, 1964.
Carew-Hunt, R. N., *The Theory and Practice of Communism*, Harmondsworth: Pen-
   guin, 1983.
Chamberlain, H. S., *The Foundations of the Nineteenth Century* (1899), New York:
   Fertig, 1977.
Chamberlain, R., *Charlemagne*, London: Grafton, 1986.
Churchill, W. S., *The Second World War*, 6 vols., London: Cassell, 1948.
Cipolla, C. M. (ed.), *The Fontana Economic History of Europe*, 6 vols., Glasgow:
   Fontana/Collins,
—— vol. 1 *The Middle Ages* (1972)
—— vol. 2 *The Sixteenth and Seventeenth Centuries* (1977)
—— vol. 3 *The Industrial Revolution* (1976)
—— vol. 4 *The Emergence of Industrial Societies* (1973)
—— vol. 5 *The Twentieth Century* (1977)
—— vol. 6 *Contemporary Economics* (1976)
Cobban, A., *A History of Modern France: vol. 1 1715–1799, Vol. 2 1799–1871; Vol. 3
   1871–1962* Harmondsworth: Penguin, 1973.

Cobban, A., *National Self-Determination*, London: Oxford University Press, 1944.

Colley, L., *Britons*, London: Pimlico, 1994.

Conquest, R., *The Great Terror*, Harmondsworth: Penguin, 1971.

Corbett, J. A., *The Papacy*, London: Macmillan, 1956.

Craig, G. A., *The Politics of the Prussian Army*, Oxford: Clarendon, 1926.

Cross, G. & Hand, G. J., *The English Legal System*, 5th ed., London: Butterworth, 1971.

Crump, C. G., *The Legacy of the Middle Ages*, Oxford: Clarendon, 1926.

Davis, R., *The Rise of the Atlantic Economies*, London: Weidenfeld & Nicolson, 1973.

Davis, R. H. C., *A History of Medieval Europe*, London: Longman, 1957.

De Burgh, W. G., *The Legacy of the Ancient World*, Harmondsworth: Penguin, 1955.

De Gaulle, C., *Discours et Messages*, vol. 4, Paris: Plon, 1970.

De Gobineau, A., *Essay sur l'Inegalité des Races Humaines* (1854), Paris: Firman–Didot, 1940.

De la Mahotière, S., *Towards One Europe*, Harmondsworth: Pelican, 1970.

Derry, T. K. *A. History of Scandinavia*, Minneapolis: University of Minnesota Press, 1979.

Deutscher, I., *Stalin*, Harmondsworth: Penguin, 1966.

Dickens, A. G., *The English Reformation*, Glasgow: Fontana/Collins, 1972.

Dickinson, G. L., *The Greek View of Life*, London: Methuen, 1912.

Dickinson, H. T., *Bolingbroke*, London: Constable, 1970.

Dinan, D., *Ever Closer Union?* London: Macmillan, 1994.

Doherty, M., *Brittany – An Example of the Continuing Strength of French Centralism*, M.Phil. thesis, University of Ulster, 1990.

Dowley, T., (ed.), *The History of Christianity*, Berkhamstead: Lion Publishing, 1977.

Droz, J., *Europe Between Revolutions 1815–1848*, Glasgow: Fontana/Collins, 1977.

Duchene, F. & Shepherd, G. (eds.), *Managing Industrial Change in Western Europe*, London: Pinter, 1987.

Dyson, K., *The State Tradition in Western Europe*, Oxford: Robertson, 1980.

Dyson, K., & Wilks, S., (eds), *Industrial Crisis: A Comparative Study of the State and Industry*, Oxford: Robertson, 1983.

Elliott, J. H., *Imperial Spain 1469–1716*, Harmondsworth: Penguin 1970.

Ellis, S. G., *Tudor Ireland*, London: Longmans, 1985.

Elton, G. R., *Reformation Europe 1517–1559*, Glasgow: Fontana/Collins, 1971.

Encounter, London, vol. 57, nos. 2&3.

European Commission, *Agreement on the European Economic Area*, Luxembourg, Office for the Official Publications of the European Communities, 1992.

—— *Official Journal*, Series C., Series L., Luxembourg, Office for Official Publications of the European Communities.

—— *Treaties Establishing the European Communities* (1987 ed.), Office for Official Publications of the European Communities, 1987.

European Court of Justice, *Court Reports*, Series, 1954–1995, Luxembourg, Office for Official Publications of the European Communities.

Feuchtwanger, E. J., *Prussia – Myth and Reality*, London: Wolff, 1974.

Fisher, H. A. L., *A History of Europe*, 2 vols., Glasgow: Fontana/Collins, 1986.

Freeman, M., *Edmund Burke and the Critique of Political Radicalism*, Oxford: Blackwell, 1980.

Freymond, J., *The Saar Conflict 1945–1955*, New York, Praeger, 1960.

Fuller, J. F. C., *The Decisive Battles of the Western World* (ed. J. Terraine), 2 vols, London: Paladin, 1970.

Fursdon, E., *The European Defence Community*, London: Macmillan, 1980.
George, S., *An Awkward Partner – Britain in the European Community*, Oxford: University Press, 1990.
German Comments, Osnabruck, Fromm, n. 40 (1995).
Graduate Institute of International Studies, *The European Free Trade Association and the Crisis of European Integration*, London: Michael Joseph, 1968.
Grant, M., *The World of Rome*, New York: Mentor, 1964.
—— *The Fall of the Roman Empire*, London: Nelson, 1976.
Grey, I., *Ivan III and the Unification of Russia*, Harmondsworth: Pelican, 1973.
Guenée, B., *States and Rulers in Later Medieval Europe*, Oxford: Blackwell, 1985.
Guroff, G. and Carstenson, F. V., *Entrepreneurship in Imperial Russia and the Soviet Union*, Princeton: University Press, 1983.
Halle, L. J., *The Cold War as History*, New York: Harper & Row, 1967.
Hay, D., *The Renaissence Debate*, New York, Holt, Rinehart & Winston, 1965.
Heater, D., *The Idea of European Unity*, Leicester: University Press, 1992.
Henderson, W. O., *The Zollverein*, London: Cass, 1968.
Heer, F., *The Holy Roman Empire*, London: Weidenfeld & Nicolson,, 1968.
Hitler, A., *Mein Kampf* (1925), trans. J. Murphy, London: Hurst & Blackett, 1939.
Hobbes, T., *Leviathan*, ed. C. B. MacPherson, Harmondsworth: Pelican, 1968.
Hobhouse, H., *Seeds of Change – Five Plants That Transformed Mankind*, London: Papermac, 1992.
Hoensch, J., *A History of Modern Hungary 1867–1968*, London: Longman, 1989.
Hoffman, S. (ed.), *A la Recherche de la France*, Paris: Editions de Seuil, 1963.
Hogarth, D. G., *The Ancient East*, Oxford: Home University Library, 1950.
Holmes, G., *Europe: Hierarchy and Revolt 1320–1450*, Glasgow: Fontana/Collins, 1975.
Hosch, E., *The Balkans*, London: Faber, 1972.
Howard, M., *War in European History*, Oxford: University Press, 1984.
Hufton, R., *Europe: Privilege and Protest 1730–1789*, Glasgow: Fontana/Collins, 1980.
Hughes, K., *The Church in Early Irish Societies*, London: Methuen, 1966.
Jayne, K. G., *Vasco da Gama and His Successors*, London: Methuen, 1970.
Johnson, D., *The Interwar Economy in Western Europe*, Dublin: Gill & Macmillan, 1973.
Jones, A. M. H., *The Decline of the Ancient World*, London: Longman, 1968.
Jones, G., *A History of the Vikings*, Oxford: University Press, 1984.
Kam, V., *Accounting Theory*, New York: Wiley, 1990.
Keegan, J., *A History of Warfare*, London: Hutchinson, 1993.
Keen, M., *The Pelican History of Medieval Europe*, Harmondsworth: Penguin, 1987.
Keesings, *Record of World Events*, vols. 38–40.
Keith, D., *A History of Scotland*, 2 vols., Edinburgh: Paterson, 1886.
Kennedy, P., *The Rise and Fall of the Great Powers*, London: Unwin, 1988.
Killen, W. D., *Ecclesiastical History of Ireland*, London: Macmillan, 1875.
Kochan, L., *The Making of Modern Russia*, Harmondsworth: Penguin, 1971.
Kohn, H., *Prelude to Nation States*, New York: Van Nostrand, 1967.
Kolodsiej, E. A., *French International Policy under De Gaulle and Pompidou*, London: Cornell, 1974.
Kuitenbrouwer, M., *The Netherlands and the Rise of Modern Imperialism*, Oxford: Berg, 1991.

Landes, D. S., *The Unbound Prometheus*, Cambridge: University Press, 1969.
Lee, S. J., *Aspects of European History 1494–1789*, London: Methuen, 1984.
—— *Aspects of European History 1789–1980*, London: Methuen, 1982.
Liddell-Hart, B., *History of the First World War*, London: Pan, 1970.
Lincoln, B., *Red Victory*, London: Sphere Books, 1991.
Lipgens, W. (ed.), *Documents on the History of European Integration*, Berlin: De Gruyter, 1985, vol. 1.
Llobera, J. R., *The God of Modernity*, Oxford: Berg, 1994.
Locke, J., *Two Treatises of Government*, London: New English Library, 1965.
Longman Handbook of European History 1763–1991, ed. C. Cook & J. Stevenson, London, Longman, 1992.
Louis, J. V., *The Community Legal Order*, Commission of the European Communities, Luxembourg, 1990.
Lovell, C. R., *English Constitutional and Legal History*, Oxford: University Press, 1962.
Lyons, F. S., *Ireland Since the Famine*, Glasgow: Collins, 1973.
Mackenzie, Lord T., *Studies in Roman Law*, London: Butterworth, 1862.
Mannion, A. M., *Agriculture and Environmental Change*, Chichester: Wiley, 1995.
Marjolin, R., *Le Travail d'une Vie*, Paris: Laffont, 1986.
Marx, K. and Engels, F., *The Communist Manifesto*, ed. A. J. P. Taylor, Harmondsworth, Penguin, 1967.
Massie, R. K., *Dreadnought*, London: Cape, 1992.
—— *Peter the Great*, London: Gollancz, 1981.
Mathias, P., *The First Industrial Nation*, London: Methuen, 1969.
Mattingley, G., *The Armada*, Boston: Houghton Mifflin, 1959.
Mayne, R., *The Recovery of Europe*, London: Weidenfeld & Nicholson, 1970.
Mayr-Harting, H., *The Coming of Christianity to Anglo-Saxon England*, London: Batsford, 1972.
McEvedy, C. (ed.), *The Penguin Atlas of Ancient History*, Harmondsworth: Penguin, 1967.
—— *The Penguin Atlas of Medieval History*, Harmondsworth: Penguin, 1961.
—— *The Penguin Atlas of Modern History (to 1815)*, Harmondsworth: Penguin, 1972.
McGrath, A. E., *A Life of John Calvin*, Oxford: Blackwell, 1993.
McSweeney, B., *Roman Catholicism*, Oxford: Blackwell, 1980.
Microsoft (R), Encarta (R) 96, *Encyclopaedia*, Microsoft Corporation.
Milward, A. S., *The Reconstruction of Western Europe 1945–51*, London: Methuen, 1984.
Monnet, J., *Memoirs* (trans. R. Mayne), London: Collins, 1978.
Moorehead, A., *The Russian Revolution*, Glasgow: Collins–Hamish Hamilton, 1958.
Morison, S. E., *The Two Ocean War*, New York: Ballantine, 1963.
Mowat, R. C., *Creating the European Community*, London: Blandford, 1973.
Moynahan, B., *The Claws of the Bear*, London: Arrow, 1990.
Newhouse, J., *De Gaulle and the Anglo-Saxons*, London: Deutsch, 1970.
Nicolson, H., *The Congress of Vienna*, London: Constable, 1946.
Norwich, J. J., *Byzantium – The Early Centuries*, London: Penguin, 1990.
—— *Byzantium – The Apogee*, London: Penguin, 1993.
—— *Byzantium – The Decline and Fall*, London: Penguin, 1996.
—— *The Normans in the South*, London: Longmans, 1967.
Nugent, N., *The Government and Politics of the European Union*, 3rd ed., London: Macmillan, 1994.
O'Sullivan, N., *Conservatism*, London: Dent, 1976.

Parker, G., *Europe in Crisis 1598–1648*, Glasgow: Fontana/Collins, 1979.
Pearson, R., *National Minorities in Eastern Europe, 1848–1945*, London: Macmillan, 1983.
—— *The Rise and Fall of the Soviet Empire*, London: Macmillan, 1997.
Penguin Atlas of World History, 2 vols., Harmondsworth, 1974.
Philip Morris Institute for Public Policy Research, *Is the West Doing Enough for Eastern Europe*, Discussion Paper n. 5, Brussels, November, 1994.
Plato, *The Republic*, trans. B. Jowett, New York: Random House, 1992.
Pollard, S., *The Idea of Progress*, Harmondsworth: Penguin, 1971.
Pounds, N. J. G., *An Economic History of Medieval Europe*, London: Longmans, 1974.
—— *An Historical Geography of Europe*, Cambridge: University Press, 1990.
Procacci, G., *History of the Italian People*, Harmondsworth: Penguin, 1970.
Roberts, S. H., *The History of French Colonial Policy 1870–1925*, London: Cass, 1963.
Roerig, F., *The Medieval Town*, London: Batsford, 1967.
Rudé, G., *Revolutionary Europe 1783–1815*, Glasgow: Fontana/Collins, 1964.
Sabine, G. H., and Thorsen, T. L., *A History of Political Theory*, 4th ed., Orlando: Harcourt Brace, 1973.
Scott, J. B., *President Wilson's Foreign Policy*, New York: Oxford University Press, 1918.
Spaak, P-H., *Combats Inachevés*, 2 vols, Paris: Fayard, 1969.
Spear, P., *A History of India*, vol. 2., Harmondsworth: Penguin, 1984.
Spielvogel, J. J. (ed.), *Western Civilisation*, New York: West Publishing Co., 1994.
Starr, C. G., *The Roman Empire 27BC–476AD*, Oxford: University Press, 1982.
Stearns, P., *The Industrial Revolution in World History*, Oxford: Westview, 1993.
Stone, L., *The Causes of the English Revolution 1529–1642*, London: Routledge & Kegan Paul, 1972.
Stubbs, W., *The Constitutional History of England*, 5th ed., 3 vols., Oxford: Clarendon, 1903–6.
Sumner, B., *Survey of Russian History*, London: Methuen, 1961.
Tawney, R. H., *Religion and the Rise of Capitalism*, Harmondsworth: Penguin, 1975.
Taylor, A. J. P., *The Struggle for the Mastery of Europe 1848–1918*, Oxford: University Press, 1971.
—— *The Origins of the Second World War*, Harmondsworth: Penguin, 1973.
—— *The Course of German History*, London: Methuen, 1961.
Terraine, J. (ed.) and Fuller, J. F. C., *The Decisive Battles of the Western World*, London: London, Granada/Paladin, 1970, 2 vols.
Thomas, H., *The Spanish Civil War*, Harmondsworth: Penguin, 1965.
—— *The Suez Affair*, Harmondsworth: Penguin, 1970.
Thomson, D., *Europe Since Napoleon*, Harmondsworth: Penguin, 1974.
Tilly, C. and Blockmans, W. P., *Cities and the Rise of States in Europe AD 1000–1800*, Oxford: Westview, 1994.
Tipton, C. L., *Nationalism in the Middle Ages*, New York: Holt, Rinehart & Winston, 1972.
Toland, J., *The Rising Sun*, New York: Bantam, 1970.
Treasure, G., *The Making of Modern Europe*, London: Methuen, 1985.
Trevelyan, G. M., *England Under Queen Anne*, vol. 1 (Blenheim), London: Collins/Fontana, 1965.
Trevor-Roper, H., *The Rise of Christian Europe*, London: Thames & Hudson, 2nd ed., 1966.

Tuchman, B. W., *A Distant Mirror*, Harmondsworth: Penguin, 1979.
Ulam, B., *Lenin and the Bolsheviks*, Glasgow: Collins/Fontana, 1965.
Ullman, R. H., *Intervention and the War*, Princeton: University Press, 1961.
Vernadsky, G. and Karpovich, M., *A History of Russia*, New Haven: Yale, 5th ed., 1961.
Vernadsky, G., *A History of Russia – Vol. 3: The Mongols*, New Haven: Yale, 1948.
Virginia Quarterly Review, vol. 38, n. 4, 1962.
Von Leyden, W., *Hobbes and Locke*, London: Macmillan, 1987.
Warrender, H., *The Political Philosophy of Hobbes*, Oxford: Clarendon, 1970.
Watt, R. M., *The Kings Depart*, Harmondsworth: Penguin, 1973.
Weber, W., *The Protestant Ethic and the Spirit of Capitalism*, London: Routledge (reprint), 1992.
Wedgwood, C. V., *The Thirty Years War*, London: Cape, 1968.
—— *William the Silent*, New York: Norton, 1968.
Werth, A., *De Gaulle*, Harmondsworth: Penguin, 1965.
—— *Russia at War 1941–45*, New York: Avon, 1964.
Whitelock, D., McKitterick, R. and Dunville, D., *Ireland in Early Medieval Europe*, Cambridge: University Press, 1982.
Wilson, E., *To the Finland Station*, London: Macmillan, 1972.
Wilson, H., *The Labour Government 1964–1970*, London: Weidenfeld & Nicolson and Michael Joseph, 1971.
Wilson, K. and van der Dussen, J., *The History of the Idea of Europe*, London: Routledge, 1993.
Woolf, S., *European Fascism*, London: Weidenfeld & Nicolson, 1968.
Wordsworth, W., *The Prelude*, ed. E. de Selincourt, Oxford: Clarendon, 1959.
Yacono, X., *Histoire de la Colonisation Française*, Paris: Presses Universitaires de France, 1979.
Yanov, A., *The Origins of Autocracy*, London: University of California Press, 1981.
Ziegler, P., *The Black Death*, London: Collins, 1969.

Index